Network
Management
Standards

Uyless Black Series on Computer Communications

Network Management Standards

The OSI, SNMP and CMOL Protocols

Uyless Black

McGraw-Hill, Inc.

New York St. Louis San Francisco Auckland Bogotá
Caracas Lisbon London Madrid Mexico Milan
Montreal New Delhi Paris San Juan São Paulo
Singapore Sydney Tokyo Toronto

Library of Congress Cataloging-in-Publication Data

Black, Uyless D.
    Network management standards / the OSI, SNMP and CMOL protocols /
Uyless Black.
        p.   cm. — (Uyless Black series on computer communications)
    Includes index.
    ISBN 0-07-005554-8
    1. Computer networks—Management.   2. Computer network protocols—
Standards.   I. Title.   II. Series.
TK5105.5.B563   1992
004.6′5—dc20   91-34707
                                                                   CIP

McGraw-Hill Series on Computer Communications,
Uyless Black, Series Advisor

    3 4 5 6 7 8 9 0   DOC/DOC   9 8 7 6 5 4 3 2

ISBN   0-07-005554-8

The sponsoring editor for this book was Neil Levine, the editing
supervisor was Peggy Lamb, and the production supervisor was
Suzanne W. Babeuf. It was set in Century Schoolbook by
McGraw-Hill's Professional Book Group composition unit.

Printed and bound by R. R. Donnelley & Sons Company.

To Steve and Ceil Malphrus. Their kindness and friendship to me surely demonstrates the adage, friends in need are friends indeed.

ABOUT THE AUTHOR

Uyless Black is president of Information Engineering Incorporated, a Virginia-based telecommunications consulting firm, He has designed and programmed many data communications systems and voice and data networks. As a former senior officer for the Federal Reserve, he managed numerous large-scale data communications systems. He has advised many companies, including Bell Labs, AT&T, Bell Northern Research, and BellCore, on the effective use of computer communications technology. He is the author of ten books and numerous articles, including *The X Series Recommendations* and *The V Series Recommendations,* both published by McGraw-Hill. He is also a series advisor for the *McGraw-Hill Series on Computer Communications*.

Contents

Preface

The idea for this book originated from a client who asked my advice about using a vendor-specific network management package instead of a package that operated with multivendor protocols. This query was posed more than three years ago, so my answer was easy to formulate: Go with the vendor-specific solution, the multivendor packages are not available.

If this query were posed today, the answer would be: Look for one of the multivendor packages now available in the marketplace. Indeed, scores of vendors offer powerful products that operate with network management standards that are published by recognized standards organizations.

The purpose of this book is to describe and analyze three prominent network management standards. First, the Open Systems Interconnection (OSI) Model protocols are examined. They are usually grouped under the names of Common Management Information Protocol (CMIP) and Common Management Information Service Element (CMISE). However, OSI also provides standards on five functional areas in network management: alarm, performance, configuration, accounting, and security. This book also covers those areas.

Second, the Internet protocols are examined. The focus is on the Simple Network Management Protocol (SNMP), which is the most widely used protocol of any discussed in this book. The CMIP over TCP protocol (CMOT) is also analyzed, but not in any great detail, since its implementation has been limited.

Third, the Institute of Electrical and Electronics Engineers (IEEE) local area networks/metropolitan area networks (LAN/MAN) standards are examined. The informal title is CMIP over LLC (CMOL), although the IEEE approach can be implemented without the use of CMIP.

The book also contains considerable information on management information bases (MIBs). These conceptual information repositories provide the foundation for the description of the managed resources in a network, as well as the network management databases. Several vendor implementations are also discussed, with emphasis on the IBM, AT&T, and DEC approaches.

It is assumed that the reader has a basic level of understanding of data communications systems and data networks. For the uninitiated reader, this book contains brief tutorials on OSI, TCP/IP, and the IEEE LAN/MAN architectures.

I wish space were available to acknowledge and thank all the organizations and individuals who have contributed to this book. Many of the ideas for the book emanated from feedback received from the delegates that attended several lectures I conducted in Europe, Canada, and the United States. I owe my thanks to Suzanne Mayhew, Lucinda Tosh, and Amanda Stuart of IBC London, England, for their support and friendship during the European lectures. Kathy Ste. Marie and Rosemary Aguilar of Bell Northern Research (BNR) have been equally supportive in some of my North American endeavors.

My McGraw-Hill support has been superlative. Thank you Neil Levine, Peggy Lamb, and Suzanne Babeuf.

During the period that I wrote this book, I had the good fortune to learn more about the professional work of two of my personal friends, Paul Lombardi and Rich DeRose. I gained a better understanding of why they are so good at what they do.

Holly Waters has made immeasurable contributions to this book. She not only prepared and edited the lecture material that led to this book, but also provided valuable input to the book itself. Not only is she a great editor, she is a terrific wife.

Uyless Black

Introduction to the Network Management Standards

Introduction

A network is of little long-term value if it cannot be managed properly. One can imagine the difficulty of trying to interconnect and communicate among different machines such as computers, switches, and private branch exchanges (PBXs), if the conventions differ for managing the use of alarms, performance indicators, traffic statistics, logs, accounting statistics, and other vital elements of a network. The difficulty of managing these resources is becoming increasingly complex as networks add more components, more functions, and more users.

In recognition of this fact, the International Standards Organization (ISO) has been working on the development of several Open Systems Interconnection (OSI) network management standards for a number of years. Some of the documents have completed the draft proposal (DP) stage; others have completed the draft international stage (DIS). Most are slated for final approval as an international standard (IS) during the years of 1990 to 1994.

A large number of suppliers and vendors have participated in the development of these standards since 1979. Companies such as AT&T, Digital Equipment Corporation (DEC), and British Telecom have all made major contributions to the OSI standards discussed in this book. In addition, over 15 countries have provided input into these specifications.

Another major thrust into network management standards has been through the Internet activities. These initial efforts were organized through the ARPANET research project that originated in the United States. In 1971 the Defense Advanced Project Research

Agency (DARPA) assumed the work of this earlier organization. DARPA's work in the early 1970s led to the development of the Transmission Control Protocol and the Internet Protocol (TCP/IP).

In the last few years, the Internet Activities Board (IAB) has assumed the lead in setting standards for the Internet and has fostered two network management standards. One protocol is intended to address short-term solutions and is called the *Simple Network Management Protocol (SNMP)*. The other protocol proposes to address long range solutions and is called *Common Management Information Services and Protocol over TCP/IP (CMOT)*.

The Institute of Electrical and Electronics Engineers (IEEE) has assumed the lead role in defining network management standards for local and metropolitan area networks (LANs and MANs). The work under way is a draft standard titled *LAN/MAN Management*. It is published as part of the IEEE 802.1 standards. Some people refer to this standard as *Common Management Information Protocol (CMIP) over Logical Link Control (LLC)*, or *CMOL*. This latter title is not entirely correct, since some of the IEEE LANs may not use CMIP, but this distinction will be explained in more detail later.

Material is also included in this book that describes several vendor products as well as a survey of the use of these standards in vendor product lines. All these standards and products are covered in later chapters. For the present, it is necessary to establish some definitions of a number of terms and concepts that will be used in this book.

Network management defined

Different organizations have different views on network management and, therefore, employ different definitions of the term. Perhaps the most useful approach is to borrow a business school definition of management, because the definition is applicable to network management.

It is commonly accepted today that management involves the planning, organizing, monitoring, accounting, and controlling of activities and resources. This definition can certainly be applied to network management. However, the OSI and Internet network management structures are focused principally on monitoring, accounting, and controlling network activities and resources. The other two aspects of network management, those of planning and organizing, are not involved in the OSI/Internet scheme, but they are the most important aspects of network management and consume most of the organization's talents and resources. Indeed, if the network is not planned and organized properly, any amount of monitoring, accounting, and controlling is futile.

Why network management standards are needed

Figure 1.1 illustrates the principal problem that occurs when management standards are not used, as well as the potential benefit that can be derived from their use. In the past, each vendor developed and sold proprietary network management packages. A number of these sys-

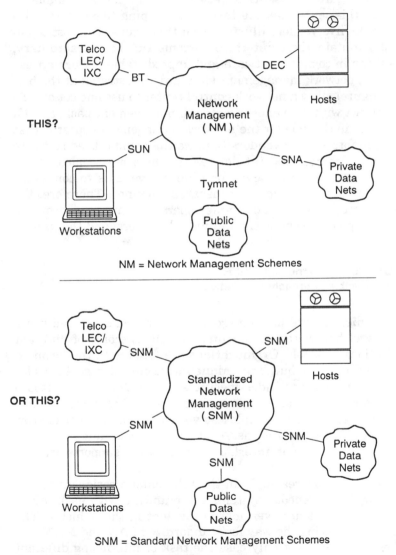

Figure 1.1 Network management alternatives.

tems are functionally rich and perform well within the vendor's network. With some exceptions, they are designed to interact with a specific vendor's hardware and software. Consequently, the use of these network management products to "oversee" other vendors' architectures is quite difficult.

The top part of Fig. 1.1 shows the typical approach without the use of network management standards. Assuming that the "cloud" in the middle of the figure represents a network and its network management center, this center has the task of developing five different interfaces for the five vendors illustrated in this figure. The cost to develop and maintain these interface systems can be extraordinary, often resulting in complex software and unpredictable performances.

In contrast, network management standards (illustrated at the bottom of the figure) allow a network control center to use one set of software to interact with the vendors' network management packages. Of course, the ace in the hole for the network management center is that this approach forces these vendors to place the standardized software in their own machines—a point not realized by some people. Nevertheless, the approach still allows the different vendors to communicate with each other in a more transparent manner. Therefore, the benefits of decreased costs and simpler operations are reaped by the network management center, the individual vendors, and the users.

Why the OSI Model, Internet, and IEEE standards are viable approaches to network management

Many companies operate in a heterogeneous environment and use a wide variety of hardware components, as well as scores of different communications protocols. Organizations are faced with the formidable technical problem of building unique interconnection packages for each of their customer's vendor-specific systems. Not only is this a complex undertaking, it also requires substantial resources. The picture will only become more complex as voice and data networks grow within and between organizations. As client, customer, and vendor relationships grow, different interface and protocol supports will be needed.

OSI is being used increasingly in the telecommunications industry to define how heterogeneous systems communicate with each other. The Internet protocols are even more prevalent in the industry. The IEEE efforts are paving the way for standardized LAN and MAN systems. These standards not only ease the task of interfacing different computers, terminals, multiplexers, PBXs, etc., but they also give the network user more flexibility in equipment and software selection because they define standard interfaces and protocols between the different vendors. Therefore, the potential purchaser has less concern that the acquisition of a component, for example, from vendor A might not interconnect with a component from vendor B.

Of equal importance is the fact that these standards allow a common platform for the implementation of user applications, support software, and network management applications. This approach simplifies the interfaces between the network control center and the user's managed network resources.

Moreover, the OSI network management standards are organized around *object-oriented design* (OOD) techniques. Fortunately, this places them in the mainstream of modern design concepts. OOD is also an excellent tool for managing multivendor devices. In an environment such as a network control center, OOD gives network engineers considerable flexibility in devising network management schemes. (Appendix A provides a brief tutorial on OOD.)

The acceptance and use of a standard often leads to lower costs because a widely accepted standard can be mass-produced and perhaps implemented in very large-scale integrated (VLSI) chips or in off-the-shelf software. This approach frees a company's personnel to use this resource as a platform to design and implement value-added services for customers.

Even if an organization sees no technical reason to use OSI, its management must face the fact that the software and hardware systems of the 1990s will make use of the OSI standards, because many companies and government agencies already require OSI's use. Regardless of one's view of OSI, it is here and it is going to be a dominant force in the computer and communications industry. On the other hand, there is little resistance to the use of TCP/IP and the IEEE standards for reasons that are examined later in this book.

Several national governments are implementing a *Government Open Systems Interconnection Profile* (GOSIP; the term varies from country to country). This profile plays a major role in the future of the data communications industry. GOSIP represents the final conventions on a set of OSI protocols for computer networking. Its importance lies in the fact that it is used by government agencies for product and services acquisition. GOSIP provides implementation specifications from standards issued by the ISO, Comité Consultatif International Télégraphique et Téléphonique (CCITT), IEEE, American National Standards Institute (ANSI), Electronic Industries Association (EIA), and others and is structured around the OSI Model.

In the United States, the National Institute of Standards and Technology (NIST) has implemented the OSI standards forum. The forum is represented by private companies and government agencies.

Through this forum, the NIST sponsors a series of workshops on the use of the network management standards. The NIST workshop agreements on network management state that the OSI network management standards must support systems operating in a multivendor environment.

The NIST OSI workshop counterpart in Europe working under the Standards Promotion and Applications Group (SPAG) is the European Workshop for Open Systems (EWOS). In Asia, the SPAG equivalent is Promotion for OSI (POSI) and its workshop is named the Asian-Oceanic Workshop (AOW). These three workshop groups coordinate their activities and often exchange liaison leaders with respect to conformance testing.

In view of these important activities, an organization should look upon network management standards as a positive factor and develop plans to exploit them. To this end, we devote the remainder of this chapter to a general introduction to the network management standards.

Integrated network management

An important goal of network management is to support an integrated approach to the management of a network (or networks) which contains multivendor computers, software packages, and carriers. Several key points about integrated network management must be emphasized.

- Integrated network management is needed to reduce the cost of interfacing different systems.

- Because integration is needed, network management requires uniformity in the exchange of management information between different vendors' product lines.

- Integrated network management does not mean that services are the same for all users. It does mean that a basic level of management service is the same for the definitions of network performance, accounting, configuration, security and fault criteria, and the exchange of common protocol data units.

- Integration and uniformity does not preclude value-added services within the context of these standards.

To place these points into perspective, imagine the potential benefits of using common network management approaches with Ethernet, TCP/IP, voice telephone, Fiber Distributed Data Interface (FDDI), and Integrated Services Digital Network (ISDN) networks. Presently, the vast majority of management packages differ across these networks. The key goal of network management standards is to develop an integrated set of procedures and standards that apply equally well across different vendors and networks.

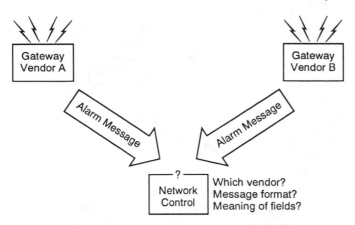

Figure 1.2 Resolving different vendors' network management protocols.

To illustrate how this goal can be met, consider Fig. 1.2. A network control facility is monitoring two different gateways. Gateway A is manufactured by one vendor, gateway B is manufactured by another, and neither is using common management protocols. Messages (for example, alarm messages) are sent to network control by either gateway. In order to interpret these messages properly, network control must:

- Be aware of which vendor's machine is sending the alarm message.
- After determining the vendor, network control must then execute a unique, vendor-specific software routine to decode the bits and fields of the alarm message since each vendor uses a unique message alarm format.
- After the bits and fields have been decoded, other special routines specific to a vendor must be executed to determine the meaning of the fields in the alarm messages.

Moreover, although the fields in the message may state they are the same, they may not be. For example, the alarm message might have a severity code of 3. This value could mean something different to vendor A than it does to vendor B or to the network control center.

Consider the alternative illustrated in Fig. 1.3. If the network control center receives standardized messages between vendor A and vendor B gateways, it need only execute one standardized routine to decode the bits and fields of the message.

Furthermore, with standardized messages, the fields in the messages have the same or at least nearly the same meaning. A severity field value means the same to each gateway. Therefore, the use of

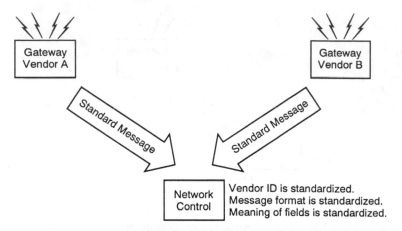

Figure 1.3 Using standardized network management protocols.

standardized messages and the standard protocol for interpreting these messages allows an integrated management approach because it allows network control to determine (with a relatively small amount of software) what the message is, what is its form, and what does it mean. Network management then need not execute two completely different sets of software systems to process the two vendors' alarm messages.

Does this really matter? The answer is, absolutely yes. One of the most expensive aspects of network management is network management software, not just in its acquisition and/or development, but in its maintenance. Common software can lead to substantially reduced costs and a less complex environment.

With these ideas in mind, the next section examines some of the basic concepts of network management as implemented in the OSI Model and to a lesser extent, in the Internet and IEEE models. These concepts are introduced here and described in more detail in subsequent chapters.

Key Terms and Concepts

OSI network management is constrained to the services and functions that are used to supervise and control the interconnection activities of data processing and data communications resources. Therefore, OSI network management is not concerned with resources that do not interconnect. Moreover, since OSI network management is an extension of OSI, it is concerned only with the communications aspects of management and not the internal operations of, say, a modem or a switch.

To a more limited extent, these principles also apply to the Internet standards, except that Internet does not consider itself an extension of OSI. However, like the OSI Model, the Internet network management standards are concerned with interconnection activities. The same holds true for the IEEE network management standards.

Network management components

The OSI, Internet, and IEEE network management standards define the responsibility for a *managing process* (called a *network management system* in some vendors' products) and a managing agent (also known as an agent process). In the strictest sense, a network management system really contains nothing more than protocols that convey information about network elements back and forth between various agents in the system and the managing process.

One other component is vital to a network management system. It is called the *management information base* or *library* (hereafter called an MIB). This conceptual object is actually a database that is shared between managers and agents to provide information about the managed network elements. We summarize these important concepts with the following notations:

- *Agent:* Reports to the managing process on the status of managed network elements and receives directions from the managing process on actions it is to perform on these elements

- *Managing process:* Directs the operations of the agent

- *MIB:* Used by both the agent and managing process to determine the structure and content of management information

Where do these components reside? The OSI, Internet, and IEEE network management standards do not require that they be placed at a particular location in the network. However, Fig. 1.4 shows a typical configuration in a LAN showing the location of the managing process, the agent software, and the MIB. In current implementations, the agent software is usually placed in components such as servers, gateways, bridges, and routers. Typically, a network control station (NCS) acts as the managing process. The MIB is usually located at the NCS and the part of the MIB that is pertinent to the agent is also located at the agent.

Object-oriented design

The OSI network management standards use many of the concepts of OOD. To a lesser extent, the Internet and IEEE model also use OOD concepts. Therefore, it is useful to discuss OOD as it pertains to net-

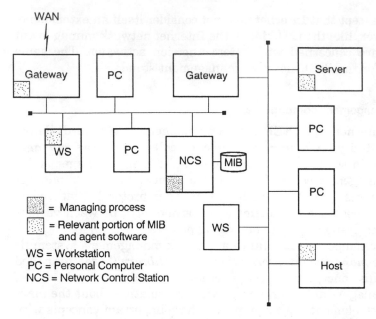

Figure 1.4   Location of network management components.

work management. The concept of OOD originated in the early 1970s. The notion of an object as a construct for manipulation (in effect, a programming construct) was first found in Simula, which was a language used to program computer simulations.

A significant event in the early history of OOD occurred in 1983, with the implementation of the Smalltalk language. Smalltalk operates on software objects. The idea of OOD (and Smalltalk) is that a program operates on an object without knowledge of the internal operations of that object. This idea is shown in Fig. 1.5. Two objects are communicating with each other. The two objects do not know about the internal operations of each other. They operate at the visible interface by passing messages (shown in the picture as operations). The

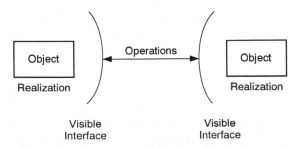

Figure 1.5   Object-oriented design concepts.

internal realization (i.e., the operations within the objects) are hidden from other objects (or the Smalltalk software). The notion of OOD and operations on objects is found in OSI network management's use of managed objects.

Managed objects

As shown in Fig. 1.6, the resources that are supervised and controlled by network management are called *managed objects*. A managed object can be anything deemed important by organizations that are using the OSI network management standards. As examples, hardware such as switches, workstations, PBXs, PBX port cards, and multiplexers can be identified as managed objects. Software, such as queuing programs, routing algorithms, and buffer management routines, can also be treated as managed objects.

From the OSI perspective, managed objects are classified by how they fit into the OSI layers. If they are specific to an individual layer, they are called (*N*)-layer managed objects. If they pertain to more than one layer, they are called system managed objects.

As Fig. 1.6 illustrates, the agent process stands between the managed objects and the network control system (or managing process). However, the term *network control system* has been renamed in this figure to that of a *management functional domain (MFD)*. This OSI term is used (in an abstract way) to describe that the management system can be clustered into agent processes reporting to the MFD. In turn, multiple MFDs can exist in an enterprise or indeed within a country. The Internet and IEEE standards do not use these concepts.

Several other important aspects of managed objects are:

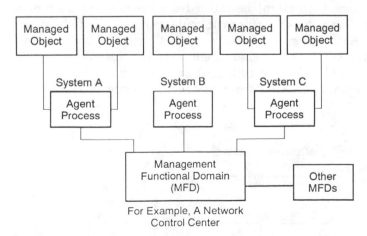

Figure 1.6 Network management terms and concepts.

- The permissible management operations that can be performed on a managed object must form part of its definition.
- The definition of a managed object may also include the effect that these operations have on related system resources.
- The state of the managed object or its properties may determine the type of operation that can be performed on the managed object.

Defining OSI managed objects

From the OSI perspective, a managed object is described and defined by four aspects of network management (see Fig. 1.7):

- Its *attributes* (characteristics) that are known at its interface (visible boundary)
- The *operations* that may be performed on it
- The *notifications* (reports) it is allowed to make
- Its *behavior* that is exhibited in response to operations performed on it

Attributes. Managed objects have certain properties that distinguish them from each other. These properties are called *attributes*. The purpose of an attribute is to describe the characteristics, current state, and conditions of the operation of the managed objects. Associated with the attributes are attribute values. For example, an object (such as a PBX line card) may have an attribute called status with a value of "operational."

Each attribute consists of one type and one or more values. For example, an integer type might be labeled the operational state of a packet switch. The values for this type could be disabled, enabled, active, or busy. As another example, the packet switch might have an octet string type labeled the management state and the values for this attribute type could be locked, unlocked, or shutting down.

OSI network management places a restriction on how attributes are

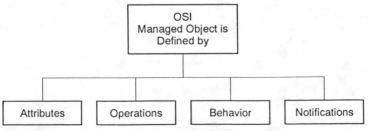

Figure 1.7 How managed objects are defined.

manipulated. Attributes cannot be created, deleted, or named during the existence of an instance of a managed object (instances are described shortly).

Operations. OSI network management establishes the permissible operations that can be performed on a managed object. The operations are:

- *Create:*   Creates a new managed object
- *Delete:*   Deletes a managed object
- *Action:*   Performs an action (operation) on a managed object
- *Get Value:*   Obtains a value about an attribute of the managed object
- *Add Value:*   Adds a value to an attribute of the managed object
- *Remove Value:*   Removes a value from a set of values about a managed object
- *Replace Value:*   Replaces a value or values for an attribute of a managed object
- *Set Value:*   Sets default values for an attribute of a managed object

Notifications. Managed objects are permitted to send reports (notifications) about events that occur on it. The nature of the notification depends on how the managed object is classified within the managed network.

Behavior. A managed object may also exhibit behavioral characteristics. These include (1) how the object reacts to operations performed on it and (2) constraints placed on its behavior.

The behavior of a managed object defines the conditions under which the values of the attributes may be altered by stimuli. Two kinds of stimuli can occur in relation to a managed object. First, external stimuli can occur through operations on the managed object. As we learned earlier, external stimuli consists of messages being passed to the visible boundary of the object. Second, the behavior of the managed object may be affected by internal stimuli. In this situation, the managed object does not have a message passed to it, but its behavior is affected by events such as internal timers.

Also, the behavior of a managed object is defined by the notifications it is allowed to create and send to some other entity. So, notifications are related to behavior. For example, it may not be allowed to report on a condition until the condition reaches or exceeds a certain threshold [such as an excessively busy central processing unit (CPU) at a switch].

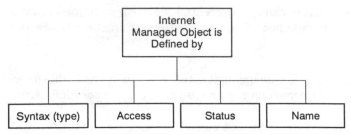

Figure 1.8   Internet managed object.

Defining Internet managed objects

From the Internet perspective a managed object is described in a less abstract manner. As shown in Fig. 1.8, a managed object is described by:

- The *syntax* used to model the object
- The level of *access* permitted to the object
- The requirement for the implementation of the object; its *status*
- An unambiguous *name* of the object

Syntax.   In the Internet model, the syntax defines the data type. In contrast to OSI network management, the Internet types are quite limited. They are defined with Abstract Syntax Notation 1 (ASN.1) types with either INTEGER, OCTET STRING, SEQUENCE, or SEQUENCE OF. In addition, the Internet MIB clarifies the use of OCTET STRING in the context of when it can be used as printable characters. Consequently, a display string can also be identified as an OCTET STRING in which ACSII character sets are defined.

Access.   The access definition provides information on how a managed object may be accessed. The following operations are permitted on a managed object:

- *Read only:*   Object instances may be read but not set.
- *Read write:*   Object instances may be read or set.
- *Write only:*   Object instances may be set but not read.
- *Not accessible:*   Object instances may neither be read nor set.

Status.   The status of the object is currently defined as (1) *mandatory,* each managed node is required to implement its managed object; (2) *optional,* nodes are required to implement the object; or (3) *obsolete,* managed object is no longer defined and the nodes need not implement it.

Name. The definition of name is an ANS.1 OBJECT IDENTIFIER, which is used to unambiguously identify a managed object. We shall see shortly in this chapter how a name is derived from a naming hierarchy used in Internet and the ISO.

OSI contrasted with Internet

The Internet model does not make a distinction between objects and attributes. Consequently, the reuse of attributes for other objects is not permitted. For example, generic attributes such as "shutting down," "operational," etc., can be applied to any object in the OSI Model. This notion does not exist in the Internet model.

Defining IEEE managed objects

The IEEE standards adhere closely to the OSI Model in regard to defining managed objects. Indeed, several of the OSI documents are included in the IEEE 802.1 LAN/MAN Management standards.

However, the IEEE operations may differ. It is possible that the operations cited in the OSI section above may be used. But the IEEE operations also include:

- *Get operation:* This operation is used to obtain a value of an identified object.

- *Set operation:* This operation is used to set a value on an object.

- *Compare and set operation:* This operation is used to perform a set of tests and, if the tests are successful, the object will be set to a particular value.

- *Action operation:* This operation is used to perform a sequence of operations on an object and/or to require the object to transit to an identified state. This operation requires that information be returned regarding the success or failure of the operation.

- *Event operation:* This operation is not initiated from a service user; rather it is a locally initiated event by the layer management entity (LME) (something like an unsolicited message—an interrupt).

OSI object classes and Internet groups

From the OSI perspective, managed objects that have similar characteristics are grouped into an *object class,* which is called a *managed object class* (MOC). In OSI, the characteristics used to determine an object class are attributes, operations, and notifications. MOCs provide a convenient means to group related resources together, and through the use of hierarchical naming techniques (described later in the chapter), it is possible to derive new classes from existing classes. This means that it is possible to encapsulate (or contain) objects within other objects and, in so doing, invoke operations or receive notifications only on the relevant "layer" of the encapsulated objects.

The Internet model does not deal with object classes in the same manner as the OSI Model. The closest approximation to an object class in Internet is a *group*. For purposes of classification, Internet managed objects are clustered into groups. For example, the interfaces group includes all objects that pertain to a physical or data link layer interface, such as Ethernet, Synchronous Data Link Control (SDLC), etc. As another example, all objects that pertain to network management protocols are classified in the SNMP group. Later chapters explain object classes and groups in more detail.

OSI management and agent processes

As discussed earlier, managed objects are managed by a *management process,* which is an application process (a network management program). As shown in Fig. 1.9, the management process is categorized as either (1) a *managing process* or (2) an *agent process.* A managing process is defined as part of an application process that is responsible for management activities (a broad definition, to be sure). An agent process performs the management functions on the managed objects at the request of the managing process.

The communications between the managing process, the agent process, and the managed objects consists of (1) management operations and (2) notifications. The agent process need not know about the specifics of the management operations it receives or the notifications it sends (although it could have this knowledge). For example, the agent process may send a notification with a value in it. The agent process need not know if the value is for an alarm, a performance parameter, etc.

Practically all management systems for communications networks support the transfer of different types of information about a managed object. OSI network management classifies this information as:

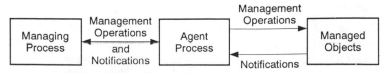

Figure 1.9   OSI management processes.

- *Data:*   This type of exchange embodies the acquisition of information by an initiator to a responder. It could be information on the status of a communication link; such as, (1) link inoperable, (2) link in standby mode, (3) link in operation.

- *Control:*   This type of exchange between two users of the OSI management services changes the attributes or status of a managed object. For example, control information could change a communications link from standby to active.

- *Events:*   This type of exchange is used to notify a user of an event that is happening. Typically, it is accompanied by the time the event occurred and the time it is being reported. For example, an event exchange could notify the user that a link was changed from standby to active and the time this event occurred.

The non-OSI resources are called a *local systems environment* and are outside the OSI standards. The user is free to design and implement the resources in any manner. The Internet and IEEE models do not enter into discussions about these subjects.

Management Information Tree and Domain Name System

Figure 1.10 shows one of the key concepts of OSI network management and the Internet standards. In the OSI Model, it is called the management information tree (MIT); in the Internet it is called the domain name system (DNS). It is used as the foundation for the identification and management of resources (objects) in a network. The tree is a hierarchical taxonomy. At the top of the tree is the root, also known as a base object. Descending down in the tree (through the *branches*) are nodes identified as level 1, 2, 3, and so on.

These nodes are considered subordinate to the nodes above them. The other term to describe this superior-subordinate relationship is

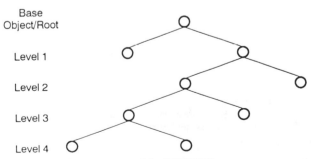

Figure 1.10   Generic view of the MIT/DNS.

the parent-child tree. Nodes in the midlevels could be children to a node above and parents to nodes below.

The idea of the hierarchical tree is to provide a framework for the identification and naming of objects. In the next sections, this generic example will be explained in more detail. For future reference, the reader should note that those nodes without subordinate entries (that is to say, the end of the hierarchical relationship) are called leaf entries.

Relative distinguished name and distinguished name

Figure 1.11 presents the MIT/DNS with a slightly modified view. The basic tree structure remains but the right-hand part of the figure contains identifiers at each node level. In our example, the highest level is designated as a country (Country), which, in this illustration, is the base object. Level 1 identifies a network (Network id) that operates within the country. Level 2 is the next subordinate level and identifies a subnetwork (Subnetwork id) identification. Level 3 identifies a node within a network (Node id). Finally, the lowest level of this tree identifies the component located at a node (Component id). The left side of the figure replaces the level designators with specific values attached to each node. These designators are called *labels*.

The base object identifies the country—in this example, the United

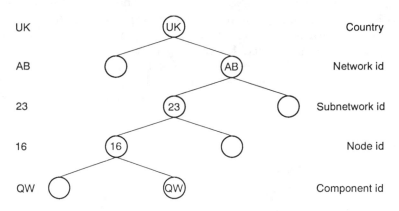

Relative Distinguished Name

Distinguished Name: Country = UK Network id = AB,
Subnetwork id = 23, Node id = 16
Component id = QW

Or: UK. AB. 23.16.QW

Figure 1.11   Object naming.

Kingdom (UK). The next subordinate entry identifies network AB. The next level identifies subnetwork 23 as part of network AB. Continuing down the tree, the Node id is identified as 16 and the Component id is identified as QW.

Each level's label is known as the *relative distinguished name* (RDN). This term is quite helpful because it allows the use of the labels within the hierarchy as appropriate to achieve an unambiguous identification. For example, in Fig. 1.11 the relative distinguished name, QW, is certainly sufficient to unambiguously identify the Component id within a node. On the other hand, the Component id, QW, is probably insufficient to uniquely identify the component across different networks.

The network administrator can use the lower-level RDNs within a specific subdomain of a network and need not be concerned with the lengthy names (and burdensome directory searches) associated with upper-level identifiers.

The full identifier for the tree in these figures is known as a *distinguished name* (DN). It is so designated because it allows the completely unambiguous identification of an object throughout the hierarchy. The creation of the DN is a very simple process (as indicated in Fig. 1.11 with the light circles). The traversal down the tree allows us to concatenate the labels associated with each node to produce the DN of: UK.AB.23.16.QW.

OSI network management and the Internet standards use the hierarchical naming scheme for searching the MIB and libraries to access information about managed objects. If the entire tree is to be searched (which might be a lengthy process), the search commences at the root of the tree. It is not necessary in many instances to search from the root. It may be possible to begin the search at some middle node in the tree with an RDN. Notwithstanding, the OSI term *base managed object* refers to that part of the subtree where a search commences.

Absolute name and relative name

The Internet standards use the same concepts of RDN and DN but use different terms. Each Internet domain (part or all of a tree) is identified by an unambiguous domain name. A domain space consists of the hierarchical space that is at the same level or below the level of the domain name which specifies the domain. Because of the hierarchical nature of the DNS, a domain may also be a subdomain of another domain. Subdomains are achieved by the naming structure, which allows encapsulation of naming relationships. In our example (Fig. 1.11), Component id is a subdomain of Node id.

The DNS provides two ways of viewing a name. One is called an *ab-*

solute name, which consists of the complete name in the DNS. In the example in Fig. 1.11, an absolute name is UK.AB.23.16.QW. In contrast a *relative name* consists of only a part of the name within a complete entry in the DNS. For example, in Fig. 1.11, QW would be used to define a relative name. The terms *absolute* and *relative names* are quite similar to the OSI Model's description of a RDN and a RN, respectively.

Inheritance and Containment

At this point in the discussion, it is appropriate to introduce two important components of OSI network management: (1) inheritance and (2) containment. These ideas are not found in the Internet suite.

From the context of OOD, inheritance means the sharing of attributes between objects. Inheritance provides a reusability function, because the lower-level nodes in an MIT must exhibit the behavior of their parent. In OOD terminology, this idea refers to encapsulating the lower-level objects into the higher-level parent objects.

OOD uses the idea of *class inheritance* to define how new classes inherit properties from existing classes (see Fig. 1.12). In so doing, there can be single or multiple inheritance. With single inheritance, an object inherits attributes from a single parent class. A more complex form of inheritance is multiple inheritance, which allows the inheritance of a subclass from more than one parent class. Not all object-oriented systems permit multiple inheritance; although it is a powerful facility, it does create considerable complexity in a software system. OSI network management has not yet defined uses for multiple inheritance.

OSI network management views inheritance in a similar way to the view in artificial intelligence (knowledge representation). A managed

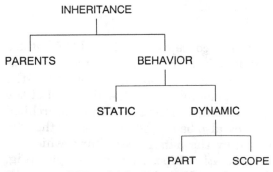

Figure 1.12   OOD and inheritance.

object subclass has all the properties of its parents. In effect, the lower-level of the hierarchy tree is really nothing more than a specialized aspect of the parents. Therefore, each attribute and instance of the subclass is a member of the parent class.

Inheritance can also be described by how classes inherit properties from the parents and how these properties can be changed. OOD uses two new terms to describe this aspect of inheritance: *static inheritance* and *dynamic inheritance*. Static inheritance requires that once the class is defined, the type values for the class do not change. On the other hand, dynamic inheritance permits the objects to alter their behavior based on operations from an outside entity or through internal stimuli. The reader may recognize that this latter aspect pertains to OSI network management.

Finally, to complete our description of inheritance, dynamic inheritance is further described as *part-inheritance* and *scope-inheritance*. Part-inheritance systems allow an object to change its behavior by receiving operations from other objects. With OSI network management, this means that the messages are passed to the managed object, which we have learned is also called *external stimuli*. In contrast, scope-inheritance establishes that an object's behavior is determined by its environment and may be altered by its environment. In OSI network management, this idea is referred to as *internal stimuli*. For example, a multiplexer may exhibit scope-inheritance even though it is receiving no messages from other objects because its software may fail, timers may expire, etc. Consequently, OSI network management allows dynamic part-inheritance and dynamic scope-inheritance.

As illustrated in Fig. 1.11, it is quite possible to obtain new object classes from existing object classes. For example, some of the characteristics of Component id can be derived from Node id. After all, they belong to the same node and network. This gives rise once again to the idea of parent and children classes.

It should also be emphasized that it is permissible to allow a subclass to override certain characteristics that are defined in a superior class. For example, a default value of "ready" for a class of "PBX Port" could be overridden by a subclass of say, "PBX Port Linecard" in which the value is something else, such as "not ready."

To summarize the major concepts of OOD's inheritance scheme, Fig. 1.12 shows the simplified taxonomy of parents, behavior, and stimuli.

The idea of containment is somewhat similar to that of inheritance, except that containment deals only with naming. Using Fig. 1.11 to demonstrate the concept of containment, the RDN of Node id implies the containment of Component id. Therefore, each object's RDN must include the names at each node, down to the object of interest. Containment naming is a very useful and flexible approach to the identification of managed objects.

Polymorphism

OSI network management also uses the OOD concept of polymorphism. A polymorphic function is one that can be applied to more than one object. This concept has been around for many years; it is used in the OSI Model with polymorphic primitives, service definitions, and PDUs. As we shall see, OSI network management uses common management information service element (CMISE) and CMIP for polymorphic operations such as get, set, create, etc. These operations can be applied to a number of managed objects.

The reader might now understand that class inheritance must be associated with polymorphism. This means that the operations that apply to a parent must also apply to the child classes.

The concept of polymorphism and class inheritance is the key to building a reusable software system, because such an approach makes it possible to build generic software logic that can be applied to a wide range of managed objects. It also allows the addition of managed objects at a later time. Therefore, many of the OSI network management standards can be used to code *application-neutral* software that can be used by different network modules, such as fault management, performance management, etc.

If the reader has difficulty grasping the idea of class inheritance and its association with polymorphism, think of a sort routine which has been around for many years. The sort routine should be able to sort any list of objects whether they are bit string, integer, floating point, ASCII string, etc.

Since the Internet model does not use the concept of inheritance, an SNMP developer cannot take advantage of generic attribute descriptions.

OSI attributes and values and Internet types and instances

The OSI MIT can be applied to the concept of attributes and attribute values. As illustrated in Fig. 1.13, each node in the tree is called an entry, which, in the context of OSI network management, is a managed object. One entry is "exploded" in order to examine its contents. It contains an attribute or attributes. Each attribute is identified by its type, which can be used as an identifier (like an Attribute id). Following the type are the attribute value(s).

The Internet concepts are quite similar to those of OSI, except the

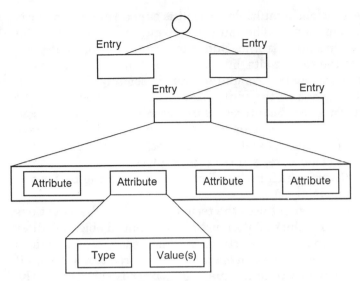

Figure 1.13   Attribute and attribute values.

terms *object types* and *instances* are used. An object type is the definition of a managed object (its syntax, access modes, etc.). An object instance is an occurrence or instantiation of the object type. For example, an object type may be defined for an interface table, and the entries in the table are an instance of the type.

Filters and Scoping

Filters

The concept of a *filter* is quite common in OSI network management systems (see Fig. 1.14) but are not employed in Internet and IEEE network management. Filters are used to determine which events in a network are to be acted upon or reported. Filters are vital in network management schemes. They prevent the network from becoming overburdened with nonessential reports on trivial events, and of more importance, they permit the reporting of critical information.

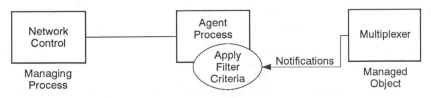

Figure 1.14   Filter operations.

For example, consider a multiplexer that is supporting a number of terminals at a remote site. The multiplexer may have its buffer (or buffers) filled by incoming traffic. Buffer overrun could present problems, not only at the remote site, but it also may have implications for data integrity at the central computer (that is sending data to a remote terminal attached to the multiplexer). On the other hand, the central computer may not be interested in a problem such as local congestion at each multiplexer site because many multiplexers have rather elaborate flow-control and error-check schemes built into their line control cards. Therefore, a filter can be placed into the network management software which makes decisions on reporting buffer saturation (or not reporting it).

OSI network management uses the term *filter* to describe assertions about the presence of values of attributes in a managed object. A filter may contain more than one assertion, in which case, the assertions are grouped together with boolean operators. A filtered test succeeds if the test is true, at which time the managed object is selected for the invocation of an operation.

Scoping

The term *scoping* can be used in conjunction with the containment tree and filters. Scoping describes the selection of a set of the managed objects in the MIT to which a filter is to be applied.

Scoping works as follows. OSI network management permits the definition of levels of managed objects. Again, this is implemented in the form of a hierarchy, as discussed earlier. The base object is the higher-level identifier in the identification tree. The scoping permits a managing process to specify the level of detail of the objects in the tree. Remember that this tree is defined as a containment tree. Therefore, identifiers are passed which allow the protocols to describe the level that is affected by the operation. It might be the base object only, it might be the entire MIT, or it might be down to an nth level.

As part of this process the return of information about the scoping operation may require multiple reporting transactions. Consequently, the scoping effect might also require multiple replies. These replies are called *linked replies*. They allow an agent process to report on actions or events on all or selected objects within the base object tree, without continuous queries from the managing process.

Synchronization

The OSI network management user may define the types of synchronization desired when managed objects have been selected for retrieval operations (for example, with the scope and filter mechanisms). Two types of synchronization are available to the user:

- *Atomic:*   All retrievals are performed or none are performed.

- *Best effort:*   Retrievals are performed if possible. If any retrieval is unsuccessful, the others are still attempted.

Event Forwarding Discriminator

The Event Forwarding Discriminator (EFD) is another aspect of OSI that is not employed in the Internet and IEEE models (see Fig. 1.15). Its purpose is to direct the notifications created by the managed objects to the proper destination. Moreover, the EFD can use filtering and apply criteria to determine if an event report using CMISE should be generated. Therefore, a managed object can be thought of as generating events or at least reporting on events. In turn, the managed object sends notifications to the agent process. One object of the agent process, the EFD, makes decisions about whether to generate a report. It should also be emphasized that an EFD is also a managed object because a managing process can exercise control over it. Of course, even as a managed object, an EFD can send its own notifications.

OSI Management Structure

As shown in Fig. 1.16, OSI (ISO 7498-4) defines three structures for OSI management protocols: (1) systems management, (2) (*N*)-layer management, and (3) (*N*)-layer operation. The Internet SNMP does not use any of these ideas, but CMOT includes them in its operations. The ideas are found in the IEEE architecture.

Systems management

Systems management is used to manage an entire OSI system. It provides mechanisms to manage multiple OSI layers and is accomplished through application layer protocols. The use of application layer pro-

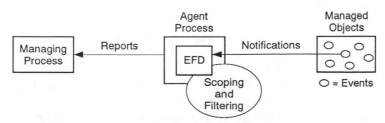

Figure 1.15   The event forwarding discriminator.

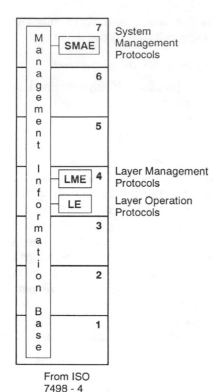

Figure 1.16   The OSI MIB.

From ISO
7498 - 4

tocols is necessary because network management needs services such as end-to-end reliability, context negotiation, etc. It assumes that the underlying OSI layers are available although an actual implementation may not use all layer functions. Systems management communications occurs through the systems management application entity (SMAE). Systems management is the preferred approach to managing an OSI-based network. It is receiving the greatest amount of attention from the standards bodies.

The OSI systems management pertains to all seven layers of OSI. This approach presents an interesting situation for the management of routers, gateways, and internetworking equipment because it is quite common for some of these devices to contain network management software.

If such a relay system is to exchange OSI-type management information through the full systems management model, it must include all seven layers of OSI. This requirement seems a bit onerous; it could be overkill in the functions provided. Of course, as a mitigating factor, one of the advantages of using the OSI stack is that the upper layers can be subsets (kernel) of the full layer protocol.

(N)-layer management

Prior to the development of the OSI network management standards, a number of layers were built with their own internal management schemes. These operations are considered to be management protocols unto themselves, although they generally operate only within a single OSI layer. An example of this approach is found in the ISO 9542 specification, which deals with end-system-to-intermediate-system connections (ES-IS). Recognizing that these management protocols were not going to go away, the OSI network management model includes a category called (N)-layer management.

The (N)-layer management structure is used to manage communication activities of (N)-layer managed objects within one OSI layer; although it can manage multiple instances of communication. It relies on the support of the (N − 1)-layer protocols. The OSI Model recommends that these (N)-layer activities do not replicate any functions at any of the upper layers. Indeed, it is planned that the (N)-layer management operations be used only if upper-layer protocols are not available.

(N)-layer operations

The third category of OSI management is called (N)-layer operations. Again, the reason for this category is recognition of the fact that some layer protocols, even though they may not be management protocols, actually contain some management information. For example, the high-level data link control (HDLC) frame reject frame (FRMR) certainly contains management information. As another example, an X.25 Reverse Charge packet contains management information as well. Consequently, the (N)-layer operation category allows the continued use of existing protocols to support specific layer activities. The (N)-layer operation manages a single instance of management communication within one layer.

Management Information Base

The MIB was introduced earlier. It is a composite of management information about the open system (that portion of the organization's system that adheres to the OSI standards). This idea has also been adapted by the Internet standards, and many of the OSI MIB structures are also found in the CMOT and SNMP MIBs.

The MIB consists of a set of managed objects and their attributes. The MIB is used by the system management entities in the application layer to communicate with each other and the (N)-layer management entities. An (N)-layer may be given some of the OSI management functions.

The idea of the MIB is to link systems management, layer management, and layer operations together. It is also intended to be used to prevent unnecessary information from being sent to the upper layers. For example, consider the X.25 Reverse Charge call. This activity resides as an (N)-management function in the network layer. These call charges need not go up into the OSI network management protocols in the application layer. Rather, they can be replaced in an MIB repository at the network layer. Later, the network administrators can define the conceptual MIB as a specific database and a managed object. Therefore, this managed object can be accessed through system management to find out about the actual cost of the X.25 calls.

The OSI MIB is conceptual in nature and to a lesser extent so is the Internet MIB. (As of this writing, the IEEE has not defined an MIB.) Despite this abstract aspect of MIBs, they form the key component of network management. After all, it is in the MIB where the managed objects are defined. The MIB contains their names, their permissible behavior, and the operations that may be performed upon them. We will return several times to analyze the MIB in more detail. In subsequent chapters, a number of examples are provided of the OSI and Internet MIBs as well as how the managed objects defined in these MIBs can be used in an actual operating network.

Open naming conventions

The MIB may contain the names and configuration relationships of the network. Many networks now use standard naming conventions for the identification of components such as packet switches, modems, and multiplexers. This idea is called *open naming* conventions. It allows an unambiguous identification of managed objects within a heterogeneous, multivendor environment.

Most network naming systems are hierarchical, and OSI and Internet use a hierarchical scheme. This means that a name at a higher level is applied across organizations, networks, and vendors, whereas the lower-layer names permit specific identification within a vendor's products and/or within networks.

Open naming conventions still require that individual data fields contain standard values. As an example, reconfiguring packet-switch ports would require standardized field values in the reconfiguration of messages even though the reconfiguration operations span across different vendors' products.

Layer Architecture of OSI Network Management

Chapter 3 provides a tutorial on the OSI Model. For obvious reasons, it forms the underlying structure for the OSI network management standards. It is used considerably in CMOT; however, its use in SNMP is quite limited. The IEEE model includes many of the OSI concepts. For our purposes in this chapter, we will restrain the discussion to a general view of the subject.

An application-entity is involved in OSI management. It is called the *SMAE*. It is responsible for implementing the OSI System Management activities. A SMAE is a collection of cooperating application service elements (ASEs).

The OSI network management model is consistent with the overall OSI application layer architecture. One configuration is shown in Fig. 1.17. Other configurations are permissible.

The systems management application service element (SMASE) creates and uses the protocol data units (PDUs) that are transferred between the management processes of the two machines. These data units are called management application data units (MAPDUs) and are examined later in the book.

The SMASE may use the communications services of ASEs or CMISE. As shown in the figure, the use of CMISE implies the use of the remote operations service element (ROSE) and the association control service element (ACSE).

In accordance with OSI conventions, two management applications

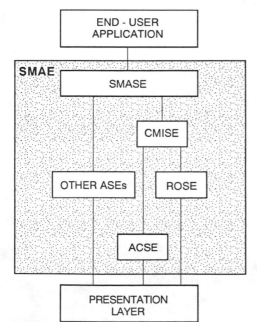

Figure 1.17 The OSI management structure.

in two open systems exchange management information after they
have established an application context. The application context uses
a name that identifies the service elements needed to support the association. ISO 10040 states that the application context for OSI management associations implies the use of ACSE, ROSE, CMISE, and
SMASE.

In later chapters, this subject is examined in more detail and discussions on the use of all these service elements will be expanded considerably.

Layer Architecture for Internet Network Management

Figure 1.18 shows the internet layers for the network management
standards. Obviously, the layering for the internet suite is simpler
than the OSI suite. The SNMP forms the foundation for the internet
architecture. The network management applications are not defined
in the internet specifications. These applications consist of vendor-
specific network management modules such as fault management, log
control, security and audit trails, etc. As illustrated in the figure,
SNMP rests over the User Datagram Protocol (UDP). UDP in turn
rests on top of IP, which then rests upon the lower layers (the data
link layer and the physical layer).

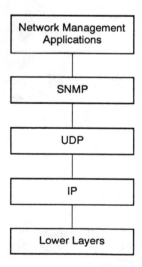

Figure 1.18 The internet network management layers.

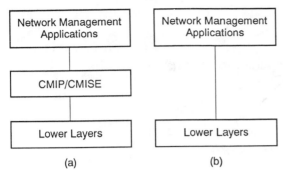

Figure 1.19   The IEEE LAN/MAN management
layers.

Layer Architecture for IEEE LAN/MAN Network Management

Figure 1.19 shows the architecture for the IEEE LAN/MAN network management standards. Principally, this work is being sponsored by the IEEE 802.1 committee and it is finding its way into vendor products. As we shall see in later chapters, its main attraction is the simplicity and efficiency of the protocol suite. As shown in Fig. 1.19a, the architecture consists of CMIP over the IEEE lower layers. (In an IEEE LAN/MAN there are only lower layers. That is to say, only the physical and data link layers are incorporated into the IEEE LAN/MAN standards.)

Alternately, the LAN/MAN management may occur without the use of CMIP, as illustrated in Fig. 1.19b. Therefore, the LAN/MAN management standards will give an implementor the option of placing CMIP over the lower-layer network management layers or invoking network management schemes within the lower two layers.

The ISO Use of the Registration Hierarchy

The ISO and CCITT have jointly developed a scheme for naming and uniquely identifying objects, such as standards, member bodies, organizations, protocols—anything that needs an unambiguous identifier. The scheme is a hierarchical tree structure wherein the lower leaves on the tree are subordinate to the leaves above. The upper branches identify the authorities as CCITT (0), ISO (1), or an object that is developed jointly by these organizations (2).

The example in Fig. 1.20 shows the ISO approach. The ISO uses four arcs below the root to identify standards, registration authorities, member-bodies, and organizations. Below these four arcs are other

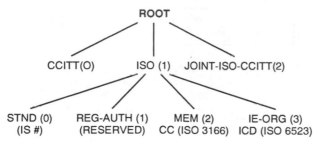

Figure 1.20   The ISO registration hierarchy.

subordinate definitions that are chosen to further identify some type of object.

We use this figure later in the book to explain some registration conventions for the OSI network management standards and the Internet standards.

The Internet Domain Name System

The idea of naming was discussed earlier in this chapter, with a comparison of the OSI MIT and the Internet DNS. This section expands on the previous discussion.

In the Internet, the organization and managing of names was provided originally by the Stanford Research Institute (SRI) Network Information Center. However, as the Internet grew, the administration became a very big job. In recognition of this problem, the Internet administrators decided in 1983 to develop a system called the DNS.

Like many addressing schemes (such as the ISO and CCITT standards), DNS uses a hierarchical scheme for establishing names and is part of the ISO addressing domain (more on this later).

The concept of the DNS is shown in Fig. 1.21. Like the OSI MIT, it is organized around a root and tree structure. A root has no higher entry and is also called a parent to the lower levels of the tree. The tree consists of branches which connect nodes. Each label of a node in the tree at the same node level must be completely unambiguous and distinct. That is to say, the label must be a relative distinguished name—distinguishable relative to this node level.

The hierarchical naming is established by moving down through the tree, selecting the names attached to each level, and concatenating these level names together to form a distinguished name—distinguishable at all levels in the tree.

For example, the first node level under the root of the tree contains several names, and we will work with COM. Proceeding down the tree to the next level, several other names are listed, in our example,

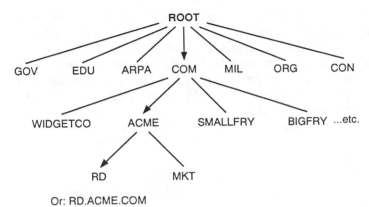

Or: RD.ACME.COM

Figure 1.21   The DNS.

ACME. Finally, RD is the lowest-level node in this tree. It is called a leaf node because it has no dependent nodes. The concatenated name is shown at the bottom of the figure as RD.ACME.COM.

The reader may be wondering about the notation in this example. The tree shows the hierarchy pursuing the route down to the bottom of the leaf. However, the actual address is written with the local label first and the top-most domain label last. This approach is different from the practice of other standards and it does take some adjustment if the reader has been using other naming standards.

Top level domains

Presently, the DNS contains seven top-level domain names. They are shown in Fig. 1.21 and are as follows:

GOV	Identifies any government body
EDU	Identifies an educational institution
ARPA	ARPANET-Internet host identification
COM	Any commercial enterprise
MIL	Military organizations
ORG	Any other organization not identified by previous descriptors
CON	Identification of countries using the ISO standard for names of countries (ISO 3166)

Summary

The OSI network management standards represent the first world-wide effort to establish a set of conventions for the management of communications networks. The standards reflect the thinking and experience of organizations with extensive experience in network management. They are founded on the concepts of the OSI Model and have been designed as application layer service elements.

The TCP/IP-based network standards found in the Internet protocols were not written with the intent of becoming worldwide standards. Yet, because of their prevalence in the industry, they have become standards, albeit in a de facto role, and outnumber their OSI counterparts in actual implementations. The Internet network management standards are modeled somewhat on OSI concepts, although many differences exist between the two suites.

The IEEE plays a major role in LAN/MAN management standards. The work by the IEEE 802.1 Committee forms the foundation for these standards.

Overview of OSI, Internet, and IEEE Network Management Standards

Introduction

The goal of this chapter is to help the reader to gain a general understanding of the OSI, Internet, and IEEE network management standards. Later chapters delve into greater detail about each standard. The reader who is familiar with the basic organization and concepts of these standards can skip this chapter.

The reader will notice that this chapter contains more material on the OSI standards than it does on the Internet and IEEE standards. It is not the author's intent to short-shrift the Internet and IEEE standards. Rather, this amount of material simply reflects the number and complexity of each of the protocol suites in the various standards.

The standards creation process for OSI network management standards

An ISO standard becomes a standard after undergoing a lengthy process of designs, writings, reviews, votes, rewritings, etc. Figure 2.1 illustrates the process involved in the development of an ISO standard. The first step entails the development of a *new work item*. This item can take the form of a working paper from any interested party that believes a standard is needed on a topic. The new work item is reviewed by ISO members and other interested parties. If it is deemed of sufficient merit to warrant further analysis and review, it then becomes a *working draft (WD)*. At this time, a working group is assigned to refine the material.

The working draft is usually taken through several cycles of revi-

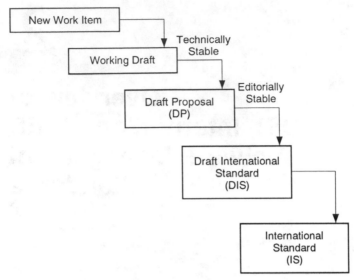

Figure 2.1   The ISO standards development process.

sion and enhancement. Eventually, it is considered technically stable and becomes a *draft proposal (DP)*. At this point in the process, the draft usually goes through still more cycles of changes. It is also registered and given an identifier. Upon being declared editorially stable, it becomes a *draft international standard (DIS)*. It is now considered technically and editorially stable. Typically, after a short delay it is voted to become an *international standard (IS)*. This complete process takes about 3 to 4 years.

Since the OSI network management documents are undergoing changes, the document numbers cited in this chapter may not be completely accurate. Also, the WD, DP, and DIS prefixes may have changed. Eventually, each document will be assigned a permanent number preceded by IS.

The standards creation process for the Internet standards

The process for creating and approving standards in the Internet world is much faster and simpler than in the OSI world. These standards are known as Requests for Comments, or RFCs.

RFCs can come about in a number of ways. An individual with a keen idea is welcome to submit a manuscript which could be accepted as an RFC. This simple process is performed by coordinating the idea with the RFC editor of Internet, also called the Deputy Internet Architect.

RFCs also stem from the International Activities Board (IAB) which may levy tasks on Working Groups within Internet, notably the Internet Research Task Force (IRTF) and the Internet Engineering Task Force (IETF). Additionally, organizations themselves may work on a problem which eventually finds its way into an RFC.

RFCs do not go through as much of a formal process as the OSI standard. OSI standards, by virtue of their extensive working groups and review process, actually go through a considerable amount of referring. Comparable RFC documents do not go through the formal referee process, although they receive considerable comment from Internet members.

The standards creation process for the IEEE standards

The Institute of Electrical and Electronics Engineers (IEEE) is a large professional society. It is organized around several boards. The Standards Board is responsible for the development of the IEEE standards and the LAN/MAN management standards are created and published through the IEEE 802 committee, IEEE Communications Society, and IEEE Computer Society.

The American National Standards Institute (ANSI) usually adopts the IEEE 802 standards as national standards for the United States and submits them to the ISO as international standards. These standards are then published by the ISO under the 8802 standards.

Organization of the OSI network management standards

Figure 2.2 provides a general view of how the OSI network management standards are organized. This view is the author's interpretation, but it reflects how the ISO has structured and arranged the documents. If the reader's time is limited, it is recommended that the management overviews be read first, followed by a review of the structure of management information (SMI) material and then the application service elements (ASEs) and the protocol. These documents provide sufficient information to give the reader an idea of the major concepts of the standards.

The SMI documents contain information that describes the model for the network management standards. Also included in SMI are definitions that are used in all the other documents.

The functional area standards are published under five categories.

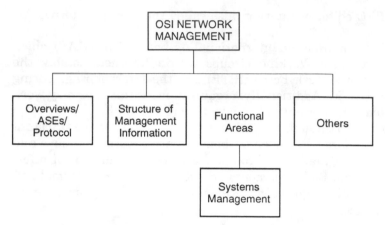

Figure 2.2 The organization of the OSI network management standards.

They define the most common network management operations: performance, fault, configuration, accounting, and security. They have received most of the attention from the user community.

As the standards have evolved, the five functional areas have been divided into more detailed specifications. They are published under the systems management documents. This material is quite important to the network manager and designer. They contain the detailed descriptions of the five functional areas.

Finally, the "others" category is used in this book to place (and describe) the other standards that do not fit neatly into the aforementioned categories.

Table 2.1 provides a summary of the ISO network management standards. The table shows the title of each standard, the ISO number, and the targeted dates for them to become DISs or ISs. Several of the standards are in the embryonic stages and will not become final ISs for several years.

With the introduction behind us, we now take a look at each of the categories and the standards that comprise them.

OSI Management Framework and Overview

The ISO documents IS 7498-4 and IS 10040 provide general overviews of the OSI management standards (see Fig. 2.3). They establish the overall structure for the OSI management operations. They are essential reading for any user of the OSI network management standards.

TABLE 2.1   Structure and Schedule for ISO Network Management Standards

Title	DIS	IS
	Dates	
Management Framework (7498-4)	6/87	10/88
Systems Management Overview (10040)	6/90	7/91
Structure of Management Information		
Part 1: Management Information Model (10165-1)	6/90	7/91
Part 2: Definition of Management Information (10165-2)	6/90	8/91
Part 4: Guidelines for Definition of Managed Objects (10165-4)	6/90	7/91
Common Management Information Service Element (CMISE)(9595)		1/90
Amendment 1: CancelGet	9/89	11/90
Amendment 2: Add/Remove	9/89	11/90
Amendment: Support for Allomorphism	11/91	11/92
Amendment: Access Control	11/91	11/92
Common Management Information Protocol (CMIP)(9596)		1/90
Amendment 1: CancelGet	9/89	11/90
Amendment 2: Add/Remove	9/89	11/90
Amendment __: State Table	7/92	7/93
Amendment __: Support for Allomorphism	11/90	11/92
Amendment __: PICS *Pro forma*	6/91	6/92
Systems Management-Configuration Management		
Part 1: Object Management Function (10164-1)	6/90	7/91
Part 2: State Management Function (10164-2)	6/90	7/91
Part 3: Relationship Management Function(10164-3)	6/90	7/91
Systems Management-Fault Management		
Part 4: Alarm Reporting Function (10164-4)	6/90	7/91
Part 5: Event Report Management Function (10164-5)	6/90	7/91
Part 6: Log Control Function (10164-6)	6/90	7/91
Part __: Confidence & Diagnostic Test Classes (10164- __)	8/91	8/92
Part __: Test Management Function (10164- __)	8/91	8/92
Systems Management-Security Management		
Part 7: Security Alarm Reporting Function (10164-7)	6/90	7/91
Part 8: Security Audit Trail Function (10164-8)	4/91	4/92
Part 9: Objects & Attributes for Access Control (10164-9)	4/91	4/92
Systems Management-Accounting Management		
Part 10: Accounting Metering Function (10164-10)	4/91	4/92
Systems Management-Performance Management		
Part 11: Workload Monitoring Function (10164-11)	4/91	4/92
Part __: Software Management Function (10164- __) 7/93	7/94	
Part 13: Measurement Summarization Function (10164-13)	8/91	8/92
Part __: Time Management Function (10164- __)	8/92	8/93

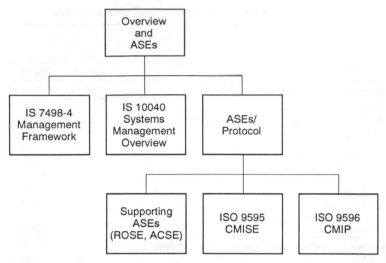

Figure 2.3   The overview standards and the ASE standards.

IS 7498-4   Management Framework

The basic foundation OSI management document is IS 7498-4. It provides the concepts and definitions for OSI management. It also introduces the five major functional components of OSI management: fault, accounting, configuration, security, and performance. In addition, it explains the concepts of individual layer management and the concepts of managed objects, which were introduced in Chap. 1. In an appendix (which is not considered part of the standard) IS7498-4 describes the OSI management structure.

IS 10040   Systems Management Overview

Another foundation document is 10040. This standard identifies the underlying OSI services used by the management entities. It also describes the concepts of distributed systems management, introducing the agent and management processes (see Chap. 1). IS 10040 also establishes the structure for the applications layer interactions among the ASEs.

IS 10040 defines the concepts of administrative management domains, which are similar to the administrative domains found in X.400. Real systems are organized into sets to: (1) meet certain requirement functions, such as fault management, accounting management, etc., (2) assign the roles of the agent and manager, and (3) establish control over the process.

These sets were described in Chap. 1. They are called *functional management domains.* The functional management domains are under the control of a *management administrative domain,* which is responsible for the transfer of the control of resources between the functional management domains.

Application Service Elements and Protocols

These standards are considered to be some of the more important parts of OSI management because they describe the service definitions (primitives), the protocol, and the protocol data units (PDUs) for the management operations. Because of their importance, Chap. 3 is devoted to them.

ROSE and ACSE

The remote operations service element (ROSE) and the association control service element (ACSE) are not part of the OSI network management standards per se. Rather, they are standards published by the ISO and CCITT for use as general software support systems for other applications. For example, the X.400 Message Handling System (MHS) standards use ROSE and ACSE, as does the file transfer and access management (FTAM) standard. Chapter 3 explains these standards and their relationships to the network management standards.

9595   Common Management Information
Service Element (CMISE)

The CMISE is defined in document 9595; it identifies the service elements (primitives) used in communications between the CMISE modules and their service users and providers. CMISE is organized around two types of services:

1. The *management notification* services can be used to report any event about a managed object that the CMISE user chooses to report.

2. The *management operation* services define the operations to create, retrieve, modify, delete, or perform other actions on a managed object.

9596   Common Management Information
Protocol (CMIP)

The ISO 9595 standard describes the protocol specification for CMIP. CMIP is the protocol counterpart to CMISE. It accepts the primitives from a network management application as defined by CMISE, constructs the appropriate application protocol data unit (APDU), and sends it (through the lower layers) to the peer CMIP user. Using the CMISE primitives, the receiving peer CMIP passes the APDU to the receiving network management application.

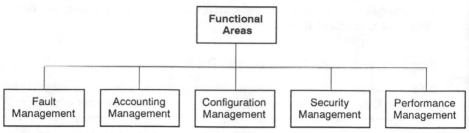

Figure 2.4   The OSI network management functional areas.

OSI Management Functional Areas

Presently, five OSI management functional areas have been defined by the ISO (see Fig. 2.4). These functional areas are scheduled to become finalized ISs in 1994. They are stable enough for organizations to review and for the purpose of strategic planning for their use. This section introduces the functional areas and subsequent chapters examine them in more detail.

Fault management

Fault management is used to detect, isolate, and repair problems. It encompasses activities such as the ability to trace faults through the system, to carry out diagnostics, and to act upon the detection of errors in order to correct the faults. It is also concerned with the use and management of error logs. Fault management also defines how to trace errors through the log and time stamping of the fault management messages.

Accounting management

This facility is needed in any type of shared resource environment. It defines how network usage, charges, and costs are to be identified in the OSI environment. It allows users and managers to place limits on usage and to negotiate additional resources.

Configuration management

This facility is used to identify and control managed objects. It defines the procedures for initializing, operating, and closing down the managed objects, and the procedures for reconfiguring the managed objects. It is also used to associate names with managed objects and to set up parameters for the objects. Lastly, it collects data about the operations in the open system in order to recognize a change in the state of the system.

Security management

This facility is concerned with protecting the managed objects. It provides the rules for authentication procedures, the maintenance of access control routines, the support of the management of keys for encipherment, the maintenance of authorization facilities, and the maintenance of security logs. Security management is in the formative stages, but it is certain that the standard will rely extensively on the Directory Service Standards for security support.

Performance management

As suggested in the title, performance management supports the gathering of statistical data and applies the data to various analysis routines to measure the performance of the system. It permits the use of models to determine if a system is (1) meeting the required throughput, (2) providing adequate response time, (3) approaching overload, and/or (4) if a system is being used efficiently.

The performance management facility relies on many definitions and concepts that have been developed for the other layers of OSI, such as residual error rate, transit delay, connection establishment delay, etc. Many of these definitions are widely used in X.25 and Internet Protocol (IP) networks. In addition, this standard provides directions on how to apply sampling formula to the analysis.

Systems Management—10164

The ISO 10164 Systems Management Standards are shown in Fig. 2.5.

10164-1   Object Management

10164-1 lays the foundations for several of the other network management standards. It defines managed objects and describes the operations for the creation and configuration of managed objects. It defines the rules for the creation, deletion, renaming, and listing of managed objects. It also defines how to delete and make attribute changes to objects.

10164-2   State Management

This standard identifies the state model for the managed objects. The OSI management standards permit two major state classifications: ad-

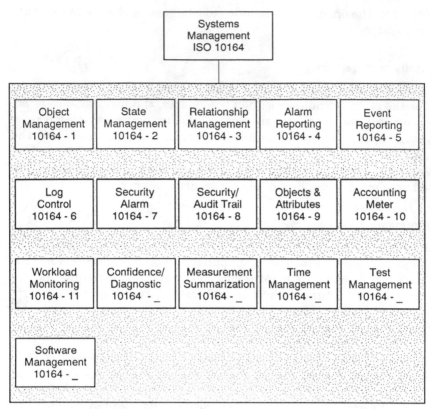

Figure 2.5   Systems management standards.

ministrative and operational. Within these states an object can be defined as busy, active, enabled, or disabled within the operational state. Within the administrative state, the substates may be shutting down, unlocked, or locked. The 10164-2 specification also defines the rules for entering and leaving these states.

10164-3   Relationship Management

This specification defines the relationships of the managed objects. The standard establishes the following relationships:

- *Direct:*   Some portion of information associated with one managed object expressly identifies the other managed object.
- *Indirect:*   A relationship is deduced between two managed objects by the concatenation of two or more direct relationships.
- *Symmetric:*   Interaction rules between two managed objects are the

same. For example, an interaction rule could stipulate the right to change an attribute of an object.

- *Asymmetric:* Interaction rules between two managed objects are different.

In addition to these definitions, relationship management defines the service aspects of the management relationships with the create, get, and set services.

10164-4 Alarm Reporting

This document defines and identifies five basic categories of errors (notification types), which comprise the kernel functional unit:

- Communications
- Quality of service
- Processing
- Equipment
- Environment

In addition to these five notification types, alarm reporting provides information on: (1) the probable cause of the alarm, (2) the severity of the alarm, (3) the backup status (if any), (4) threshold values (if any exist), (5) proposed repair actions, (6) indications if the alarm created state changes at the monitored object, and (7) optional textual information about the alarm.

10164-5 Event Reporting

This standard establishes the components to support remote event reporting and local event processing. The standard is formed around the concept of a set of *discriminators*. As an example, the event forwarding discriminator is responsible for filtering events based on a number of selection criteria and deciding if the event is to be reported. In so doing, the discriminator uses a discriminator construct which establishes the thresholds and other criteria which must be satisfied for the event to be forwarded.

10164-6 Log Control Function

As the title suggests, 10164-6 defines the log control operations for a network management system. This specification defines how to preserve information about events and operations on managed objects. The standard also specifies mechanisms to control times for when logging occurs, for resuming logging, and for suspending logging. In addition, it defines operations for retrieving and deleting log records, as well as the modification of criteria that are used in creating the logging records.

10164-7   Security Alarm Reporting Function

This document defines procedures for the security management user to receive notifications on various types of alarms on managed objects. The standard specifies five types of security alarms:

- An *integrity* violation indicates that there has been a potential interruption in information flow. The information may have been deleted, inserted with other information, or modified in a way that is not permitted.

- An *operational* violation indicates that a requested service was not obtained because of a malfunction or otherwise incorrect invocation of a service.

- A *physical* violation indicates that a breach of a physical resource (for example, the tapping of a channel) has been detected.

- A *security service* violation indicates that some security device in the network has detected a security attack.

- The *time-to-remain* violation indicates that some event has occurred outside a permitted time threshold.

In addition to the security alarm types, this standard defines a number of causes which relate to the alarm types. Some examples follow:

- An indication that information was not expected but has been received

- An indication that information that is expected has not been received

- An indication that information that has been received has been modified illegally

- An indication that information has been received more than once, thereby alerting the user to a replay attack

- An indication that a communications medium has been tapped

10164-8   Security Audit Trail Function

This specification is similar to the log control function, except that it provides audit trail logs which are a record of historical events that relate to the security measures. It provides support on auditing information related to accounting, security utilization, disconnections, connections, and other management operations.

10164-9   Objects and Attributes
for Access Control

The purpose of this document is to allow the network administrator to prevent unauthorized access to certain managed objects. It defines access control mechanisms based on a knowledge of a user's profile. In addition, this standard defines rules to allow or deny access to the managed objects.

10164-10   Accounting Meter Function

This standard defines how charges, costs, and usage are identified and recorded in the managed network. In addition, it provides thresholds which limit the user's use of certain of the managed objects.

10164-11   Workload Monitoring Function

This standard defines a workload monitoring model for a managed resource. It establishes procedures for feedback to the user in order to determine trends regarding the performance of the managed objects. It measures threshold values for reporting on early warning and severe warning conditions. It defines how to measure resource utilization and how to clear various conditions relating to the managed objects. It also provides definitions for gauges, thresholds, counters, etc.

10164-__   Other Functions

The remainder of the 10164 standards shown in Fig. 2.5 are either not yet written in sufficient detail or are too unstable to warrant discussion.

Structure of Management Information
DP10165

The SMI standards are divided into four parts (see Fig. 2.6). These parts are described in the following documents.

10165-1   Management Information Model

SMI part 1 identifies the attributes of the managed objects that can be manipulated. It also identifies the operations of object attributes such as get, set, add, and remove and the operations that may apply to the object itself, read, delete, and action.

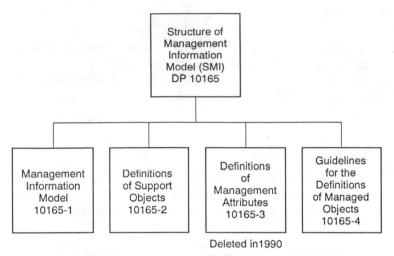

Deleted in1990

Figure 2.6   Structure of management information.

10165-2   Definitions of Support Objects

This specification identifies common object classes used by OSI management. At the present time, it only defines the object class for discriminators: event, report, and service access.

10165-3   Definitions of Management
Attributes

Document 10165-3 (now deleted from this standard) defined management attributes, and as the title suggests, it specified the attributes used by management: state change, error cause state, configuration state, object class distinguished name (DN), counters log, definitions, severity, trend indication, etc. Most of this information was moved to the other 10165 documents.

10165-4   Guidelines for the Definitions of
Managed Objects

This document provides some very useful definitions of terms. It contains information on how to define objects, events, attributes, and actions. Additionally, it contains the rules on how to create and use templates.

CCITT and the Network Management
Standards

It might be surprising to the reader to learn that CCITT was not a forerunner in the network management standards arena. After all, CCITT concerns itself extensively with networks.

TABLE 2.2   Relationship of the X.700 Series and the ISO Standards

Title	ISO	CCITT
Management Framework	7498-4	X.700
Systems Management Overview	10040	—
Structure of Management Information		
Part 1: Management Information Model	10165-1	X.720
Part 2: Definition of Management Information (10165-2)	10165-2	X.721
Part 4: Guidelines for Definition of Managed Objects (10165-4)	10165-4	X.722
Common Management Information Service Element (CMISE)	9595	X.710
Common Management Information Protocol (CMIP)	9596	X.711
Systems Management-Configuration Management		
Part 1: Object Management	10164-1	X.730
Part 2: State Management	10164-2	X.731
Part 3: Relationship Management	10164-3	X.732
Systems Management-Fault Management		
Part 4: Alarm Reporting	10164-4	X.733
Part 5: Event Reporting Management	10164-5	X.734
Part 6: Log Control Function	10164-6	X.735
Part __: Confidence and Diagnostic Test Classes	10164-__	X.737
Part __: Test Management	10164-__	—
Systems Management-Security Management		
Part 7: Security Alarm Reporting Function	10164-7	X.736
Part 8: Security Audit Trail Function	10164-8	X.740
Part 9: Objects & Attributes for Access Control	10164-9	X.741
Systems Management-Accounting Management		
Part 10: Accounting Metering Function	10164-10)	X.742
Systems Management-Performance Management		
Part 11: Workload Monitoring Function	10164-11	X.739
Part __: Measurement Summarization Function	10164-__	X.738
Part __: Software Management Function	10164-__	—
Part __: Time Management Function	10164-__	—

CCITT has been working recently on network management standards. The standards are published in CCITT's X.700 series. The relationships of the CCITT and ISO network management documents are summarized in Table 2-2. They are technically aligned with the ISO standards (unless the author missed something in the analysis of the CCITT specifications), and they are identical to the ISO specifications.

The Internet Network Management Standards

Table 2.3 lists and describes the titles of the RFCs pertinent to the Internet network management standards. The RFCs are the Internet equivalent to formal standards.

TABLE 2.3   The Internet Standards for Network Management

RFC number	Date	Title
1052	April 1988	IAB Recommendations for the Development of Internet Network Management Standards
1155	May 1990	Structure and Identification of Management Information for TCP/IP-based Internets
1213	March 1991	Management Information Base for Network Management of TCP/IP-based Internets: MIB II
1157	May 1990	A Simple Network Management Protocol (SNMP)
		Others
1095	April 1989	The Common Management Information Services Protocol over TCP/IP (CMOT)
1085	December 1988	ISO Presentation Services on top of TCP/IP-based Internets

RFC 1052 provides useful information on the background of the development of these standards. The standards themselves are contained in three documents. RFC 1155 contains common definitions and identification of information used on Transmission Control Protocol/Internet Protocol- (TCP/IP) based networks. It is similar in intent to the OSI Network Management Standard IS 7498-4 and IS 10040.

RFC 1213 contains information dealing with an Internet Management Information Base (IMIB). This document is the second release of the MIB, which is known as MIB II.

The other important document is RFC 1157, which describes the Simple Network Management Protocol (SNMP). Although subsequent RFCs contain additional information for the use of SNMP, the reader may find that RFC 1215 (a convention for defining traps for use with the SNMP) and RFC 1187 (bulk table retrieval with the SNMP) are useful documents for ancillary information on SNMP. Additionally, RFC 1212 (concise MIB definitions) is a very useful document that provides information on producing MIB modules.

Two other RFCs are listed in Table 2.3. These RFCs deal with the Common Management Information Services and Protocol over TCP/IP (CMOT) and the Lightweight Presentation Protocol (LPP). As described earlier in this book, the CMOT approach has not proven to be successful. It is listed in this table in case the reader wants to analyze these documents for historical reasons.

The IEEE Network Management Standards

The IEEE standards are listed in Table 2.4. As the table indicates, several of the standards are from the ISO standards. The key docu-

TABLE 2.4   The IEEE Standards for Network Management

Number	Date	Title
802.1B/D	March 1990	LAN/MAN Management
802.1E/D	July 1989	System Load Protocol
802.1/F/D4	March 1990	Guidelines for Layer Management Standards
802.1	February 1990	SMI, Part 1 of ISO DP 10165
802.1	December 1989	SMI, Part 2 of ISO DP 10165
802.1-90	November 1989	SMI, Part 4 of ISO DP 10165

ment is titled *LAN/MAN Management*. It describes the protocols and service definitions for LAN/MAN management. The *System Load Protocol* standard describes the procedures to transfer a block of information from one machine to another. The other standards are taken from the ISO SMI specifications that were discussed earlier in this chapter.

Summary

The OSI, Internet, and IEEE network management standards are considered to be the authoritative specifications for network management protocols. The OSI and IEEE standards are designed to operate with OSI-based systems and networks, although the IEEE standards may also operate with non-OSI environments. The Internet standards are designed to operate with TCP/IP-based systems.

These standards use relatively simple protocols to convey management information between agents and managing processes. The OSI Model uses CMIP, the Internet model uses SNMP, the IEEE may or may not use CMIP.

3

Overview of
OSI, Internet, and
IEEE 802 Standards

Introduction

The majority of the readers of this book are likely to be familiar with
the concepts of the OSI Model, the Internet standards, and the IEEE
802 Standards. Therefore, this chapter reviews in a general way the
OSI, Internet, and IEEE terms that pertain to network management.
The reader may wish to obtain a copy of *OSI: A Model for Computer
Communications Standards* (Uyless Black, Prentice Hall, Inc. 1990).
It is a more detailed treatment of the OSI Model and is highly recom-
mended by the author. Also included in this McGraw-Hill series is
TCP/IP and Related Protocols (Uyless Black, McGraw-Hill, Inc, 1992).
Naturally, it is also highly recommended.

OSI Network Management's Use of OSI
Services

OSI network management uses several of the OSI application, presentation, and session layer service definitions and protocols. It may also
use the other lower-layer standards, but in the spirit of OSI, network
management does not know or care about the lower-layer activities or
how they provide services to network management.

The OSI network management standards are rather tightly coupled
with several applications layer protocols and the presentation and session layers. Therefore, Chap. 4 is devoted to these layers. They are described in general terms in this chapter.

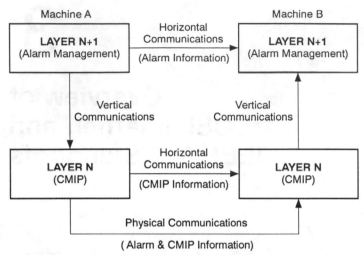

Figure 3.1 Horizontal and vertical communications.

Horizontal and vertical communications

The relationship of these layers is shown in Fig. 3.1. Each layer contains entities that exchange data with and provide functions (horizontal communications) to peer entities at other machines. For example, layer $N + 1$ in machine A (for example, an alarm management application) communicates logically with layer $N + 1$ in machine B, and the N layer (for example, Common Management Information Protocol, CMIP) in the two machines follow the same procedure. Entities in adjacent layers in the same computer interact through the common upper and lower boundaries (vertical communications) by passing parameters to define the interactions.

Components of layered communications

Several components are involved in the layer's communications process (see Fig. 3.2). Their functions are:

- *Service data unit (SDU):*   Consists of user data and control information created at the upper layers which is transferred transparently by layer N to layer $N - 1$. The SDU identity is preserved from one end of an (N)-connection to the other.

- *Protocol control information (PCI):*   Information exchanged by peer (the same) entities at different sites on the network to instruct an entity to perform a service function (that is, headers and trailers).

- *Protocol data unit (PDU):*   The combination of the SDU and PCI.

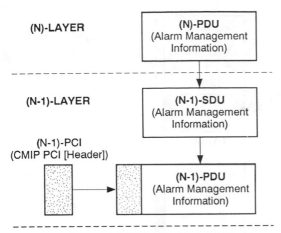

Figure 3.2 The use of SDUs, PDUs, and PCIs.

To summarize the OSI layering concepts, the following actions constitute a typical operation. When the PDU from layer N passes to layer $N - 1$, it becomes the SDU to that layer (see Fig. 3.2). The SDU at layer $N - 1$ has a PCI added to it to become a full PDU to be passed through the next layer. In effect, this scenario entails adding a header at each layer (except at the physical layer, and some would argue that synchronization bits, such as the flag in a megastream or a T1 carrier, are actually physical layer PCIs).

The header is used by the peer layer entity at another machine to invoke a function, and the contents of the header determine the function that is invoked. The peer entity at the receiving machine receives the SDU that is created at the transmitting peer entity. As with all layered protocols, the process repeats itself through each layer.

Encapsulation and decapsulation

Figure 3.3 shows how the layers of OSI communicate. At a transmitting computer, user data are presented by a user application to the upper layer (application). This layer adds its PCI (which the reader probably knows as a header) to the user data and performs some type of support service to the user. It then passes its header and the user data to the next lower layer, which repeats the process.

Each layer adds a header to the data unit received from the adjacent upper layer (in many systems a header is not added at the physical layer). This concept is somewhat inaccurately called *encapsulation*

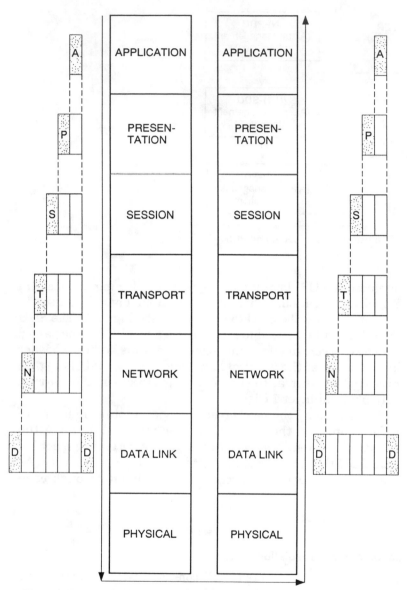

Figure 3.3 Encapsulation and decapsulation.

(the data from the upper layers are only encapsulated at one end). The only layer that completely encapsulates the data is the data link layer, which adds both a header PCI and a trailer PCI.

The fully encapsulated data unit is transported across the communications circuit to a receiving station. As shown on the right side of

Fig. 3.3, the process is reversed; the data goes from the lower layers to the upper layers, and the header created by the transmitting peer layer is used by the receiving peer layer to invoke service functions for (1) the transmitting site and/or (2) the upper layers of the receiving site. As the data goes up through the layers, the headers are stripped away after they have been used. This process is called *decapsulation*.

Communications between layers

Figure 3.4 shows a layer providing a service or a set of services to users A and B. The users communicate with the service provider through an address, or identifier, commonly known as the *service access point* (SAP). Through the use of four types of transactions, called *primitives* (Request, Indication, Response, and Confirm), the service provider coordinates and manages the communications process between the users. (Some sessions do not require all primitives):

- *Request:* A primitive by the service user to invoke a function
- *Indication:* A primitive by the service provider to (1) invoke a function or (2) indicate a function has been invoked at a SAP
- *Response:* A primitive by the service user to complete a function previously invoked by an Indication at that SAP
- *Confirm:* A primitive by the service provider to complete a function previously invoked by a request at that SAP

A primitive is coded with a specific format. For example, let us assume we wish to establish a *connection* to a network in order to access

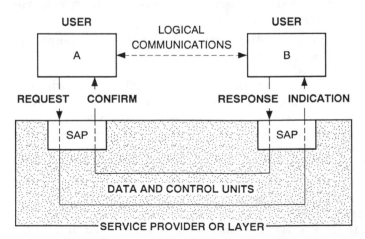

Figure 3.4 OSI primitives and service provisions.

a computer in another city. Let us also assume that we communicate with the network through primitives. We could request the connection with the following primitive:

N-CONNECT request (called address, calling address, quality of service parameters, user data)

This is a request primitive, or more precisely, a network layer (the letter N is for network) connect-request primitive. Notice the parameters associated with the connect request. The addresses are used to identify the called and calling parties. The quality of service (QOS) parameters are translated into services for the user; these services are called *facilities*. They inform the service provider about the type of services that are to be invoked (expedited delivery, for example). It is possible that the primitive could contain many QOS parameters to invoke many facilities. The last parameter, user data, contains the actual data to be sent to the called address.

The primitive is used by the layer to invoke the services within a layer (called *service entities*) and to create any headers that will be used by the peer layer entity in the remote station. This point is quite important. The primitives are used by adjacent layers in the local site to create the headers used by peer layers at the remote site.

Service Definitions and Protocol Specifications

The CCITT and ISO use two OSI-based terms in describing many of the X Series Recommendations:

- *Service definitions:*   Defining the services between the layers, typically with the use of primitives

- *Protocol specifications:*   Actions taken within the layer and between peer layers as a result of the service definitions.

The previous section explains the concepts of vertical and horizontal communications between layers. A convenient way to think of service definitions is that they provide vertical communication services. The protocol specifications provide horizontal communication services.

The service definitions are usually depicted with time transition diagrams, as shown in Fig. 3.5. For example, the figure shows that a request primitive is issued before an indication primitive (although exceptions do exist). The response and confirm primitives used are based on the earlier request and indication primitives. Typically, they are employed to (1) confirm that something has happened and (2) inform the other user about the results of the happening.

Other scenarios are common in the use of the OSI network manage-

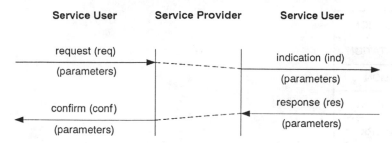

Figure 3.5 Typical sequence for the issuance of primitives.

ment protocols. For example, Fig. 3.6 shows that a network manage-ment service may not be confirmed or that the service provider chooses to send an unsolicited indication primitive.

A Review of the OSI Layers

The seven OSI layers are shown in Fig. 3.7. These layers are summa-rized in this section. We also use this section to introduce some impor-tant attributes of the layers and the relationships of the layers to each other.

The lowest layer in the model is called the *physical* layer. The func-tions within this layer are responsible for activating, maintaining, and deactivating a physical circuit between a data terminal equip-ment (DTE) and a modem, multiplexer, or some other similar device. The layer also identifies the bits (as 0s or 1s).

This layer is concerned with the nature of the signals. Conse-quently, it must be able to distinguish between different levels of volt-ages and the direction and intensities of currents. It has the task of

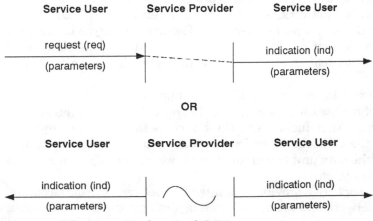

Figure 3.6 Other scenarios of service definitions.

APPLICATION
PRESENTATION
SESSION
TRANSPORT
NETWORK
DATA LINK
PHYSICAL

Figure 3.7   The OSI Model.

sending and receiving electromagnetic signals. It is also responsible for creating and interpreting the optical signals in the optical fibers. This layer is also responsible for defining the cabling and wiring between machines (if any exist). It also contains the specifications for the physical connectors used to attach cables and wires to the computers (which some people simply call plugs).

The *data link layer* is responsible for the transfer of data over the channel. It provides for the synchronization of data to delimit the flow of bits from the physical layer. It also provides for the identity of the bits in regard to the delineation of the bits within successive PDUs. It ensures that the data arrives safely at the receiving computer or terminal. It provides for flow control to ensure that the computer does not become overburdened with too much data at any one time. One of its most important functions is to provide for the detection of transmission errors and to provide mechanisms to recover from lost, duplicated, or damaged data.

The *network layer* specifies the interface of the user DTE into a packet-switched network, as well as the interface of the DTEs with each other through a packet network. The network layer is the layer responsible for routing. In a packet switch, this routing function is called *packet* switching; in a circuit switch network, it is called *circuit* switching.

The network layer is responsible for supporting the end user's negotiation of services with a network. These services are referred to as QOS features. They include functions such as the reverse-charging of calls (like the call collect service in a telephone system), negotiating the size of the data unit traversing the network, providing for security features, and so on.

The *transport layer* provides the interface between the data communications network and the upper three layers. It is the layer that gives the user options in obtaining certain levels of quality (and cost) from the network itself (i.e., the network layer). It is designed to keep the user isolated from some of the physical and functional aspects of the packet network. It also provides for end-to-end integrity of the transfer of user data.

The transport layer can recover from the potentially destructive actions of clear, reset, and restart packets, which are used at the network level. For example, a network level reset might require the transport level to maintain copies of the user data, and after the network reset is complete (with the possible loss of data in the network), the transport layer could perform certain functions to recover this data.

Despite this recovery mechanism, it must be emphasized that the transport layer may also perform destructive operations. This event occurs when a user requests a disconnect at the transport layer. That is to say, the user asks the transport layer to release its session. The transport layer might then request the network layer for the release. The transport layer does indeed recover from lower-layer destructive operations, but it does not recover from its own disconnect. In other words, a disconnect at the transport layer may also be destructive.

The *session layer* serves as the user interface into the transport service layer. This layer provides for an organized means to exchange data between end-user applications. The users can select the type of synchronization and control needed from the layer. To cite some examples: (1) Users can establish an alternate two-way dialogue or a simultaneous two-way dialogue, or (2) synchronization points can be established to recover from file and data transfer problems.

One of the most important functions of the session layer is the provision for a "graceful close" between the user applications. This service ensures that all data are received before a connection is released at any of the lower layers. The session layer either (1) recovers from a lower-layer destructive operation or (2) prevents the transport layer disconnect from being destructive. Therefore, this layer provides for absolute end-to-end integrity of the transfer of data between different computers.

If the user applications reside in the same machine, the session layer can be invoked to provide for data transfer integrity. Indeed, if the two applications reside in the same computer, it generally is not necessary to invoke the operations of the lower four layers.

The *presentation layer* is used to assure that user applications can communicate with each other, even though they may use different representations for their PDUs (packets or messages). The layer is concerned with the preservation of the syntax of the data. For example, it can accept various data types (character, boolean, integer) from the application layer and negotiate an acceptable syntax representation with another peer presentation layer, perhaps located in another computer. It also provides a means to describe data structures in a machine-independent way. It is used to code data from an internal format of the sending machine into a common transfer format and then decode this format to a required representation at the receiving machine.

The *application layer* is concerned with the support of an end-user application process. This layer contains service elements to support application processes such as job management, file transfers, electronic mail, and financial data exchanges. The layer also supports the virtual terminal and virtual file concepts. Directory services are obtained through this layer.

Some additional thoughts regarding the seven layers might prove helpful. The lower three layers specify the machine-to-machine communications wherein the machines communicate directly or through intermediate systems. Generally, these intermediate systems are networks, whose operations, logically enough, reside in the network layer. Layer 4, which provides the "bridge" between the upper three layers and the lower three layers, specifies the end-system-to-end-system communications. The top three layers are concerned with end-user communications.

Application Layer Architecture

Figure 3.8 shows the relationship of the major components in the application layer that service OSI network management. The application process rests above the application entity (AE), the user entity

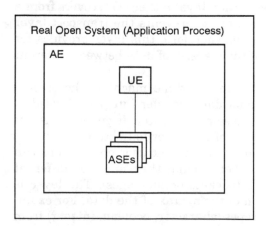

Figure 3.8 Architecture of the application layer.

(UE), and the application service elements (ASEs), because the application process is a program that uses these services.

The AE represents the application process within the OSI Model. Although it defines a set of functions needed by the application process, the application process is allowed to use more than one AE.

The ASE is really nothing more than a part of an AE that provides a specific and defined OSI capability. Simply stated, an ASE serves a specific purpose. The logical grouping of the ASEs comprises the user entity.

The AE is composed of a set of programs. Therefore, when they execute, they are *invoked*. In the context of OSI terms, an invocation is an instance of the program running. That is to say, it is an application entity invocation (AEI).

In later chapters we will see that an ASE, called the *association control service element (ACSE),* supports the establishment, maintenance, and termination of application associations. An application association is a detailed description of a cooperative relationship between two AEs through the use of presentation services within a defined application context.

An *application context* is the set of service elements and supporting information used by an application association. Essentially, it is a set of rules for communicating in a given application association and the AEs' invocations (their actions).

OSI Network Management Profiles

Invariably, the question arises as to how an end-user is to determine which part of OSI network management is being used in a product line. The question can be answered by an understanding of the concept of suites, or profiles. These two terms (they are used interchangeably) mean that a precise combination of the OSI standards is applied to a product. Invariably, the next question that arises is, "We thought these were standards; why are we using options?" The answer to this question stems from the fact that each layer of OSI provides basic subsets (generally referred to as *kernels,* or *functional units*) as well as optional services which may or may not be implemented.

In the vast majority of cases, standards groups and manufacturers are building and publishing stacks of OSI protocols, which use a subset of the full OSI standards. These subsets are called *profiles,* or *suites.*

OSI Network Management's Use of Encapsulation and Mapping

The discussions in this chapter have emphasized the importance of encapsulation in the OSI Model. While encapsulation is still used by the

OSI network management standards, OSI also makes extensive use of a concept called the mapping of services. (Mapping and encapsulation are not at odds with OSI, since the Model uses the same approach in its upper layers.) The distinction between encapsulation and mapping can be seen in Fig. 3.9. A fault management module receives an INITIATE request primitive from its user and sends an alarm message to a Common Management Information Service Element (CMISE) module. This action is shown as the ACTION request service definition. This service definition contains a number of parameters that define the exact nature of the alarm. These parameters are treated as data by CMISE; and, as in the typical OSI Model operation, CMISE encapsulates its PDU around the alarm (user) data. However, the service definition also contains parameters that are not encapsulated. These parameters are mapped directly to a CMISE service as well as to a service definition parameter for the CMISE to the remote operations service element (ROSE) operation.

For example, the receipt of the ACTION primitive from fault management causes CMISE to map some parameters in this prim-

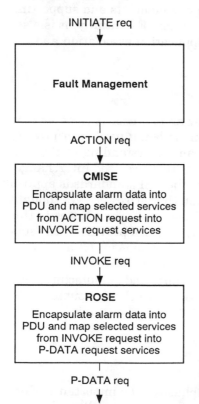

Figure 3.9 Encapsulation and mapping.

itive *directly to parameters* in the INVOKE request service definition primitive.

The reader should keep these distinctions between encapsulation and mapping in mind. They will aid in understanding several discussions in later chapters.

Placement of OSI Network Management in the Layers

Several discussions in Chap. 1 emphasized that OSI network management modules are designed to reside in the application layer, and Fig. 3.10 substantiates these statements. This approach may seem quite logical for some people, but it is a source of confusion to those individuals who have been exposed to the OSI-based notion that network op-

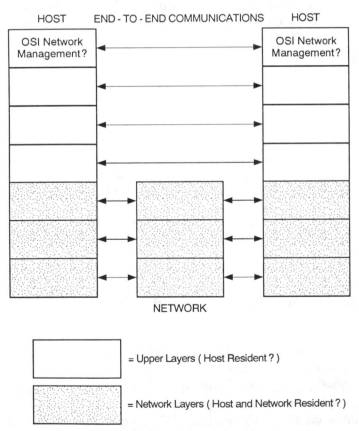

Figure 3.10   Placement of OSI network management functions.

erations reside in the lower three layers of the OSI Model and that the upper four layers reside in the user host computer. Figure 3.10 shows this relationship.

To make certain the reader is not confused, be aware that nothing precludes all layers residing in any type of machine. For example, the seven layers can be "tailored" to fit rather well into a network operations center computer.

The key word is indeed *tailored*. That is, the network manager must carefully consider what parts of the layers are needed for network management. For example, a "minimal" level of services may be needed at the transport layer because upper-layer modules do not need them and the network manager wishes to keep overhead low. As another example, the network control center may choose to use a connectionless network layer instead of a connection-oriented standard because of the nature of the traffic passed in the network management data units.

Therefore, if the selection of the entities in each layer is done with some forethought, the application layer aspect of OSI network management is not contradictory to the OSI Model, nor is it contradictory to sound design.

Overview of the Internet Protocols

Like the OSI Model, the Internet Protocol suite uses a layered architecture. However, it does not contain as many layers as the OSI Model nor does it have as many options. The internet suite is considered to be a simpler suite, easier to implement, and does not require as many central processing unit (CPU) cycles or as much random access memory (RAM).

An example of a typical internet topology and the internet layers are shown in Fig. 3.11. This example shows three computers (labeled hosts in this figure) attached to networks A and B. The two networks are connected with a gateway.

The internet standards do not address the lower layers in the host or gateway. These are usually implemented with widely known and accepted standards such as:

- At the physical level, EIA 232-D, V.24/V,28, V.35, digital systems (such as DDS or T1), or any of the CCITT V Series modems
- At the data link layer, high-level data link control (HDLC) type protocols such as Link Access Procedures Balanced (LAPB), Link Access Procedures on the D-channel (LAPD), Logical Link Control (LLC), and other proprietary protocols such as SDLC.

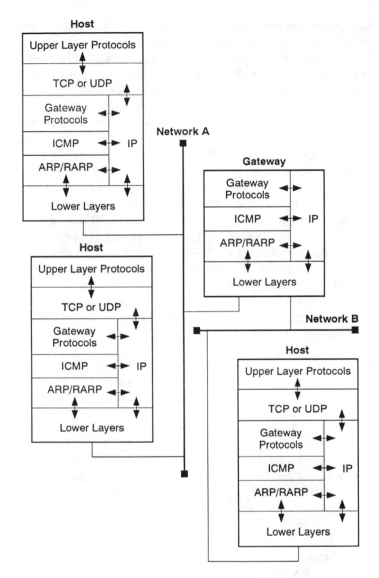

Figure 3.11 Major components of the Internet TCP/IP suite.

The Internet Protocol

The next layer in the internet suite consists principally of the Internet Protocol (IP), which is a routing and gateway protocol. This means that its principal concern is the relaying of traffic between machines.

IP is connectionless service protocol. It permits the exchange of traffic (datagrams) between machines without any prior call setup. Since the IP is a connectionless protocol, it is possible that the datagrams could be lost between the two end users' stations. For example, the IP gateway enforces a maximum queue length size, and if this queue length is violated, the buffers will overflow. In this situation, the additional datagrams are discarded in the network. For this reason, a higher-level transport layer is needed to recover from discarded data.

IP hides the underlying subnetwork from the end user. This aspect of IP is quite attractive because it allows different types of networks to attach to an IP gateway. As a result, IP is reasonably simple to install, and because of its datagram design, it is quite robust.

Since IP is an unreliable, best-effort datagram-type protocol, it has no reliability mechanisms. It provides no error recovery for the underlying subnetworks. It has no flow-control mechanisms. The user data (datagrams) may be lost, duplicated, or even arrive out of order. It is not the job of IP to deal with most of these problems. As we shall see later, most of the problems are passed to the next higher layer, the Transmission Control Protocol (TCP).

IP supports fragmentation operations. The term *fragmentation* refers to an operation wherein a PDU is divided or segmented into smaller pieces. This feature can be quite useful because networks do not use the same size PDU.

Without the use of fragmentation, a gateway would have the task of trying to resolve incompatible PDU sizes between networks. IP solves the problem by establishing the rules for fragmentation at the gateways and reassembly at the receiving host.

IP uses a mechanism called *source routing* as part of its routing algorithm. Source routing allows an upper-layer protocol (ULP) to determine how the IP gateways route the datagrams. The ULP has the option of passing a list of Internet addresses to the IP module. The list contains the intermediate gateways that are to be transmitted during the routing of the datagrams to the final destination. The last address on the list is the final destination.

When IP receives a datagram, it uses the addresses in the source routing field to determine the next intermediate hop. If the hop does not equal the IP module's address, the module places the next address in the route data field into the destination address field of the IP header.

The IP module then replaces the value in the source list with its own address. This address is the address known to the environment which is next receiving the datagram. Of course, it must then increment the pointer by 1 in order for the next hop to retrieve the next IP address in the route. With this approach, the datagram follows the source route dictated by the ULP and also records the route along the way. A recording is also made on the inverse path of the route.

The IP gateway makes routing decisions based on the routing list. If the destination host resides in another network, the IP gateway must decide how to route to the other network. Indeed, if multiple hops are involved in the communications process, each gateway must be traversed and the gateway must make decisions about the routing.

Each gateway maintains a routing table that contains the next gateway to the final destination network. In effect, the table contains an entry for each reachable network. These tables could be static or dynamic, although dynamic tables are stipulated in the IP standards.

The routing table contains a network number for each reachable network and the address of a neighbor gateway (that is to say, a gateway directly attached to this network). The neighbor gateway is the shortest route to the destination network. Otherwise, the IP gateway logic establishes that the gateway is directly connected to this network.

The IP routing is based on a concept called the *distance metric*. This value is really nothing more than the least number of hops between the gateway and the final destination. The gateway consults its routing table and attempts to match the destination network address contained in the IP header with a network entry contained in the routing table. If no match is found, it discards the datagram and builds an Internet Control Message Protocol (ICMP) message to send back to the IP source. This message would contain a "destination unreachable" code. If a match is found in the routing table, the gateway then uses the network address of the neighbor gateway and places this in the *local* network destination address of the datagram. If, however, the final destination is directly connected to the gateway, the destination address in the local network header is the same as the destination address in the IP header.

Companion standards to IP

Figure 3.11 also shows that there are other protocols that are considered companions to or supporters of IP. This example shows (1) gateway protocols, (2) ICMP, and (3) Address Resolution Protocol/Reverse Address Resolution Protocol ARP/RARP. A brief discussion of these protocols follows.

IP does not participate in the discovery of routes or in building routing tables. It uses the tables that are provided by the gateway protocols. These protocols are responsible for having a knowledge of the topology of a network or an internet and exchanging routing information with gateways and hosts. The gateway protocols encompass widely used standards such as the routing information protocol (RIP), external gateway protocol (EGP), and, more recently, the open shortest path first protocol (OSPF). The ICMP is also a companion protocol to that of IP. Its principal job is to provide error reports and status information between the gateways and hosts. It does not correct errors, nor does it recover from lost traffic. Its principal job is to report on problems or unusual conditions encountered by the IP module.

The ARP/RARPs provide address resolution (as their name implies) between the physical medium access control (MAC) address and IP addresses. The principal job of ARP is to obtain a MAC physical level address from an IP address. This entails a gateway or host broadcasting an ARP message to stations on the network. The message contains a destination IP address. In effect the message says "Here is an IP address. Will the station that owns this IP address please respond with its physical level MAC address?" Ideally, only one station responds with the MAC address. This response allows the inquiring station to store this address in RAM. Thereafter, it need not send broadcasts. It need only perform a table look up to match the destination IP address with the recently discovered MAC address, and then it uses the MAC address and the local area network (LAN) frame for each transmission.

RARP is used less often. Its job is just the opposite of ARP. It is used to obtain a IP address from a MAC address. This situation might occur with certain stations that have no disks. It is somewhat of a bootstrap operation.

The Transmission Control Protocol and the User Datagram Protocol

Figure 3.11 shows either the Transmission Control Protocol (TCP) or the user datagram protocol (UDP) resting above IP. The TCP protocol is a connection-oriented protocol that provides considerable integrity to an internet. One of its main jobs is to recover from traffic that may have been discarded by the connectionless-type protocol IP. However, it is possible to contain connectionless service at this level by invoking an UDP. Both these protocols are considered to be transport layer protocols. Their optional use gives a designer considerable flexibility on how to configure an internet suite.

TCP provides the following services to the upper layers. This section describes each of the services.

- Connection-oriented data management
- Reliable data transfer operations
- Stream-oriented data transfer operations
- Push functions
- Resequencing

- Flow control (sliding windows)
- Multiplexing
- Full-duplex transmission
- Precedence and security

TCP is a *connection-oriented* protocol. This term refers to the fact that TCP maintains status and state information about each user data stream flowing into and out of the TCP module. The term used in this context also means TCP is responsible for the reliable transfer of the data across one network or multiple networks to a receiving user application (or the next ULP). TCP must ensure (as shown in Fig. 3.11) that the data are transmitted and received between the two hosts across the networks.

Since TCP is a connection-oriented protocol, it is responsible for the *reliable data transfer* of each of the characters passed to it from an upper layer (characters are also called *bytes* or *octets*; the term *octet* is used in TCP). Consequently, it uses sequence numbers and positive/negative acknowledgments.

A *sequence number* is assigned to each octet transmitted. The receiving TCP module uses a checksum routine to check the data for damage that may have occurred during the transmission process. If the data are acceptable, TCP returns a positive acknowledgment (ACK) to the sending TCP module. If the data are damaged, TCP discards the data and uses a sequence number to negatively acknowledge (NAK) the data. Like many other connection-oriented protocols, TCP uses timers to ensure that the lapse of time is not excessive before remedial measures are taken for either the retransmission of data at the transmitting site or the transmission of acknowledgments at the receiving site.

TCP receives the data from an ULP in a *stream-oriented* fashion. This operation is in contrast to other "block-oriented" protocols in the industry. Stream-oriented protocols are designed to send individual characters and *not* blocks, frames, datagrams, etc. The bytes are sent from an ULP on a stream basis, byte by byte. When they arrive at the TCP layer, the bytes are grouped into TCP *segments*. These segments are then passed to the IP (or another lower-layer protocol) for transmission to the next destination. The length of the segments is determined by TCP, although a system implementor could also determine how TCP makes this decision.

In consonance with the stream transfer capability, TCP also supports the concept of a *push* function. This operation is used when an application wants to make certain that all the data that it has passed to the lower-layer TCP has been transmitted. In so doing, it governs TCP's buffer management.

To obtain this function, the ULP sends a push primitive to TCP. The operation requires TCP to forward all the buffered traffic in the form of a segment or segments to the destination. As we shall see later, the TCP user can use a close connection operation to provide the push function as well.

In addition to using the sequence numbers for acknowledgment, TCP uses them to *resequence* the segments if they arrive at the final destination out of order. Because TCP rests upon a connectionless system, it is quite possible that duplicate datagrams could be created in an internet. TCP also eliminates duplicate segments.

The TCP module is also able to *flow control* the sender's data, which is very useful to prevent buffer overrun and a possible saturation of the receiving machine. The concept used with TCP is somewhat unusual among communications protocols. It is based on issuing a "window" value to the transmitter. The transmitter is allowed to transmit a specified number of bytes within this window, after which the window is closed and the transmitter must stop sending data.

TCP also has a very useful facility for *multiplexing* multiple user sessions within a single host computer onto the ULPs. As we shall see, this is accomplished through some rather simple naming conventions for ports and sockets in the TCP and IP modules.

TCP provides *full-duplex transmission* between two TCP entities. This permits simultaneous two-way transmission without having to wait for a turnaround signal, which is required in a half-duplex situation.

TCP also provides the user with the capability to specify levels of *security* and *precedence* (priority level) for the connection. Even though these features are not implemented on all TCP products, they are defined in the TCP standard.

The Internet upper layer protocols

Finally, the ULPs are considered to be application layer protocols (in relation to the OSI Model). Protocols such as the file transfer protocol (FTP), the simple mail transfer protocol (SMTP), and the TELENET protocol are used here for providing support for file transfer, mail transfer, and virtual terminals.

The Internet encapsulation and decapsulation operations

Figure 3.12 shows the encapsulation and decapsulation of Internet PDUs in a typical protocol stack that resides in a user host machine. The model is similar to OSI, but unlike the OSI Model, the Internet model does not contain session or presentation layers.

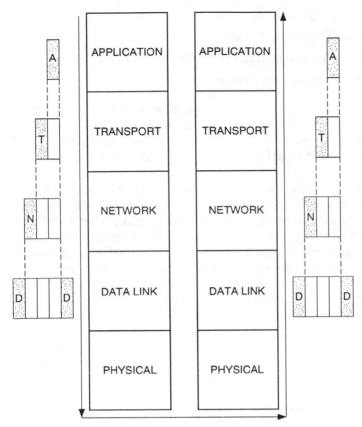

Figure 3.12 Encapsulation and decapsulation.

The IEEE 802 LAN/MAN Standards

As discussed earlier, the Institute of Electrical and Electronics Engineers (IEEE) publishes several widely-accepted LAN/MAN standards. They are organized as follows:

- IEEE 802.1   High Level Interface and Management (and MAC Bridges)
- IEEE 802.2   Logical Link Control (LLC)
- IEEE 802.3   Carrier Sense Multiple Access/Collision Detect (CSMA/CD)
- IEEE 802.4   Token Bus
- IEEE 802.5   Token Ring
- IEEE 802.6   Metropolitan Area Networks (MANs)

- IEEE 802.7   Broadband Networks
- IEEE 802.8   Fiber Optic Networks
- IEEE 802.9   Integrated Data and Voice Networks
- IEEE 802.10   Security and Privacy

The IEEE 802 layers are organized as shown in Fig. 3.13. These standards encompass only the physical and data link layers of a conventional layered model. Of course, other layers are stacked on top of these layers for added functionality, but they are not defined by the IEEE.

This figure is based on the IEEE 802 documents and should be considered as a conceptual model only. The reason for this statement is that the figure could imply (or the reader might infer) that 802.7 and 802.8 do not fit in the layers. They certainly fit in the physical layer and the MAC sublayer, but the IEEE rendition leaves them as shown in the figure. Furthermore, the 802.1 standards are quite far-reaching. They include the bridge standards, the network management standards, general statements on LANs/MANs, addressing, etc. Therefore, be aware that this figure is somewhat abstract and meant to convey a general view of the IEEE 802 architecture and not necessarily a view of how the layers actually interact (although it is close).

The IEEE efforts have emphasized the need to keep the OSI and 802 specifications as compatible as possible. The 802 committees split the data link layer into two sublayers: MAC and LLC. As illustrated in Fig. 3.13, MAC and the physical layer encompass 802.3, 802.4, 802.5,

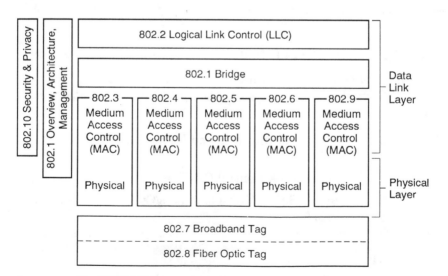

Figure 3.13   The IEEE 802 layers.

802.6, and 802.9. The LLC includes 802.2. This sublayer was implemented to make the LLC sublayer independent of a specific LAN access method. The LLC sublayer is also used to provide an interface into and out of the specific MAC protocol.

The MAC/LLC split provides several attractive features. First, it controls access to the shared channel among the autonomous user devices. Second, it provides for a decentralized (peer-to-peer) scheme that reduces the LAN's susceptibility to errors. Third, it provides a more compatible interface with wide-area networks (WANs), since LLC is a subset of the HDLC superset. Fourth, LLC is independent of a specific access method; MAC is protocol-specific. This approach gives an 802 network a flexible interface with workstations and other networks.

Connection options with LLC types 1, 2, and 3

At the onset of the IEEE 802 work, it was recognized that a connection-oriented system would limit the scope and power of a LAN. Consequently, two connectionless models are now specified, and the IEEE LAN/MAN management standards uses the connectionless options. The two options are:

- Unacknowledged connectionless model
- Acknowledged connectionless model

Let us consider the reason for this approach. First, many local applications do not need the data integrity provided by a connection-oriented network. As examples: (1) Sensor equipment can afford to lose occasional data since the sensor readings typically occur quite frequently, and the data loss does not adversely affect the information content. (2) Inquiry-response systems, such as point of sale, usually perform acknowledgment at the application level. These systems do not need connection-oriented services at the lower levels. (3) Packetized voice can tolerate some packet loss without affecting the quality of the voice reproduction.

Second, high-speed application processes cannot tolerate the overhead in establishing and disestablishing the connections. The problem is particularly severe in the LAN, with its high-speed channels and low error rates. Many LAN applications require fast setups with each other. Others require very fast communications between the DTEs.

An acknowledged connectionless service is useful for a number of reasons. Consider the operations of a LAN in a commercial bank. A data link protocol usually maintains state tables, sequence numbers, and windows for each station on the link. It would be impractical to provide this service for every station on the bank's local network. Yet, workstations like the bank's automated teller machines (ATMs) require that they be polled for their transactions. The host computer must also be assured that all transactions are sent and received without errors. The data is too important to use a protocol that does not provide acknowledgments. Additionally, the bank's alarm system needs some type of acknowledgment to assure that the computer receives notice of security breaches in the bank. It is too time-consuming to establish a "connection" before sending the alarm data.

Classes of service

The 802 LAN standards include four types of service for LLC users:

Type 1   Unacknowledged connectionless service

Type 2   Connection-mode service

Type 3   Acknowledged connectionless service

Type 4   All of the above services

All 802 networks must provide unacknowledged connectionless service (Type 1). Optionally, connection-oriented service can be provided (Type 2). Type 1 networks provide no ACKs, flow control, or error recovery; Type 2 networks provide connection management, ACKs, flow control, and error recovery. Type 3 networks provide no connection setup or disconnect, but they do provide for immediate acknowledgment of data units. Most Type 1 networks use a higher-level protocol (i.e., transport layer) to provide connection management functions.

Summary

The OSI network management standards make extensive use of the other OSI standards. They are not intended to function without the use of several of the ASEs that reside in the applications layer. They are also dependent upon the services of the presentation and session layers.

The Internet network management standards also rely on other Internet protocols. The Internet protocol Simple Network Management Protocol (SNMP) is designed to rest on top of TCP or UDP, which invokes IP. IP, in turn, invokes a variety of lower-layer protocols.

The IEE LAN/MAN standards use the LLC, MAC, and physical layers to relay network management information between LAN or MAN stations. These standards can operate with or without CMIP. Although not defined in the standard, SNMP is implemented in many LAN systems.

4

Supporting
Upper Layer Protocols
for OSI Network Management

Introduction

It is not the intent of this chapter to present an in-depth tutorial on OSI upper layer protocols. However, in order to gain a full understanding of how OSI network management standards operate, it is necessary to have a general understanding of the major operations of the presentation and session layers and several entities in the application layer. Indeed, OSI network management relies heavily on the services of these upper-layer protocols. Moreover, it is almost impossible to understand the OSI network management documents if the reader does not have some knowledge of the presentation layer. Furthermore, the Internet and IEEE standards make use of some of the OSI presentation layer conventions.

We begin our discussion with the presentation layer, since it is adjacent to the application layer in a typical protocol stack and must be understood before the application layer entities can be analyzed. After the discussion of the presentation layer, we will review the session layer. Then, the key application layer protocols will be examined.

The Presentation Layer

Introduction

To understand the value of the presentation layer, the ideas of Fig. 1.3 are presented again in Fig. 4.1. Recall that one of the major goals of standardized network management is to adapt a common convention for the exchange of messages between agents (in this figure, agents

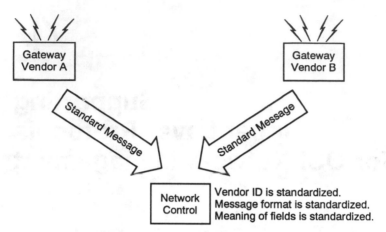

Figure 4.1 Presentation layer operations.

residing in gateways) and a managing process (in this figure, network control).

The presentation layer performs the services associated with the message data structure description and representation. It is not concerned with the meaning (that is, the semantics) of the data, but it is concerned with (1) how the type of data is identified and (2) how the bits are arranged within a data field [that is, the syntax (Webster's second definition of syntax)]. With the aid of the presentation layer, the network control center can decode the messages from vendor A and vendor B with relative ease because the messages and related protocols are standardized.

The presentation layer can accept various data types from a user application (such as integer, ASCII strings, boolean, etc.) and, if necessary, negotiate with another presentation layer on how the data will be represented during the communications process. In performing these services, the two presentation layers are concerned with (1) the syntax of the data of the sending application, (2) the syntax of the data of the receiving application, and (3) the syntax used between the presentation entities that support the sending and receiving applications.

The latter service is called a *transfer syntax*. It is negotiated between the presentation entities. Each presentation entity chooses a syntax that is best for it to use in view of the user's syntax. It then attempts to negotiate the use of this syntax with the other presentation layer entity. Therefore, the two presentation entities must agree on a transfer syntax before data can be exchanged. Moreover, it may be necessary for the presentation layer to transform the data (change the syntax) in order for the users to communicate with each other.

ASN.1 and the transfer syntax

The ISO and CCITT have developed a presentation and transfer syntax to be used by application layer protocols (which includes the OSI network management standards). The ISO standard is ISO 8824, which is titled Abstract Syntax Notation 1 (ASN.1). In addition, ISO 8825 [with the Basic Encoding Rules (BER)] provides a set of rules to develop an unambiguous, bit-level description of data. That is to say, it specifies the representation of the data during the communications transfer process. In summary, ASN.1 describes an abstract syntax for data types and values, and BER describes the actual representation of the data.

Be aware that ASN.1 is not an abstract syntax unto itself but a language for describing abstract syntaxes. Some people use the term *ASN.1* to include an abstract syntax and the basic encoding rules for a transfer syntax. However, we shall see that the two are different from each other.

As a final point to this introduction, it is noteworthy to state that ASN.1 is used only in the upper three layers of the OSI Model, but it need not be restricted to these layers. It can be used at the lower layers as well, but it is unlikely that the current standards will be reissued to accommodate ASN.1. Notwithstanding, OSI now describes all data units in the upper layers in abstract syntax, and the Internet documents also use ASN.1-type notations.

Overview of ASN.1

Each piece of information exchanged between OSI users has a *type* and a *value*. The type is a class of information, such as integer, boolean, octet, etc. A type can be used to describe a collection or group of values. For example, the type integer describes all values that are whole (nondecimal) numbers. The term *data type* is a synonym for type.

The value is an instance of the type, such as a number or a piece of alphabetic text. For example, if we describe "P of type integer," and "P = 9," it means this instance of P has a value of 9. In an OSI message, for example, the fields can be defined as an integer or bit string type with an instance (or value).

In order for machines to know how to interpret data, they must first know the type of the data (values) to be processed. Therefore, the concept of type is very important to the presentation layer services.

The standards define several *built-in types,* which are summarized in Table 4.1. Built-in types are commonly used types.

Another important feature of these standards is the use of *tags.* To

TABLE 4.1   Built-In Types

Type	Function
Boolean	Identifies logical data (true or false conditions).
Integer	Identifies signed whole numbers (cardinal numbers).
Bit string	Identifies binary data (ordered sequence of 1s and 0s).
Octet string	Identifies text or data that can be described as a sequence of octets (bytes).
Null	A simple type consists of a single value. It could be a valueless placeholder in which there are several alternatives but none of them apply. A null field with no value does not have to be transmitted.
Sequence	A structured type is defined by referencing an ordered list of various types.
Sequence of	A structured type is defined by referencing a single type. Each value in the type is an ordered list (if a list exists). It can be used as a method of building arrays of a single type.
Set	A structured type is similar to the sequence type except that set is defined by referencing an unordered list of types and allows data to be sent in any order.
Set of	A structured type is similar to the sequence type except that set of is defined by referencing a single type and each value in the type is an unordered list (if a list exists).
Choice	Models a data type chosen from a collection of alternative types and allows a data structure to hold more that one type.
Selection	Models a variable whose type is that of some alternatives of a previously defined choice.
Tagged	Models a new type from an existing type but with a different identifier.
Any	Models data whose type is unrestricted. It can be used with any valid type.
Object identifier	A distinguishable value associated with an object, or a group of objects, like a library of rules, syntaxes, etc.
Character string	Models strings of characters for some defined character set.
Enumerated	A simple type, its values are given distinct identifiers as part of the type notation.
Real	Models real values (for example: $M \times B^e$, where M = the mantissa, B = the base, and e = the exponent).
Encrypted	A type whose value is a result of encrypting another type.

distinguish the different types, a structure of values (for example, a database record) or a simple element (for example, a field within the database record) can have a tag attached that identifies the type. For example, a tag for an OSI network management alarm message could be PRIVATE 22. This is used to identify the record and inform the receiver about the nature of its contents. ASN.1 provides a tag for every type.

ASN.1 defines four classes of *types*. Each tag is identified by its class and its number (as in our example PRIVATE 22). The type classes are defined as:

- *Universal:*   Application-independent types

- *Application-wide:*   Types that are specific to an application and used in other standards [OSI, X.400 Message Handling System (MHS), file transfer and access management (FTAM), etc.]

- *Context-specific:*   Types that are specific to an application and are limited to a set within an application

- *Private-use:*   Reserved for private use and not defined in these standards

Several tags are used for the universal assignment. Remember, the tag is used to identify a class. The tag has two parts, a *class identifier* and a *number*. Table 4.2 shows the universal class tag assignments.

TABLE 4.2   Universal Class Tag Assignments

UNIVERSAL 1	BOOLEAN
UNIVERSAL 2	INTEGER
UNIVERSAL 3	BITSTRING
UNIVERSAL 4	OCTETSTRING
UNIVERSAL 5	NULL
UNIVERSAL 6	OBJECT IDENTIFIER
UNIVERSAL 7	Object description
UNIVERSAL 8	EXTERNAL
UNIVERSAL 9	REAL
UNIVERSAL 10	ENUMERATED
UNIVERSAL 11	ENCRYPTED
UNIVERSAL 12-15	Reserved for future use
UNIVERSAL 16	SEQUENCE and SEQUENCE OF
UNIVERSAL 17	SET and SET OF
UNIVERSAL 18	NumericString
UNIVERSAL 19	PrintableString
UNIVERSAL 20	TeletexString
UNIVERSAL 21	VideotexString
UNIVERSAL 22	IA5String
UNIVERSAL 23	UTCTime
UNIVERSAL 24	GeneralizedTime
UNIVERSAL 25	GraphicString
UNIVERSAL 26	VisibleString
UNIVERSAL 27	GeneralString
UNIVERSAL 28	CharacterString
UNIVERSAL 29 +	Reserved for additions

ASN.1 rules

ASN.1 imposes a set of rules for the programmer. They are simple but quite important. The rules relevant to our discussion are summarized below:

- Several built-in types are included in the standard.

- Names of all types must begin with an uppercase letter.

- Reserved words are all uppercase and have special meaning within the standard.

- Certain names must begin with a lowercase letter. These names are inserted to assist a person in understanding the use of the ASN.1 notation. They have no effect on any further coding.

ASN.1 notation symbols.   The pair of angle brackets (< >) is a notation as a placeholder for an actual item such as type name, module name, a type definition, or a module body. The :: = means "defined as."

The following notation describes the rules for representing a *module* (which is one of several ASN.1 forms we will examine in this chapter).

```
< module name >  DEFINITIONS :: =  BEGIN
< module body >  END
```

The module name identifies the module. It is an ASN.1 identifier. The DEFINITIONS indicate the module is defined as the ASN.1 definitions that are placed between the BEGIN and END words. In other words, a module contains other ASN.1 definitions.

Within the modules are definitions of types. They have the following form:

```
< type name >  :: =  < type definition >
```

This notation is an example of a *simple type*. It is so named because it directly specifies the set of its values. The type name is the identifier of the type. The type definition describes the class and several other attributes which will be explained shortly.

The next example shows how three type definitions are coded within a module:

```
< module name >  DEFINITIONS :: = BEGIN
        < type name >  :: =  < type definition >
        < type name >  :: =  < type definition >
        < type name >  :: =  < type definition >
END
```

This example is called a *structured type*. It contains a reference to one or more other types. The types within the structured type are called *component types*.

Summary of ASN.1 structure

Figure 4.2 summarizes the major aspects of ASN.1. The ASN.1 tags are categorized by four classes; each class is assigned a number. The four classes can be coded with a *simple* structure (a coding in which the type does not include other types) or a *more complex* (a coding that includes other types) structure. The *other* category is not defined in the standard.

Examples of OSI network management ASN.1 coding

A few simple examples should help us in tying together some of the pieces of information about ASN.1. The examples use ISO 9596 Common Management Information Protocol, or (CMIP). This standard is examined in considerable detail in Chap. 6. However, our examples do not require the reader to know CMIP. Other examples of ASN.1 usage with OSI, Internet, and IEEE network management are used throughout the remainder of this book.

Figure 4.3 shows an example of the definition of a base managed object (explained in Chap. 1). Please examine the coding in Fig. 4.3 that is enclosed with the square bracket and numbered 1. BaseManagedObject is defined as a SEQUENCE type, which is an or-

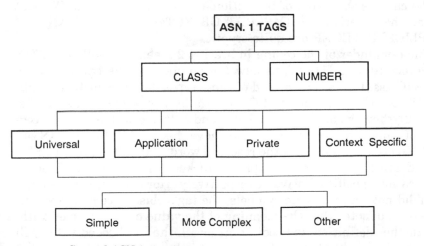

Figure 4.2 General ASN.1 structure.

```
┌ BaseManagedObject ::= SEQUENCE {
1 │    baseManagedObjectClass          ObjectClass,
  └    baseManagedObjectInstance       ObjectInstance }
```

```
┌ ObjectClass ::= CHOICE {
2 │    globalFormnon               [0] IMPLICIT OBJECT IDENTIFIER,
  └    nonSpecificForm             [1] IMPLICIT INTEGER }
```

```
┌ ObjectInstance ::= CHOICE {
  │    distinguishedName           [2] IMPLICIT DistinguishedName,
3 │    nonSpecificForm             [3] IMPLICIT OCTET STRING,
  └    enumerateForm               [4] IMPLICIT INTEGER }
```

Figure 4.3   Defining the base managed object.

dered list of types. These types are defined inside the curly brackets as ObjectClass and ObjectInstance. Notice that ObjectClass and ObjectInstance are assigned the names baseManagedObjectClass and baseManagedObjectInstance, respectively. These names are inserted for the convenience of the reader. They have no effect on the coding of the value of the type and must begin with a lowercase letter.

The type name ObjectClass is defined further in the part of Fig. 4.3 labeled 2. It is defined as a CHOICE. This notation means that the value of a CHOICE type must be only one of the alternatives inside the curly brackets. In this example it must be one of the types identified with the optional names of globalForm or nonSpecificForm. Also, as Table 4.2 indicates, CHOICE has no tag. Therefore, every element in a choice module must be tagged.

We can see the value of the optional names in bracket 2. Without them, the notations [0] IMPLICIT OBJECT IDENTIFIER AND [1] IMPLICIT INTEGER are quite cryptic.

The remainder of the coding in bracket 2 means the following. The notations [0] and [1] assigns new tag numbers to the two choices of ObjectClass. Hereafter, instead of these types being identified as OBJECT IDENTIFIER and INTEGER with the values of 6 and 2 (see Table 4.2), they are now identified as 0 and 1. It is possible that the coding of these tagged types could have been [APPLICATION 4], [PRIVATE 6], and so on. If the reserved words APPLICATION or PRIVATE are included in the square brackets, the type is defined as application-specific or private, respectively. However, since the notation did not contain these symbols, the tag's class is context-specific. The term denotes that the meaning of the value can be derived without further definition and coding. After all, the final coded value will be tagged as either 0 or 1. Therefore, it is known from the context of the tag what type is used.

The IMPLICIT notation is optional but quite useful. If it is present, the original tag's value will not appear in the encoded value. If it is not present, both tags are present in the encoded value, which of course requires extra bits to represent the redundant information.

The OBJECT IDENTIFIER type in bracket 2 is a value distinguishable from all other such values and is used to unambiguously identify any object. Typically, it is used to assign a unique identifier to something such as a protocol data unit (PDU), file, module in a library, etc. It is used extensively by the ISO and Internet in their naming conventions (see Chap. 1). The tag of [0] serves to identify the specifics of the object identifier.

The ObjectInstance type is defined further in bracket 3 of Fig. 4.3. The only new notation in this coding is DistinguishedName. Recall from Chap. 1 that OSI network management uses a distinguished name for the unambiguous identification of an object throughout the management information tree (MIT).

To obtain more information about the distinguished name, the reader of CMIP must refer to another part of the CMIP ASN.1 definitions. Figure 4.4 is an example of the CMIP code that defines the distinguished name. Well, it does and it doesn't. Notice that the coding uses the IMPORTS reserved word. This feature of ASN.1 is used to list the types that are defined elsewhere and referenced in this definition. It is very useful in that it obviates coding the type twice. However, the reader must then obtain the document (or computer printout) that describes the definition of distinguished name (which we shall do next).

The coding in the top box in Fig. 4.4 uses the CCITT and ISO naming convention to identify the object as joint-iso-ccitt ds(5) modules(1) information-framework(1). This notation can be traced down the tree to the leaf entry to yield the distinguished name value of 2511.

Figure 4.5 provides an example of the OSI Directory tree (introduced in Chap. 1) and how ASN.1 is used to describe the Directory entries. We use this figure to extend the discussion of distinguished names. The distinguished name is a sequence of relative distinguished names, which is a SET OF AttributeValueAssertion. The SET OF is similar to SEQUENCE except the elements in SET OF do not have to be in order, as they must be in SEQUENCE.

Finally, the attribute type and value are defined as OBJECT IDENTIFIER and ANY DEFINED BY types. This latter type is also coded as simply ANY and is used when the type does not have to be specified; in other words, any ASN.1 defined type can be used. The ANY type is quite general, and not used in some OSI standards, although OSI network management makes rather extensive use of it.

The generality of ANY bothered some people, so the ASN.1 standard was amended to permit an ANY DEFINED BY. This notation

--Directory Service Definition

IMPORTS DistinguishedName FROM Information-Framework

{ joint-iso-ccitt ds(5) modules (1) information-framework (1) }

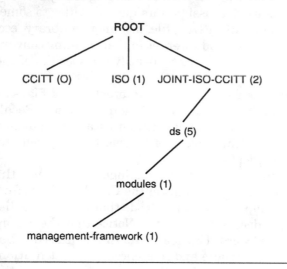

Therefore, abstract syntax name =
joint-iso-ccitt 2 ds 5 modules 1 management-framework 1

or: 2 5 1 1

Figure 4.4   Use of the IMPORTS statement.

uses <name> to identify a required element of the SEQUENCE to provide information about what type the ANY may assume. In Fig. 4.5, the ANY DEFINED BY really means OBJECT IDENTIFIER because the <name> is replaced by attributeType, which is an OBJECT IDENTIFIER. To be sure, it is a circuitous way to define a type.

This brief discourse on ASN.1 and some of the OSI network management definitions is sufficient for the present. Additional ASN.1 rules will be explained when they are encountered in the context of the discussions on OSI network management.

Basic Encoding Rules

X.209 and ISO 8825 describe the encoding rules for the types and their values in contrast to X.208 and ISO 8824, which are concerned with

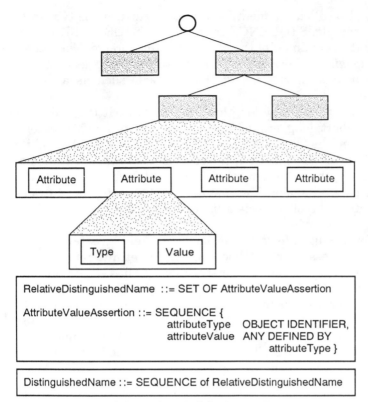

RelativeDistinguishedName ::= SET OF AttributeValueAssertion

AttributeValueAssertion ::= SEQUENCE {
                    attributeType   OBJECT IDENTIFIER,
                    attributeValue   ANY DEFINED BY
                                              attributeType }

DistinguishedName ::= SEQUENCE of RelativeDistinguishedName

Figure 4.5 Using ASN.1 to identify directory entries.

the abstract description of objects. These BER provide the conventions for the transfer syntax conventions.

The rules require that each type be described by a well-formed, specific representation. This representation is called a *data element* (or just an *element*). As shown in Fig. 4.6, it consists of three components, type, length, and value (TLV), which appear in the following order:

Type Length Value

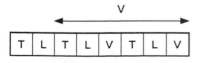

Where:
T = Type (identifier)
L = Length
V = Value (contents)

Figure 4.6 BER format for the transfer element.

The *type* is also called the identifier. It distinguishes one type from another (for example, SEQUENCE from OBJECT IDENTIFIER) and specifies how the remainder of the element is interpreted. The length specifies the *length* of the value. The *value* (also known as contents) contains the actual information of the element, such as a distinguished name.

The length (L) specifies the length of the contents. It may take one of three forms: short, long, or indefinite. The short form is 1 octet long and is used when L is less than 128 octets. Bit 8 is always 0, and bits 7 through 1 indicate the length of the contents. The length value defines only the length of the contents (value) and does not include the octets that comprise the identifier and the length octets. As an example, a contents field of 22 octets is described in the L field as 00010110_2.

The long form is used for a longer contents field: greater than or equal to 128 and less than 2^{1008} octets. The indefinite form can be used when the element is a constructor. It has the value of 1000000_2, or 80_{16}. For the indefinite form, a special end-of-contents (EOC) element terminates the contents. The representation of EOC is 00000000_{16}.

The contents (value) is the actual information of the element. It is described in multiples of 8 bits and is of variable length. The contents are interpreted based on the coding of the identifier (type) field. Therefore, the contents are interpreted as bit strings, octet strings, etc.

As shown in Fig. 4.6, the transfer element can consist of a single TLV or a series of data elements, described as multiple TLVs. This example shows that such a construction includes one T and one L field to define the complete protocol data unit, followed by as many TLV fields as is necessary to encode the data.

The element consists of an integral number of n octets, written with the most significant bit (MSB), 8, on the left and the least significant bit (LSB), 1, on the right:

Bit Position → 8 7 6 5 4 3 2 1
Data Bits →   X X X X X X X X

Class		P/C	Tag Number				
8	7	6	5	4	3	2	1

Figure 4.7 The type and identifier format.

Note: For tag numbers greater than 30, identifier is coded with extension octets

The single-octet type or identifier is coded as shown in Fig. 4.7. Bits 8 and 7 identify the four type *classes* with the following bit assignments:

Universal	00
Application-wide	01
Context-specific	10
Private-use	11

Bit 6 identifies the *form* of the data element. Two forms are possible. A *primitive* element (bit 6 = 0) has no further internal structure of data elements. A *constructor* element (bit 6 = 1) is recursively defined in that it contains a series of data elements. For example, it can contain a "complex" series that is defined as SEQUENCE.

The remaining 5 bits (5 through 1) distinguish one data type from another of the same class by the use of a *tag number*. For example, the field may distinguish boolean from integer types (see Table 4.2). If the system requires more than 5 bits (a tag number greater than 30), bits 5 through 1 of the first octet are coded as 11111_2 and bit 8 of the subsequent octets are coded with a 1 to indicate more octets follow and with a 0 to indicate it is the last octet.

Relationship of ASN.1 to the BER.   To the uninitiated reader, the relationship of ASN.1 to BER is probably far from obvious. Therefore, this section provides a tutorial on how the ASN.1 definitions are used to specify the rules of how the data elements are encoded (to the bit level) for transmission across the communications channel.

Figure 4.8 shows that several ASN.1 definitions are applied to the BER type-length-value structure. To facilitate the analysis, the figure is divided into three boxes. At the top of each box is the relevant ASN.1 code used to encode the bit stream for transmission across the communications channel. The subsequent entries in each box show how the BER standard uses the ASN.1 notations to encode the protocol data unit for transmission. The reader should relate this picture to the ASN.1 code in Fig. 4.3.

Figure 4.9 continues the analysis to a finer level of detail. We have disposed with the ASN.1 notations and have added the hexadecimal equivalents to the 4-bit "nibbles" of each 8-bit octet. The reader may find this figure helpful because a number of documents and vendors' specifications use the hexadecimal notations.

Finally, Fig. 4.10 shows an even finer level of detail in this analysis. The top part of the figure shows the bits and their symbolic hexadec-

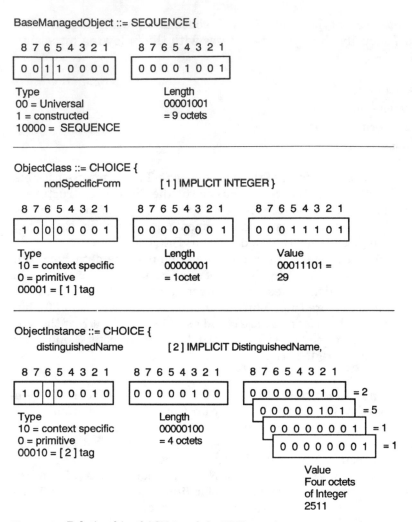

Figure 4.8 Relationship of ASN.1 and the TLV notations.

imal identifiers that are transmitted across the communications channel. The bottom part of the figure shows the actual bits that are sent across the channel. Of course, these bits represent physical signal states. For example, the binary 0 may be encoded by the modem or line driver as a positive voltage and the binary 1 may be encoded as a negative voltage.

Figure 4.11 illustrates the encoded bits for a digital channel transmission. The scheme uses a positive voltage for binary 0s and a negative voltage for binary 1s. The voltage level returns to zero voltage in between successive signals. Of course, a presentation layer protocol is

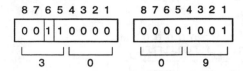

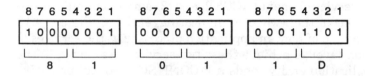

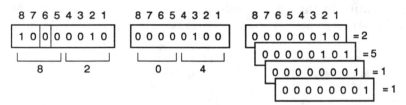

Figure 4.9   Hexadecimal and binary equivalents from Fig. 4.8.

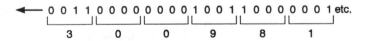

The bits that are transmitted
across the communications channel:

◄——— 0 0 1 1 0 0 0 0 0 0 0 0 1 0 0 1 1 0 0 0 0 0 0 1 etc.

Figure 4.10   The bits transmitted across the communications channel.

not concerned with physical signaling, but its coding decisions ulti-
mately determine what is sent on the physical medium.

Example of syntax negotiation

We mentioned earlier in this discussion that OSI network management relies on the presentation layer for two critical operations: (1) a

The bits that are transmitted
across the communications channel:

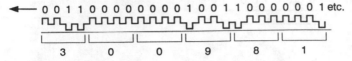

Figure 4.11   A digital signal on the channel.

abstract syntax agreement between the OSI network management entities [or its application service element (ASE) service provider, association control service element (ACSE)], and (2) agreement on a transfer syntax between the two communicating entities. Figure 4.12
provides an example of how an application process uses the services of
the presentation layer to achieve these two services. As shown in the
figure, the application entity sends a P-CONNECT request primitive
to the presentation layer. Some of the parameters in this primitive
contain the abstract syntax identifications (ABSYNA, ABSYNB). The
presentation entity receives this information and decides if it can support these syntaxes with the use of a transfer syntax. It then encodes
a connection request presentation PDU (CA PPDU) to send to the presentation entity in the other machine. Included in the PDU are the
proposed abstract syntaxes (ABSYNA, AYSYNB) as well as the pro-

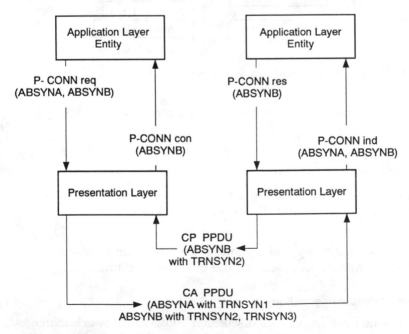

Figure 4.12   Negotiating presentation contexts.

posed transfer syntax(es) (TRNSYN1, TRNSYN2, TRNSYN3) it is able to support, for each abstract syntax presented to it from the user application entity.

In actual situations, it is unlikely that more than one transfer syntax would be proposed, but it is conceivable that a machine might offer more than one. For example, X.209 and the External Data Representation protocol (XDR) might be supported by a computer.

The receiving presentation entity receives the PDU. It then issues a P-CONNECT indication primitive to its application layer. Although not shown in Fig. 4.12, the ACSE acts as the agent for the OSI ASE. The proposed syntaxes to be used during the communications process are in this primitive.

As we see in the figure, the application entity sends back a P-CONNECT response primitive. This primitive contains the names of the abstract syntaxes it is able to use during the process (only ABSYNB). It cannot negotiate new abstract syntaxes at this time. It must use at least one of the abstract syntaxes it received in the P-CONNECT response primitive or refuse the connection. Of course, it can use them all if it wishes.

The remote presentation entity receives this primitive and maps a PDU from the parameters. As shown in the figure, it indicates in the PDU the transfer syntax that is to be used during the communications process (ABSYNB with TRNSYN2).

Finally, the local presentation entity receives the PDU and examines the proposed transfer syntax. If it accepts the proposals, it maps these fields to the P-CONNECT confirm primitive and sends it to the local application entity.

In summary, these operations resulted in the negotiation of the abstract syntax and the transfer syntax between the pair of communication entities. The final negotiated agreement is called a *presentation context*. Furthermore, the current presentation context containing the specific abstract syntaxes and transfer syntaxes is called the *defined context set*.

Figure 4.13 also shows other terms that are used in the standards for the description of these operations.

Use of templates in OSI network management

In an effort to simplify (and make less rigorous) some shorthand notations for network management macros, PDUs, etc., the concept of templates was devised. Templates can be translated into ASN.1 macro notations and they serve a very useful function with the OBJECT

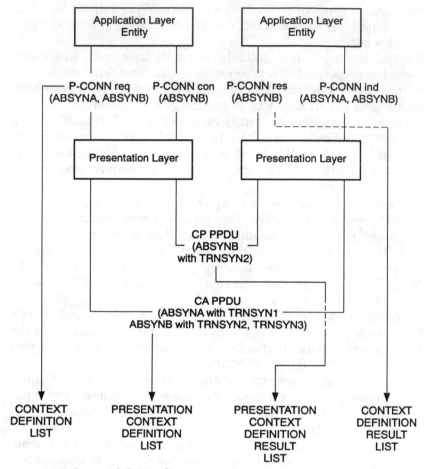

Figure 4.13 Context definition lists.

IDENTIFIER (at the bottom of the template, see Fig. 4.14). It is used with the ISO/CCITT registration authority hierarchy to identify the organization responsible for the registration of the object.

The coding scheme for a template is shown in Fig. 4.14. It is quite similar to conventional ASN.1 coding but uses slightly different rules:

```
<template-label>          TEMPLATE NAME
      ELEMENT NAME1 [<element-definition>]
      ELEMENT NAMEn [<element-definition>]
   REGISTERED AS <OBJECT-IDENTIFIER>
```

Figure 4.14 The template format.

- Brackets ([]) delimit parts of the template that may or may not be present. Strings reside inside the brackets. If the close bracket is followed by an asterisk, the contents within the brackets may appear more than one time. The template type governs whether the parts within the brackets may be omitted.

- The placement values < > identify strings within them that must be replaced with each instance, that is to say, each time the template is used. Again, the meaning of the replacement and the structure depend on what is inside the brackets.

- Uppercase notations identify key words. Key words are required at each instance of the template use. The exception to this rule is if the key words are enclosed in braces ({}).

- The labels for templates must be unique within the OSI network management standard or, for that matter, any other standard in which they are used. As noted in our example, the last coding line of the template has a reserved word REGISTERED AS followed by OBJECT IDENTIFIER.

This last line in the template is used to identify the template with the sponsoring standard organization. As an example, the <OBJECT IDENTIFIER > for an OSI network management PDU could be replaced by:

{ISO STANDARD(0) IPS-OSI-MIPS(9596) CMIP(2) VERSION(1) EXPANDED(2) INVOKEPDU(12) CREATE(8)}

The hierarchical classification scheme, used in conjunction with the templates, provides a very valuable tool of the management of OSI resources. Later chapters show the use of ASN.1 coding as well as templates in OSI network management (as well as the Internet and IEEE standards).

The Session Layer

CCITT X.215 and X.225 define the service definitions and protocol specifications for the exchange of data between session layer users. The principal parts of X.215 describe how the users establish a session through the session layer, exchange and account for data through synchronization points, use tokens to negotiate several types of dialogues, and release the session. X.225 describes the functions and protocol data units of the session layer. The ISO publishes comparable standards as DIS 8326 and DIS 8327.

The session layer is so named because it manages the user application-to-application sessions. From the context of OSI network management, it assists the application layer service elements in their operations. From the view of the session layer, an upper-layer ASE is simply an "application."

The OSI session layer systems provide the following services:

- Coordinate the exchange of data between applications by logically connecting and releasing sessions (also called dialogues) between the applications.

- Provide synchronization points (called checkpoints in some vendors' literature) to structure the exchange of data.

- Impose a structure on the user application interactions.

- If necessary, provide a convention for users to take turns in exchanging data.

- Use a synchronization point to ensure all data units have been received by the applications before a session releases.

Major features of session layer services

Tokens. A key aspect to session level activities is the *token*. The token gives a user the exclusive right to use a service. It is dynamically assigned to one user at a time to permit the use of certain services. For example, a user can issue the Please token to another user to request the transfer of one or more tokens (that is to say, the use of a service or services). The relinquishing user may respond by passing back a Give token. If tokens are not available when the session is established between the session users, they remain unavailable for the session.

Tokens are not used for all session service functions but are invoked for four specific functions:

- Data exchange procedures
- Releasing certain user dialogues
- Supporting synchronization functions
- Supporting an activity across more than one synchronization function

Synchronization services. *Synchronization* (sync) points are another important part of the session layer. They are used to coordinate the exchange of data between session service users. Synchronization services are like checkpoints or restarts in a file transfer or transaction transfer operation. They allow the users to (1) define and isolate points in an ongoing data exchange and (2) if necessary, back up to a point for recovery purposes.

The session services do not actually save the session service data units (SSDUs) and do not perform the recovery operations. These activities are the responsibility of the application layer or the end-user application. The session layer merely decrements a number back to the sync point and the user must apply it to determine where to begin recovery procedures.

Two types of synchronization points are available, minor and major. As Fig. 4.15 illustrates, the sync points are used in conjunction with the following dialogue units and activities:

- *Major sync point:*   Structures the exchange of data into a series of dialogue units. Each major sync point must be confirmed and the user is limited to specific services until a confirmation is received. The sending user can send no more data until the receiving user acknowledges a major synchronization point. A major sync point allows related units of work to be clustered together.

- *Dialogue unit:*   An atomic action in which all communications within it are separated from any previous or succeeding communications. A major sync point delineates the beginning and ending of a dialogue unit.

- *Minor sync point:*   Structures the exchange of data within a dialogue unit. This is more flexible than a major sync point. For example, each sync point may or may not be confirmed, and it is possible to resynchronize to any minor sync point within the dialogue unit. A confirmation confirms all previous minor sync points.

- *Activity:*   Consists of one or more dialogue units. An activity is a logical set of related tasks, for example, the transfer of a file with related records. A useful feature of the dialogue unit is that it can be interrupted and later resumed. Each activity is completely independent of any other activity.

The OSI Model does not specify what types of applications are to be managed with synchronization points and dialogue units. An OSI network management function could be managed with each event from a

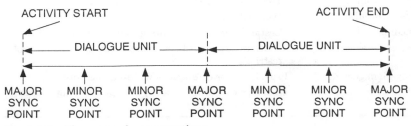

Figure 4.15   The session layer operations.

managed object considered as a dialogue unit. As another example, the completion of a *scoping operation* could be managed with the operation delineated with a major sync point.

Activity rules.   The session layer restricts a session connection to one activity at a time, but several consecutive activities can be invoked during the session connection. An activity can perform resynchronization because it can span more than one session connection. It can be interrupted and reinvoked during another session connection.

The use of activities infers a *quarantine* service capability. This term describes the process of accumulating SSDUs and releasing them only upon permission from the user. This service is not mentioned in the CCITT documents because it was realized that the activity management functions could be used to do quarantining. However, the ISO 7498 document does specify quarantine service.

Functional unit.   The *functional unit* concept is a key aspect of the session layer. It is used to define and group related services offered by the layer. Presently, the session layer provides 12 functional unit services. (Note: The kernel is actually not a functional unit but is so described to provide continuity to our analysis.) Table 4.3 briefly describes these units.

TABLE 4.3   Session Services (SS) Functional Units

Kernel	Provides five nonnegotiable services
Half-duplex	Alternate two-way transmission of data between SS users, data sent by owner of data token
Duplex	Simultaneous two-way transmission of data between SS users
Typed data	Transfer of data with no token restrictions
Exceptions	Reports of exceptional situations by either SS user or SS provider
Negotiated release	Releases a session through orderly (normal) measures or by passing tokens
Minor synchronize	Invokes a minor sync point
Major synchronize	Invokes a major sync point
Resynchronize	Reestablishes communications and reset connection
Expedited data	Transfers data that is free from token and flow control restrictions
Activity management	Provides several functions within an activity
Capability exchange	Exchanges a limited amount of data while not operating within an activity

Example of session layer operations

Figure 4.16 illustrates some of the major features of the session layer. The contents of the figure are largely self-explanatory, except for the last notation in the figure, "A 'special' data unit is sent to B." This operation allows a machine to send a small amount of data even though it does not have the token rights. This feature could be quite

Figure 4.16   Major features of session layer.

important for network management, for example, if a station needs to send an unsolicited alarm message.

Contribution of the Application Layer to OSI Network Management

The remainder of this chapter is devoted to an examination of the support the OSI network management standards receive from ASEs residing in the application layer. Emphasis is placed on the following protocols:

- Association control service element (ACSE)
- Remote operations service element (ROSE)
- File transfer and Access management (FTAM)

ACSE and ROSE are required by OSI network management. FTAM is not cited in the standards but is used by a number of vendors for the transfer and management of files, such as performance and alarm logs.

Overview of Key Terms

Before proceeding further with the explanation of the application layer, a few terms introduced in Chap. 3 must be reexamined. The ISO provides these definitions in its 7498 and 9545 standards. Please refer to Fig. 4.17 during this discussion.

- *Real open system:*   A system that complies with OSI in its communications with other real open systems.
- *Application process (AP):*   AP is a component within a real open system. It is an abstract representation of the elements of the open system which performs processing for a particular application.
- *Application entity (AE):*   AE represents the AP within OSI and provides a set of OSI communications capabilities for the AP.
- *Applications service element:*   ASEs are part of an applications entity that provides a defined OSI capability for a specific purpose. It permits the interworking of AEs of the same kind with the use of application protocol data units (APDUs).
- *User entity (UE):*   A UE is a logical grouping of ASEs.

The idea of the ASE is to provide a defined set of services that are needed by a number of applications. In a sense, the ASE is like a common software subroutine that has been written to satisfy a community

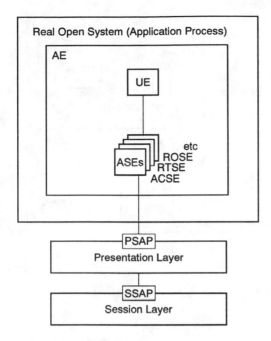

Figure 4.17 ASE relationships.

of users. The advantage of such an approach is that each application or other ASE need not write its own duplicate subroutine; it merely invokes the services of the ASE.

An AE consists of one user element and one or more ASEs, and operates through a single Presentation Service Access Point (PSAP) address with the presentation layer. In turn, the PSAP is mapped directly onto a Session Service Access Point (SSAP).

It is quite possible that an end-user application could use more than one application-level protocol in a single session. As a consequence, the supporting AE to the application process can contain multiple ASEs. This means that ASEs can be used in a variety of combinations to support the user application process.

Application associations and application contexts

The ACSE supports the establishment, maintenance, and termination of *application associations*. An application association is a detailed description of a cooperative relationship between two AEs through the use of presentation services within a defined *application context*. In turn, an application context is the set of ASEs and supporting information used on the application association. Essentially, it is a set of rules for communicating in a given application association and the

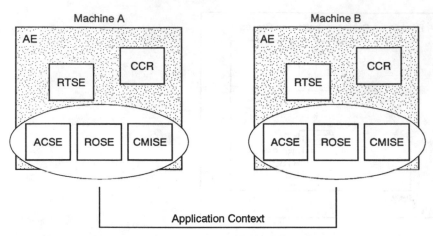

Figure 4.18 The application context.

AEs' invocations (their actions). See Fig. 4.18 for an illustration of the application context.

In a sense, the application association and application context are like a "cataloged procedure" found in the IBM large-scale computer environment, because, like a cataloged procedure of Job Control Language (JCL), they identify all the programs, files, databases, directories, and supporting system software needed for the user application to execute properly.

The application context must include a set of ASEs and also may include a description of:

- The relationships and dependencies of the ASEs
- The optional features that may be invoked by the ASEs
- The logical structure of information to be exchanged between the co-operating entities
- The interleaving of service requests and PDUs
- The rules for mapping the AE's protocol control information (PCI; header) onto the presentation layer or another ASE
- Any additional rules or any modification or deletion of rules

The final point about the general architecture of the application layer is that the end user still has the task of developing an interface that can communicate with the service elements (SEs) in the AE. The interface can be a system furnished by a vendor, or it can be developed by an organization's system personnel. Indeed, nothing precludes this interface from using the service definitions of the ASEs.

Our approach in the following two sections is to examine the ACSE and ROSE standards and recommendations as they pertain to OSI network management.

Association Control Service Element

The ACSE provides several very basic and important functions to AEs. It provides services needed between applications processes that are independent of any application-specific needs. In other words, it supports the use of common services.

The ISO and CCITT publish the following standards and recommendations for ACSE:

- Service definitions: CCITT X.217; ISO 8649
- Protocol specifications: CCITT X.227; ISO 8650

ACSE's main task is to support the associations between applications. In so doing, it performs four services:

- A-ASSOCIATE
- A-RELEASE
- A-ABORT
- A-P-ABORT

The *A-ASSOCIATE* service sets up the application association between the applications by using the ASE procedures that are identified by an application context name. It is responsible for performing the following services:

1. Supporting AE titles (optional)
2. Supporting the application context name (required)
3. Providing the presentation context (optional)
4. Providing a result of the operation (required)

As might be expected, the *A-RELEASE* service provides an orderly release of the association of the two applications. It can use the session layer orderly release to ensure that both applications agree to the release. Otherwise, the association continues.

The *A-ABORT* and *A-P-ABORT* services cause the termination of the application, presentation, and session connections. The A-ABORT is initiated by the user or the association control service; the A-P-ABORT service is initiated by the presentation layer.

It is instructive to note that the ACSE is not involved with the transfer of user data between the application and presentation layers. This task is left to other ASEs, described later in this chapter.

On reviewing the functions of the services of ACSE, it might appear that this service element performs limited services. This supposition is correct, but upon further examination of ACSE it will become evident that its services are absolutely essential.

To illustrate this point, let us assume that two applications are executing (reading, writing, performing computations, etc.) and have not established an applications association (relationship) with each other. Further assume that an application sends data erroneously to the other application (because of problems in the code or in the way it is loaded by the operator, etc.). ACSE will not allow the data to be transferred but will require that an association be established between the applications before the data transfer can take place. It also "knows" how to refuse release requests from applications, just in case they were issued regarding two applications that had no association between them.

Every application association is named by an ASN.1 OBJECT IDENTIFIER. Also, the association control identifies with an ASN.1 OBJECT IDENTIFIER the abstract syntaxes of the application PDUs that an association can carry as a result of its use by the ASEs.

Example of an application context association creation operation

Figure 4.19 shows the operations between an application layer entity, the ACSE, and the presentation layer in the negotiation of the application context. The legend in the figure shows the parameters that are contained in the primitives between the applications layer entity, ACSE, and the presentation layer. Most of these primitives are used for naming and identification services.

Remote Operations Service Element

Up to this point in our discussion of the application layer architecture, we have not examined any services to support interactive communications between two distributed entities, yet some of the operations in this type of environment are common to many applications.

Most applications designers develop interactive applications based on two operations: (1) a transaction from an originator to the recipient which requests that an operation be performed and (2) a transaction from the recipient to the originator that describes the result of the requested operation. A third option is usually included to provide an error report about problems resulting from the transactions and to allow the transaction to be aborted, if necessary.

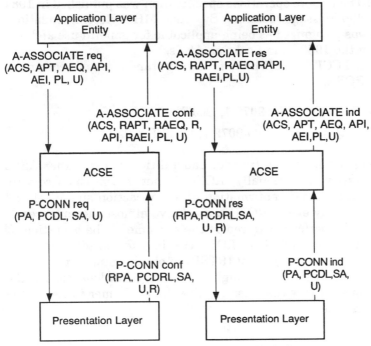

Note: Major parameters are noted; not all inclusive

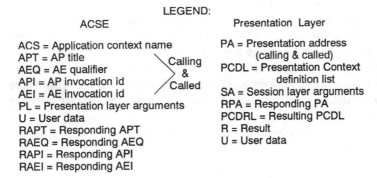

LEGEND:

ACSE

ACS = Application context name
APT = AP title
AEQ = AE qualifier
API = AP invocation id
AEI = AE invocation id
PL = Presentation layer arguments
U = User data
RAPT = Responding APT
RAEQ = Responding AEQ
RAPI = Responding API
RAEI = Responding AEI

Calling & Called

Presentation Layer

PA = Presentation address
(calling & called)
PCDL = Presentation Context
definition list
SA = Session layer arguments
RPA = Responding PA
PCDRL = Resulting PCDL
R = Result
U = User data

Figure 4.19   Creating the application context association.

As a point of emphasis, the originator (or invoker) can invoke operations in another system (the performer). Since the performer system may be different from the one in which the invoker resides, the interactive transaction may involve remote operations; hence the name *ROSE*.

The CCITT and the ISO have published the ROSE standards which define the procedures for supporting distributed, interactive applications processing. The two specifications are technically aligned with each other. The remote operations specification was published in 1984 with the X.400 Message Handling Systems (MHS) Recommendations (X.410). It was recognized as being applicable for general use and was published in the 1988 Blue Books as ASEs.

The ISO and CCITT publish the following standards and recommendations for ROSE:

- *Service definitions:*   ISO 9072-1; CCITT X.219

- *Protocol specifications:*   ISO 9072-2; CCITT X.229

ROSE does not have any transfer capabilities. It uses other ASEs for this operation. Additionally, ROSE is not a confirmed service. Some applications need confirmation of a transaction submittal and some do not. In any event, ROSE can achieve almost the same result by requiring the performer to report the outcome of the operation. If this capability is not sufficient, ROSE can invoke the services of the reliable transfer service element (RTSE) to obtain reliable transfer of its data units. However, this might be unduly burdensome for the ROSE implementations that also require the performer to report the outcome of the operation.

Major ROSE operations

ROSE bears many similarities to some of Systems Network Architecture's (SNA) services. Table 4.4 summarizes these features.

ROSE permits two modes of operation. The *synchronous mode* requires the performer to reply to the invoker before the invoker can invoke another operation, which is a common method to control interactive, transaction-based systems. The *asynchronous* mode allows the invoker to continue invoking operations without requiring a reply from the performer.

The reporting requirements are combined with the mode definitions

TABLE 4.4   Classification of ROSE Operations

Result of operation	Expected reporting from performer
Success or failure	If successful, return result. If a failure, return an error reply.
Failure only	If successful, no reply. If a failure, return an error reply.
Success only	If successful, return result. If a failure, no reply.
Success or failure	In either case, no reply.

TABLE 4.5   ROSE Operation Classes

Class number	Definition
1	Synchronous: Report success (result) or failure (error)
2	Asynchronous: Report success (result) or failure (error)
3	Asynchronous: Report failure (error) only
4	Asynchronous: Report success (result) only
5	Asynchronous: Report nothing

to define five classes of operations. These operations are summarized in Table 4.5.

ROSE also provides for the grouping of operations in the event that the performer notifies the invoker that it must also perform some operation(s). This function is called *linked operations*. The invoker of an operation invokes a parent operation which is executed by the performer (i.e., the performer of a parent operation). This AE can invoke one or more child operations, which are performed by the invoker [i.e., the performer of child operation(s)].

ROSE also uses four macros, which are defined in ASN.1. (The reader should obtain ISO 9072-1 and read Annex B. It contains useful tutorial information on the use of the ROSE macros.) The four macros are:

- *BIND:*   Allows the specification of the types of user data values to be exchanged in the establishment of the application association.

- *UNBIND:*   Allows the specification of the types of user data values to be exchanged in the release of the application association.

- *OPERATION:*   The type notation in this macro allows the specification of an operation and user data to be exchanged for a request and a positive reply. This macro can specify a list of linked child operations if the operation is a parent operation.

- *ERROR:*   The type notation in this macro allows the specification of an operation and user data to be exchanged in a negative reply.

ROSE provides five services. ROSE also makes use of ACSE and, optionally, the direct use of the presentation layer and RTSE. A brief explanation of each of these services follows.

The RO-INVOKE service allows the invoker AE to request that an operation be performed by a performer AE. This service begins when ROSE receives a request from the ROSE user (the invoker) to be performed by the other ROSE user (the performer). This service is a nonconfirmed service.

The RO-RESULT service is also a nonconfirmed service. It is used by a ROSE user in reply to a previous RO-INVOKE to notify the invoking user of the completion of a successful operation.

The RO-ERROR service is a nonconfirmed service to reply to a previous RO-INVOKE. Its purpose is to notify the user of an unsuccessful operation.

The RO-REJECT-U service is a nonconfirmed service which rejects an RO-INVOKE service. It is also used to reject a RO-RESULT and a RO-ERROR, if necessary.

Finally, the RO-REJECT-P service is used by the ROSE provider to inform the ROSE user about a problem.

Example of ROSE INVOKE and RESULT operations

Figure 4.20 shows an example of the use of the ROSE INVOKE and RESULT services. The invoking ROSE user sends the RO-INVOKE request to the ROSE provider. This primitive contains the following parameters (initials are the author's own shorthand notations for the figure):

- Operation value (OV)
- Operation class (OC)
- Argument (A)
- Invoke id (IID)
- Linked id (LID)
- Priority (P)
- Result (R)

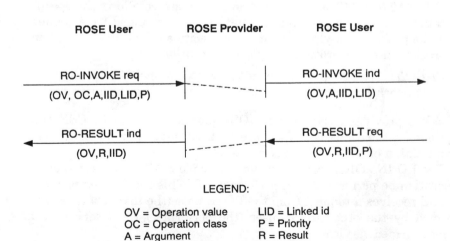

Figure 4.20   ROSE INVOKE and RESULT primitives.

The remote ROSE user receives the RO-INVOKE indication primitive. It performs the operations that are defined in the parameters. Next, it reports on the result of the operation by sending the RO-RESULT request. The ROSE provider passes this information to the invoking ROSE user with the RO-RESULT indication primitive.

FTAM in OSI Network Management

The FTAM standards are used by a number of organizations for the support of file transfer and file management operations. ROSE is not suited to this work because it is connectionless and transaction-oriented. The OSI network management standards do not cite the use of FTAM, but the OSI Model supports its use through the negotiation of an application context, which could include FTAM.

The FTAM specification is divided into four parts:

- *8571/1:*   Introduction to the FTAM concepts; discusses file transfer problems

- *8571/2:*   Explains the terms, concepts, and vocabulary used in FTAM (file name, contents, access codes)

- *8571/3:*   Describes interface required between the two entities that participate in the file transfer process

- *8571/4:*   Defines the specific rules for the activities in part 3

The FTAM virtual filestore concept

Although data usage often varies among different applications, a common model for all data files and databases can provide a common foundation for file transfer, access, and management among diverse applications. This model is called the *virtual filestore*. Virtual filestore contains the file's characteristics, structure, and attributes. Its objective is to reduce the amount of detail needed to communicate with a file located in a remote part of the network.

The basic idea of virtual filestore is to provide a mapping of file definitions to and from actual files, which are called *real filestores*. The filestore definitions form a schema (or set) of the file; subset descriptions of files form subschemas (or subsets). The concepts of schemas and subschemas are very well known and understood in the database management industry. (The terms *sets* and *subsets* are used with virtual filestore.) The set provides a map of the data, shows the names of the attributes, and establishes relationships of data elements. It provides the overall view of the database. It says nothing about the physical structure of the file or the physical access method. The subset is the specific user view of the database, that is, the user subset of the set.

Typically, organizations have hundreds of subsets and individual users often have multiple subsets to satisfy different kinds of retrieval and update requirements. This presents a challenging problem for the database and network designers: They must provide for a physical design that satisfies all user "views" at all nodes in the network. The OS standards provide methods to join different subsets between systems at the presentation layer and additional procedures to manage file service dialogue at the session layer.

File access data units

In virtual filestore, the conventional notion of a "data record" is called a *data unit (DU)*. The DUs are related to each other through a hierarchical structure called *file access data units (FADU)*. Operations on a file are performed in a FADU. The DU is considered to be the smallest amount that can be transferred.

FTAM is also organized around the concept of the *attribute,* which describes the properties of a file. Presently, four groups of attributes are defined:

- *Kernel group:*   Properties common to all files
- *Storage group:*   Properties of files that are stored
- *Security group:*   Properties for access control
- *Private group:*   Properties beyond FTAM scope

The kernel group consists of the file name, a description of the file structure (sequential, hierarchical), access restrictions (deletion, reads, etc.), location of the file user, and the identification of the AEs involved in the FTAM communications process.

The storage group describes several properties of a file. The properties are either (1) information about the ongoing characteristics of the file or (2) information about the latest operations on the file. The following properties are included in the storage group:

- Date and time of last: (1) read; (2) change; (3) attribute change
- Identification of: (1) creator; (2) last reader; (3) last modifier; (4) last attribute modifier
- Filesize and availability

- Identification of party to be charged for file storage and file access activities
- Description of any locks on the file
- Identification of initiating FTAM user

The security group includes attributes on access permission criteria, encryption procedures, and legal qualifications (trademarks, copyrights, etc.).

The private group is not defined by the FTAM standard. It is used for files beyond the virtual filestore attributes.

FTAM regimes

FTAM is organized around the concepts of regimes. The file service regimes define how FTAM primitives are used for the file activity. Regimes provide the protocol for file selection, file opens and closes, data transfer, and recovery operations. Four types of file service regimes are defined:

- The *application association regime* exists during the lifetime of application association of two file service users.

- The *file selection regime* exists during the time in which a particular file is associated with the application association.

- The *file open regime* exists during a particular set of presentation contexts, concurrency controls, and commitment controls in operation for data transfer.

- The *data transfer regime* exists when a particular access context and direction of transfer are in force.

Virtual filestore actions. Virtual filestore defines two types of "actions" on files. The first encompasses actions to the contents of a file such as locating and reaching a file. This type also describes the protocol for inserting, replacing, extending, and erasing a FADU within virtual filestores.

The second type defines actions on a complete file. For example, procedures describe the creation of a file, as well as its deletion. In addition, the read, open, close, and select attributes of the file are also defined within this action type.

File service primitives. FTAM services are managed with primitives. The ISO 8571 FTAM primitives invoke specific file services. These

TABLE 4.6   File Service Primitives

Primitive	Parameters
F-INITIALIZE	Diagnostic, called address, calling address, responding address, service type, service class, functional units, attribute groups, rollback availability, communications Quality of Service (QOS), presentation context, identity of initiator, current account, filestore password, checkpoint window
F-TERMINATE	Charging
F-U-ABORT	Diagnostic
F-P-ABORT	Diagnostic
F-SELECT	Diagnostic, filename, attributes, access control, access passwords, concur, current access structure type, current account
F-DESELECT	Diagnostic, charging
F-CREATE	Diagnostic, filename, attributes, access control, access passwords, concurrency control, commitment control, override, current account, delete password, charging
F-READ-ATTRIB	Diagnostic, attribute names, attributes
F-CHANGE-ATTRIB	Diagnostic, attributes
F-OPEN	Diagnostic, processing mode, presentation context name, concurrency control, commitment control, activity identifier, recovery mode
F-CLOSE	Diagnostic, commitment control
F-BEGIN-GROUP	Threshold
F-END-GROUP	—
F-RECOVER	Diagnostic, activity identifier Bulk transfer number, access control, access passwords, recovery point
F-LOCATE	Diagnostic, FADU identity, concurrency control
F-ERASE	Diagnostic, FADU identity, concurrency control

primitives and their associated parameters are summarized in Table 4.6.

Example of a Layering Option in the OSI Network Management Application Layer

To conclude the discussion of the ASEs that support OSI network management, Fig. 4.21 shows a possible "stack" of the ASEs in the applications layer that might comprise the application context. The figure does not show RTSE other than with the general notation of ASEs. However, remember that RTSE can be used by ROSE for certain services. If so, it would rest under ROSE in the stack.

The emphasis in the figure is on the arrows connecting the system management application service elements (SMASEs) and the common

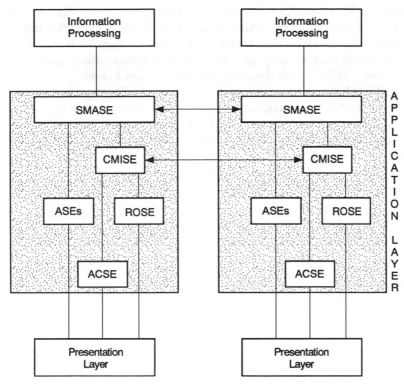

Figure 4.21 Network management application layer.

management information service elements (CMISEs) in the different machines. From the view of OSI network management, the operations of the lower-level ASEs in the application layer are a means to an end: the exchange of PDUs between the SMASEs.

Summary

The presentation layer's principal functions are syntax description, syntax negotiation, and the encoding and decoding of the data during the transfer across the communications channel. The presentation layer architecture is based on ASN.1 and the transfer syntax protocol. The OSI network management standards, the Internet management standards, and the IEEE LAN/MAN management standards use ASN.1 notation extensively.

The session layer provides OSI network management with many useful services, such as dialogue control, checkpoints, and negotiated connection disconnects. The session layer is very rich in functions and is somewhat complex. Fortunately, through the use of functional units and subsets, the user of the OSI network management standards can tailor the OSI session layer to the needs of a specific action on a managed object. The Internet standards do not use the session layer. The IEEE standards may or may not use this layer, depending upon the choice to use CMIP (which does rely on the session layer).

The OSI application layer (with ACSE and ROSE) plays an important role in the OSI network management standards, and some organizations also use FTAM for their file transfer operations. It is not used in the Internet stack, unless Common Management Information Services and Protocol over TCP/IP (CMOT) is utilized. The IEEE standards may or may not use the OSI application layer.

Management MIBs and Libraries

Introduction

Earlier discussions in Chap. 1 focused on the importance of network management information databases, often referred to as a management information base (MIB) or a management information library (MIL). This chapter examines three MIBs/MILs. The first example is the Internet MIB II. The second is the OSI MIL currently being developed by the OSI Implementors' Workshop (OIW) that is sponsored by the U.S. National Institute of Standards and Technology (NIST). The third example is the OSI/Network Management Forum Library of managed object classes (MOCs), name bindings, and attributes. The IEEE has not yet defined an MIB/MIL, but these other groups have included some local area network/metropolitan area network (LAN/MAN) objects in their work. Emphasis is placed on the Internet MIB II in this chapter since it is more widely used than the other standards.

The reader should be aware that these MIBs and MILs represent dynamic information repositories and are subject to ongoing updates. Notwithstanding, this chapter should provide the reader with an understanding of how they are used in network management.

Additionally, this chapter also includes information on the OSI and Internet structure of management information (SMI), because this information is closely related to MIBs and libraries.

The Internet MIB

The Internet SMI describes the identification scheme and structure for the managed objects in an internet. The SMI deals principally with organizational and administrative matters. It leaves the task of object definitions to the other network management Requests for Comments (RFCs). SMI describes the names used to identify the managed objects. These names are object identifiers and use the naming convention introduced in Chap. 1 and explained in more detail in the next section.

The Internet naming hierarchy

The objects within an internet have many common characteristics across subnetworks, vendor products, and individual components. It would be quite wasteful for each organization to spend precious resources and time in coding Abstract Syntax Notation 1 (ASN.1) to describe these resources. Therefore, the Internet MIB provides a registration scheme wherein objects can be defined and categorized within a registration hierarchy. This concept is founded on the ISO/CCITT agreement convention which the Internet standard uses to identify objects within a system.

Figure 5.1 shows the ISO and Internet registration tree for the Internet MIB. At the root level, three branches identify the registration hierarchy as either CCITT (0), ISO (1), or joint CCITT/ISO (2). Since the Internet activities are of concern in this chapter, Fig. 5.1 shows the ISO branch. The emphasis is branch 3, which from ISO's perspective is labeled IE-ORG. The next branch identifies the Department of Defense (DOD) with the value 6. Internet is found under this branch with a value of 1. Next within the Internet hierarchy are four nodes; one is labeled management (Mgmt) with a value of 2. The next entry of this branch is labeled mib (1). This example shows the path to a leaf entry that identifies an Ethernet interface. The complete registration number is 1.3.6.1.2.1.2.1.3.6. If an agent were to report about an Ethernet interface, it must identify the interface type with this OBJECT IDENTIFIER value.

Internet MIB syntax and types

The Internet standards use ASN.1 constructs in the MIB to describe the syntax of the object types. The full ASN.1 set is not allowed. The following primitive types are permitted: INTEGER, OCTET STRING, OBJECT IDENTIFIER, and NULL. In addition to the primitive types, these constructor types are allowed: SEQUENCE and SEQUENCE OF.

The SMI standard defines six major Internet managed objects (types). They are as follows:

- *Network Address:* This type allows a choice of the Internet family of protocols. The type is defined in the modified ASN.1 notation as

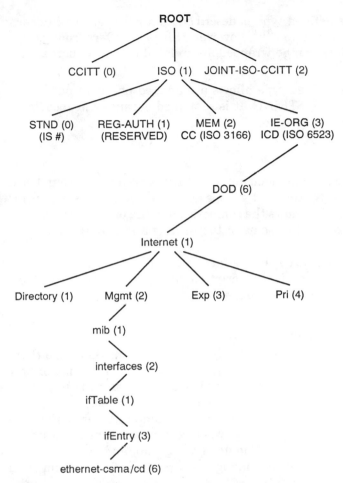

Figure 5.1 An Internet registration hierarchy example.

CHOICE, which will allow choosing the protocol within the family. Presently, only the Internet family is present.

- *IP Address:* This address is used to define the Internet 32-bit address. The ASN.1 notation is an OCTET STRING.

- *Time Ticks:* This type represents a nonnegative integer, which is used to record events such as the last change to a managed object, the last update to a database, etc. The SMI standard requires that it represent a time increment of hundredths of a second.

- *Gauge:* The SMI definition for this type is a nonnegative integer which can range from 0 to 2^{31-1}. The gauge definition does not permit counter-wraparound, and it may increase or decrease in value.

- *Counter:*   This defined type is described as a nonnegative integer, again ranging from 0 to 2^{31-1}; however, this type differs from gauge in that the values can be wrapped around and can only increase in value.

- *Opaque:*   This defined type allows a managed object to pass anything as an OCTET STRING. It is so named because the encodings are passed transparently.

The Internet MIB structure

The Internet network management structure is organized around object groups. Presently, 10 object groups have been defined as members of the MIB. Figure 5.2 shows the composition of the object groups. The reader probably recognizes some of the initials and acronyms in this figure.

Each of these object groups is defined in detail in the Internet MIB. RFC 1213 provides a detailed description (with a modified ASN.1 notation) for each of the object groups.

Overview of the object groups

Each object group is described briefly in this section. Be aware that this general explanation is to give the reader an idea of the major operations of the groups. RFC 1213 should be studied carefully to appreciate the full functions supported by the MIB definitions.

The *system* object group describes (1) the name and version of the hardware, as well as the operating system and networking software of the entity, (2) the hierarchical name of the group, and (3) an indication of when (in time) that the management portion of the system was reinitialized.

The *interfaces* object group describes (1) the number of network inter-

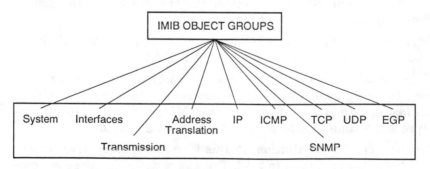

Note: Groups Transmission and SNMP have been added to MIB II

Figure 5.2   MIB object groups.

faces supported, (2) the type of interface operating below the Internet Protocol (IP) [e.g., link access procedures balanced (LAPB), Ethernet, etc.], (3) the size of datagram acceptable to the interface, (4) the speed (bit/s) of the interface, (5) the address of the interface, (6) the operational state of the interface (up, down, etc.), and (7) the amount of traffic received, delivered (unicast or broadcast), or discarded and the reasons.

The *address translation* group describes the address translation tables for network-to-physical address or physical address-to-network address translation.

The *IP* group describes (1) if the machine forwards datagrams, (2) the time-to-live value for datagrams that originated at this site, (3) the amount of traffic received, delivered, or discarded and the reasons, (4) information on fragmentation operations, (5) address tables, including subnet masks, and (6) routing tables, including destination address, distance metrics, age of route, next hop, protocol from which route was learned [routing information protocol (RIP), external gateway protocol (EGP), etc.].

The Internet Control Message Protocol (ICMP) group describes (1) the number of the various ICMP messages received and transmitted and (2) the statistics on problems encountered.

The Transmission Control Protocol (TCP) group describes (1) the retransmission algorithm and maximum and minimum retransmission values, (2) the number of TCP connections the entity can support, (3) the information on state transition operations, (4) the information on traffic received and sent, and (5) the port and IP numbers for each connection.

The User Datagram Protocol (UDP) group describes (1) information on the traffic received and sent and (2) information on the problems encountered.

The *EGP* group describes (1) information on traffic sent and received and problems encountered, (2) the EGP neighbor table, (3) addresses to neighbors, and (4) the EGP state with each neighbor.

The *transmission* group was added to the second release of the MIB (MIB II). It is intended to provide information on the types of transmission schemes and interfaces.

The Simple Network Management Protocol (SNMP) group was also added to MIB II. It contains 30 objects that are used with SNMP. Most of the objects deal with (1) error reporting capabilities and (2) statistics on SNMP traffic.

Notations for the objects

The Internet objects are described further with certain *key words* (reserved words). Five notations are used to describe the format of a managed object:

- *Object (descriptor):*   As the name implies, this field describes the object in ASCII text.

- *Syntax:*   This field describes the bit-stream representation of the object (integer, octet, etc.).

- *Definition:*   This field describes the managed object in text, to aid the reader in understanding the notation.

- *Access:*   This field describes whether the managed object can be: (1) read-only, (2) write-only, (3) read-write, or (4) not accessible.

- *Status:*   This field is used to describe information such as: (1) the object is mandatory, (2) the object is optional, (3) the object is obsolete, etc.

Templates to define objects

All object definitions are defined with templates and ASN.1 code. Templates are examined in this section. A later section examines the ASN.1 code. The template format is shown in Fig. 5.3. The fields were listed and described above.

Each of the object groups in Fig. 5.2 is defined in RFC 1213 with this standard template format. It is of little value to the reader to merely repeat these templates—they consume over 50 pages in the standard. Each group was described briefly in the previous section to give the reader an idea of their principal functions. The remainder of this section shows one example. The example is taken from the interfaces object group.

Figure 5.4 shows the template for the leaf entry of the registration tree

---

OBJECT:

    A name for the object type, with its
    corresponding OBJECT IDENTIFIER
Syntax:

    The ASN.1 coding to describe the syntax
    of the object type

Definition:

    Textual description of the object type

Access:

    Access options

Status:

    Status of object type

Figure 5.3   Template for Internet MIB (IMIB) object type definitions.

OBJECT:

    ifType {ifEntry 3}

Syntax:

    INTEGER {
        other (1),   --none of the following
        regular1822 (2),
        hdh1822 (3),
        ddn-x25 (4)
        rfc877-x25 (5),
        ethernet-csmacd (6),
        iso88023-csmacd (7),
        iso88024-tokenBus (8),
        iso88025-tokenRing (9),
        iso88026-man (10),
        starLan (11),
        proteon-10Mbit (12),
        proteon-80Mbit (13),
        hyperchannel (14),
        fddi (15),
        lapb (16),
        sdlc (17),
        t1-carrier (18),
        cept (19),   --european equivalent of T-1
        basiclsdn (20),
        primarylsdn (21),
                --proprietary serial
    --...and others not shown,
          }

Definition:
    The type of interface....immediately "below"
    the IP in the protocol stack

Access:
    read-only

Status:
    mandatory

—Note: ...means some the material of RFC is omitted.

Figure 5.4   The interface type (ifType) template.

for the TCP/IP interfaces. Be aware that several intermediate nodes in the tree are not included in this example. The notation of ifType {ifEntry 3} means the ifType belongs to parent ifEntry 3 in the tree.

The Syntax clause describes the abstract syntax (in ASN.1) of the object type. As the entry shows, the physical, data link, and subnetwork interfaces that exist below IP are described and assigned an integer value. Thus, two machines that exchange information about the interface supported below the IP layer are required to use these values. For example, ifType = 6 must be used to identify an Ethernet interface, as well as the numbers of the nodes higher in the tree (as seen in Fig. 5.1).

The high-level MIB

Figure 5.5 shows the RFC 1213 ASN.1 notation for the MIB. The code can be understood in the context of the objects illustrated in Fig. 5.2 and the naming hierarchy tree in Fig. 5.1.

The IMPORTS statement designates that a number of definitions are imported from RFC 1155 and 1212. All objects are tagged as OBJECT IDENTIFIERS and defined with another name within the naming tree ({mgmt1}, {MIB - 2 1}, etc).

Lower-level definitions. Figure 5.6 shows the next lower level of definition in relation to the MIB definition in Fig. 5.5. For convenience, this code shows at the first line the system object group, identified as MIB - 2 1.

Figure 5.6 also shows one of the objects within the system labeled as *sysUpTime*. The entries in the sysUpTime coding define the characteristics of system up time with the SYNTAX, ACCESS, and STATUS definitions explained earlier in this chapter.

```
RFC1213-MIB DEFINITIONS :: = BEGIN

IMPORTS
        mgmt, NetworkAddress, IpAddress, Counter, Gauge, TimeTicks
        FROM RFC1155-SMI;
    OBJECT-TYPE
    FROM RFC-1212;

mib - 2        OBJECT IDENTIFIER :: = {mgmt 1}
    system         OBJECT IDENTIFIER :: = {mib - 2 1}
    interfaces     OBJECT IDENTIFIER :: = {mib - 2 2}
    at             OBJECT IDENTIFIER :: = {mib - 2 3}
    ip             OBJECT IDENTIFIER :: = {mib - 2 4}
    icmp           OBJECT IDENTIFIER :: = {mib - 2 5}
    tcp            OBJECT IDENTIFIER :: = {mib - 2 6}
    udp            OBJECT IDENTIFIER :: = {mib - 2 7}
    egp            OBJECT IDENTIFIER :: = {mib - 2 8}
--  cmot           OBJECT IDENTIFIER :: = {mib - 2 9}
    transmission   OBJECT IDENTIFIER :: = {mib - 2 10}
    snmp           OBJECT IDENTIFIER :: = {mib - 2 11}
    END
```

Figure 5.5 Definition of the highest-level MIB.

```
system OBJECT IDENTIFIER ::= {mib - 2 1}      From highest-
                                              level definition;
                                              see previous figure

sysUpTime    OBJECT-TYPE          Time Ticks (.001s):
SYNTAX    TimeTicks               Time since last
ACCESS    read-only               reinitialization
STATUS    mandatory
:: = {system 3}
                                  Part of system object
                                  group with ID of 3
```

Figure 5.6   Part of the definition of the system object group.

The Internet MIB in more detail

This section provides more detailed information on the revised Internet MIB, now designated as MIB-II. The principal changes for this standard were made to reflect new requirements, principally in defining new operations and in new groups. Some editorial changes were made for technical clarity and readability, and several objects were further defined. MIB II also introduces the *deprecated* object. This term means that the object must be supported, but it will probably be removed in another version of the MIB. Presently, MIB II designates only one object, atTable, as deprecated. However, because atTable is deprecated, the complete address translation group is also deprecated. This produces no ill effects on ongoing operations because this capability is now present in the IP group.

The figures in this section are drawn to aid the reader in understanding the organization of the MIB II. As such, instead of just listing each object with a brief description, each system group is drawn with its subordinate entries listed with hierarchical indentations noted from the left to the right of the page. Where tables exist in the MIB, they are noted in these figures. It is hoped this approach will aid the reader to understand how the composition of the MIB could be used to create a logically hierarchical database.

The MIB groups are listed in the following figures:

- The *system* group in Fig. 5.7
- The *interfaces* group in Fig. 5.8
- The *address translation* group in Fig. 5.9
- The *IP* group in Fig. 5.10
- The *ICMP* group in Fig. 5.11
- The *TCP* group in Fig. 5.12

- The *UDP* group in Fig. 5.13
- The *EGP* group in Fig. 5.14
- The *SNMP* group in Fig. 5.15

The system group.   The system group contains seven objects. Its purpose is to provide general administrative information about a managed object—for example, an agent. The system group must be implemented for all objects, although all the objects do not have to have values. Figure 5.7 shows the structure of the system MIB. The objects in this group are used to perform the following functions:

- *sysDescr:*   An octet string to describe the object, such as hardware, operating system, etc.
- *sysObjectID:*   An OBJECT IDENTIFIER to uniquely identify the object (with naming hierarchy values) within the naming subtree
- *sysUpTime:*   In Time Ticks, the time since the object was declared up and running (reinitialized)
- *sysContact:*   An octet string to identify the person and/or organization to contact for information about the object
- *sysName:*   An octet string to identify a name (usually a person) that is responsible for the object
- *sysLocation:*   An octet string containing the location of the object
- *sysServices:*   An integer value that describes the service(s) offered by the object, based on the location of the service within a layer

The interfaces group.   This group is also mandatory for all systems. Its purpose is to provide information on an object's interface(s). It de-

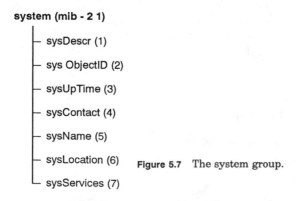

system (mib - 2 1)

├─ sysDescr (1)

├─ sys ObjectID (2)

├─ sysUpTime (3)

├─ sysContact (4)

├─ sysName (5)

├─ sysLocation (6)

└─ sysServices (7)

Figure 5.7   The system group.

scribes the type of interface, such as SDLC or Ethernet, etc., and provides statistics on the operations occurring at the interface. It also provides additional descriptors. Figure 5.8 shows the structure of the interfaces MIB. It consists of one individual entry and a 22-column table. Each row of the table contains information about one interface. Consequently, a device with multiple interfaces would have multiple row entries. The individual entries of the interface MIB are used for the following services and functions:

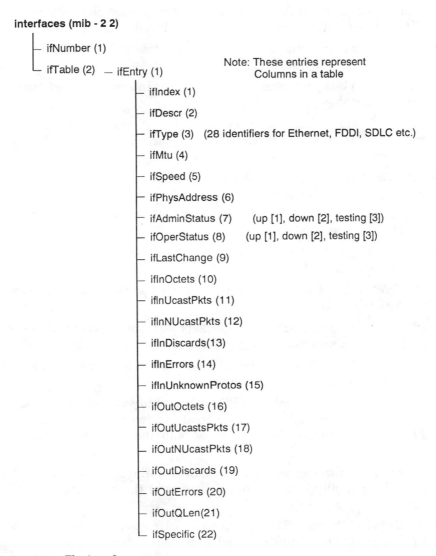

Figure 5.8   The interfaces group.

- *ifNumber:*   A value containing the number of network interfaces at this system.

- *ifIndex:*   An unambiguous value for each interface, its value can range from 1 to the value of ifNumber.

- *ifDescr:*   Textual information describing the interface, typically a product name, a manufacturer name, and a version number of the interface.

- *ifType:*   Identifies the specific type of interface, and currently contains values to identify one of 32 interface types such as Ethernet, SDLC, Fiber Distributed Data Interface (FDDI), etc.

- *ifMtu:*   The maximum size of the protocol data unit (PDU) that can be serviced at this interface, specified in octets.

- *ifSpeed:*   In bits per second, the value of the interface's speed capacity, if relevant.

- *ifPhysAddress:*   The interface address immediately below the network layer in a typical protocol stack, typically an IEEE MAC address for a LAN interface.

- *ifAdminStatus:*   Describes the state of the interface, which can be up = 1, down = 2, or testing = 3.

- *ifOperStatus:*   Describes the operational state of the interface, which can be up = 1, down = 2, testing = 3.

- *ifLastChange:*   In Time Ticks, the time the interface entered its current operational state.

- *ifInOctets:*   Total number of octets received at this interface since the last reinitialization.

- *ifInUcastPkts:*   The number of packets delivered to the next layer protocol, nonbroadcast packets only.

- *ifInNUcastPkts:*   The number of broadcast or multicast PDUs delivered to the next higher-layer protocol.

- *ifInDiscards:*   The number of PDUs discarded at this interface and not delivered to a higher-layer protocol. No errors occurred but the PDUs were discarded for other reasons (buffer space problems for example).

- *ifInErrors:*   Number of PDUs which contained errors, were ill formed, unintelligible, etc. (not delivered to the next higher-level protocol).

- *ifInUnknownProtos:*   The number of PDUs discarded because the PDU is related to an unsupported or unknown protocol.

- *ifOutOctets:* Total number of transmitted octets at this interface since the last reinitialization.

- *ifOutUcastPkts:* Total number of PDUs that the next higher-layer protocol requested this interface to transmit to a non-multicast or nonbroadcast address. This figure includes those PDUs which may have been discarded or otherwise not sent.

- *ifOutNUcastPkts:* Total number of PDUs that the next higher-layer protocol requested to be sent on a broadcast or multicast basis, including those that were discarded or otherwise not sent.

- *ifOutDiscards:* Total number of outgoing PDUs which were discarded even though they contained no errors (again, for example, buffer space problems).

- *ifOutErrors:* The total number of outgoing PDUs that contained errors and were discarded.

- *ifOutQLen:* The total length of the output queue in total number of PDUs involved.

- *ifSpecific:* A reference to a MIB definition that relates to the media used at the interface. This is used to provide additional information and may possibly not contain a value.

The address translation group. Figure 5.9 shows the organization for the address translation (AT) group which is designated as MIB - 2 3. This group consists of one table; although it will be phased out of MIB, it is still described in MIB II to provide compatibility for MIB I implementations. However, it is considered to be deprecated, in the sense that it will be excluded from future implementations. The purpose of this group is to provide a translation between physical medium access control (MAC) addresses and Internet IP addresses. The entries perform the following functions:

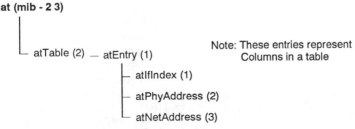

Figure 5.9   The address translation group.

- *atifIndex:* This object is the same value as the ifIndex in the interfaces group. It is a unique identifier of an interface.

- *atPhysAddress:* This identifies a MAC-type address base (a physical address).

- *atNetAddress:* Identifies an IP address which corresponds to the atPhysAddress.

The IP group. Figure 5.10 shows the structure for the IP group, which is a MIB - 2 4 entry. This group consists of several individual values,

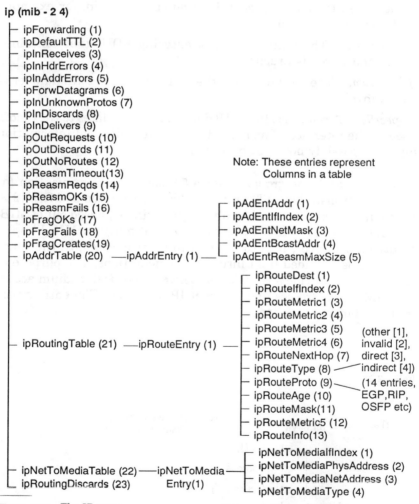

ip (mib - 2 4)
- ipForwarding (1)
- ipDefaultTTL (2)
- ipInReceives (3)
- ipInHdrErrors (4)
- ipInAddrErrors (5)
- ipForwDatagrams (6)
- ipInUnknownProtos (7)
- ipInDiscards (8)
- ipInDelivers (9)
- ipOutRequests (10)
- ipOutDiscards (11)
- ipOutNoRoutes (12)   Note: These entries represent
- ipReasmTimeout(13)   Columns in a table
- ipReasmReqds (14)
- ipReasmOKs (15)
- ipReasmFails (16)   ipAdEntAddr (1)
- ipFragOKs (17)   ipAdEntIfIndex (2)
- ipFragFails (18)   ipAdEntNetMask (3)
- ipFragCreates(19)   ipAdEntBcastAddr (4)
- ipAddrTable (20) —ipAddrEntry (1) — ipAdEntReasmMaxSize (5)

                                        ipRouteDest (1)
                                        ipRouteIfIndex (2)
                                        ipRouteMetric1 (3)
                                        ipRouteMetric2 (4)
                                        ipRouteMetric3 (5)   (other [1],
- ipRoutingTable (21) —ipRouteEntry (1) — ipRouteMetric4 (6)   invalid [2],
                                        ipRouteNextHop (7)   direct [3],
                                        ipRouteType (8) —indirect [4])
                                        ipRouteProto (9)   (14 entries,
                                        ipRouteAge (10)   EGP,RIP,
                                        ipRouteMask(11)   OSFP etc)
                                        ipRouteMetric5 (12)
                                        ipRouteInfo(13)

                                        ipNetToMediaIfIndex (1)
- ipNetToMediaTable (22)——ipNetToMedia— ipNetToMediaPhysAddress (2)
- ipRoutingDiscards (23)   Entry(1)   ipNetToMediaNetAddress (3)
                                        ipNetToMediaType (4)

Figure 5.10 The IP group.

as well as three tables. The purpose of the group is to provide information on IP operations as well as the IP routing tables and physical-to-network as well as network-to-physical address conversion values. The objects in this group are used to perform the following functions:

- *ipForwarding:* Indicates if this machine is acting as a forwarding gateway for incoming datagrams.
- *ipDefaultTTL:* Contains the default value for the time-to-live field in the IP datagrams originating at this machine.
- *ipInReceives:* Total datagrams received from lower layers, including errorred datagrams.
- *ipInHdrErrors:* Total IP datagrams discarded due to errors in the header fields of the datagram.
- *ipInAddrErrors:* Total datagrams discarded because the IP address was invalid.
- *ipForwDatagrams:* The indication of the total number of incoming datagrams whose final destination was not this machine. Consequently, no attempt was made to forward them through an internet.
- *ipInDiscards:* The value of the total incoming datagrams discarded, although no problems existed (for example, buffer space problems).
- *ipInDelivers:* The total number of incoming datagrams delivered to other protocols, including upper-layer protocols and companion protocols such as ICMP.
- *ipOutRequests:* The total number of IP datagrams requested to be transmitted from the IP module from upper-layer protocols or companion protocols.
- *ipOutDiscards:* The total number of outgoing datagrams discarded, although no problems existed (for example, buffer space problems).
- *ipOutNoRoutes:* Total number of datagrams discarded because a destination could not be found or available gateways were not operable.
- *ipReasmTimeout:* The total number of seconds the incoming received datagram fragments were held while awaiting reassembly.
- *ipReasmReqds:* The total number of fragments which were reassembled at this IP module.
- *ipReasmOKs:* Total number of IP datagrams that were reassembled successfully.

- *ipReasmFails:* The total number of reassembly failures detected during the reassembly process.

- *ipFragOks:* Total number of datagrams that were successfully fragmented.

- *ipFragFails:* The total number of datagrams that were discarded because the *don't fragment* flag was set.

- *ipFragCreates:* The total number of IP datagram fragments generated at this IP module.

The first table in the IP group is called the ipAddrTable; it consists of five columns. Their functions are as follows:

- *ipAdEntAddr:* The value of the IP address for this IP module.

- *ipAdEntIfIndex:* The index value pertinent to this interface; the same value is identified by the ifIndex in the interface group.

- *ipAdEntNetMask:* Contains the net mask value associated with the IP address for this module.

- *ipAdEntBcastAddr:* Contains the value of the least significant bit in the IP broadcast address for this IP module.

- *ipAdEntReasmMaxSize:* The size of the largest datagram that can be handled by this IP module.

The second table in the IP group is the IP routing table. Each row entry consists of 13 columns. Each row contains an entry for each route known to this IP module. The objects in the IP routing table are used to perform the following functions:

- *ipRouteDest:* Contains the destination IP address for this route.

- *ipRouteIfIndex:* The physical interface through which the next hop can be reached, the communications port. This value is the same value as the ifIndex object in the interfaces group.

- *ipRouteMetric(1-4):* Contains the routing metric used for this route [number of hops, type of service (TOS), etc.]. Values depend on specific routing protocol used.

- *ipRouteNextHop:* Contains the IP address of the next hop from this IP module.

- *ipRouteType:* Contains other = 1, invalid = 2, direct = 3, indirect = 4.

- *ipRouteProto:* Contains 1 of 14 entries to describe the routing protocol used for route discovery [(EGP, open shortest path first (OSPF), etc.].

- *ipRouteAge:* The value in number of seconds since the route was last updated.

- *ipRouteMask:* Contains the subnetwork mask for this route.

- *ipRouteMetric5:* Identifies an alternate routing metric for this route.

- *ipRouteInfo:* A reference to MIB definitions relating to a routing protocol.

The last table in the IP group is the IP address translation table. It contains four columns and is used to provide address translation from physical and network addresses. It is used in conjunction with ARP and proxy ARP for address mapping. The columns in this table are used to perform the following functions:

- *ipNetToMediaIfIndex:* Contains the value of the interface number, which is the same value of the IfIndex object in the interfaces group.

- *ipNetToMediaPhysAddress:* Contains the MAC-to-physical address for the interface.

- *ipNetToMediaNetAddress:* Contains the IP address which corresponds to the physical address.

- *ipNetToMediaType:* Describes the type of mapping used for address translation.

- *ipRoutingDiscards:* Number of routing entries discarded.

The ICMP group. The ICMP group is used to report on the operations of the ICMP module in a host or gateway. As shown in Figure 5.11, this group contains no tables, but only scalar objects. The objects perform the following functions:

- *icmpInMsgs:* Contains a count of the total number of ICMP messages received by the ICMP module

- *icmpInErrors:* Records the number of messages the ICMP has received, checked, and found to be in error

- *icmpInDestUnreachs:* Contains the total number of messages that could not be delivered because the destination was not reachable

- *icmpInTimeExcds:* Contains a value representing the total number of messages received in which the time was exceeded for their time to live in the internet

icmp (mib - 2 5)
- icmpInMsgs (1)
- icmpInErrors (2)
- icmpInDestUnreachs (3)
- icmpInTimeExcds (4)
- icmpInParmProbs (5)
- icmpInSrcQuenchs (6)
- icmpInRedirects (7)
- icmpInEchos (8)
- icmpInEchoReps (9)
- icmpInTimestamps (10)
- icmpInTimestampRep (11)
- icmpInAddrMasks (12)
- icmpInAddrMaskReps (13)
- icmpOutMsgs (14)
- icmpOutErrors (15)
- icmpOutDestUnreachs (16)
- icmpOutTimeExcds (17)
- icmpOutParmProbs (18)
- icmpOutSrcQuenchs (19)
- icmpOutRedirects (20)
- icmpOutEchos (21)
- icmpOutEchoReps (22)
- icmpOutTimestamps (23)
- icmpOutTimestampReps (24)
- icmpOutAddrMasks (25)
- icmpOutAddrMaskReps (26)

Figure 5.11   The ICMP group.

- *icmpInParmProbs:*   Records the total number of messages received in which there were parameter problems

- *icmpInSrcQuenchs:*   Contains the value of the total number of source quench messages received

- *icmpInRedirects:*   Reflects the total number of redirect messages received by the ICMP module

- *icmpInEchos:*   Contains the value of the total number of echo request messages received by the ICMP module

- *icmpInEchoReps:*   Contains the value of the total number of ICMP echo reply messages received by this module

- *icmpInTimestamps:*   Represents the value of the total number of ICMP timestamp request messages received by this module

- *icmpInTimestampReps:*   Represents the value of the total ICMP timestamp reply messages received by this module

- *icmpInAddrMasks:*   Represents the total number of address mask request messages received by this module

- *icmpInAddrMaskReps:*   Represents the total number of ICMP address mask reply messages received by this module

As Fig. 5.11 indicates, a comparable set of object groups are used to report on the number of messages sent by the ICMP module. For purposes of brevity, we will not repeat each of these items here because they simply mirror the input statistics just discussed.

The TCP group.   The TCP group is used to gather statistics and report information on each TCP connection at a TCP module. The TCP group consists of several scalar values and one table (see Fig. 5.12). The TCP group performs the following functions:

- *tcpRtoAlgorithm:*   This group identifies the algorithm used to establish the retransmission timeout value for unacknowledged traffic.

- *tcpRtoMin:*   This object contains a minimum value for this TCP module relating to the retransmission timeout.

- *tcpRtoMax:*   As a complement to tcpRtoMin, this object contains the maximum timeout value for this TCP module.

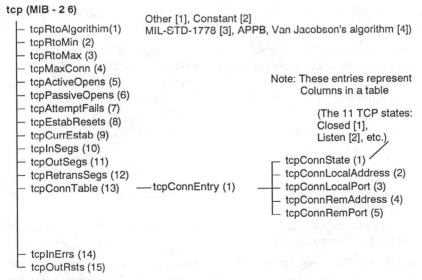

Figure 5.12   The TCP group.

- *tcpMaxConn:*   This establishes the maximum number of TCP connections the module can support.

- *tcpActiveOpens:*   This records the number of active opens that have been supported by this entity (transitions to the SYN-SENT state from the CLOSED state).

- *tcpPassiveOpens:*   This reflects the number of passive opens supported by this entity (those connections going from a SYN-RCVD state from the LISTEN state.

- *tcpAttemptFails:*   This contains the number of failed connection attempts (those potential connections moving to a CLOSED state from either a SYN-SENT state or a SYN-RCVD state).

- *tcpEstabResets:*   This object records the number of resets that have occurred at this entity (a direct transition to the CLOSED state from either an ESTABLISHED or CLOSE-WAIT state).

- *tcpCurrEstab:*   This value records the number of TCP connections in which the state is CLOSE-WAIT or ESTABLISHED.

- *tcpInSegs:*   This represents the total number of segments received by this entity.

- *tcpOutSegs:*   This value records the total number of segments sent by this entity.

- *tcpRetransSegs:*   This value records the total number of segments retransmitted.

- *tcpConnTable:*   This is the one table for the TCP group. It contains five columns which are used for the following services:

  - *tcpConnState:*   This object describes the state of this TCP connection. The following states are permitted on a TCP module: 1 = closed, 2 = listen, 3 = synSent, 4 = synReceived, 5 = established, 6 = finWait1, 7 = finWait2, 8 = closeWait, 9 = lastACK, 10 = closing, 11 = timeWait, 12 = deleteTCB.
  - *tcpConnLocalAddress:*   This value contains the local IP address for this connection.
  - *tcpConnLocalPort:*   This contains the local port number for this connection.
  - *tcpConnRemAddress:*   This object contains a remote IP address for this connection.
  - *tcpConnRemPort:*   This object contains the remote port number for this TCP connection.

- *tcpInErrs:*   This object records the total number of segments received which were in error—typically segments that reveal an erroneous check sum.

- *tcpOutRsts:* This object contains the number of TCP segments that were sent which have the RST flag on.

The UDP group. The UDP group consists of four scalar entries and one table (see Fig. 5.13). The small number of managed objects in this group reflects UDP's connectionless nature. The UDP group is used to perform the following services:

- *udpInDatagrams:* This object records the total number of UDP datagrams that have been delivered to the users of this UDP module.
- *udpNoPorts:* Records the number of UDP datagrams that were received in which an application could not be found at the destination port.
- *updInErrors:* This object records the total number of UPD datagrams received that could not be delivered because of problems other than the lack of an application.
- *udpOutDatagrams:* Contains the total number of UDP datagrams sent from this UDP entity.

The only table in this group is the *UDP listener* table. It contains two columns which perform the following services:

- *udpLocalAddress:* This object contains the local address for the UDP listener.
- *udpLocalPort:* This object contains the local port number for the UDP listener.

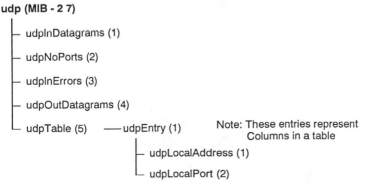

udp (MIB - 2 7)

├─ udpInDatagrams (1)

├─ udpNoPorts (2)

├─ udpInErrors (3)

├─ udpOutDatagrams (4)

└─ udpTable (5) ──── udpEntry (1)   Note: These entries represent
                                           Columns in a table
                          ├─ udpLocalAddress (1)
                          └─ udpLocalPort (2)

Figure 5.13 The UDP group.

The EGP group.   The EGP group is used to record and report information about operations at the EGP module (see Fig. 5.14). It consists of
four scalar values and a table of 15 columns. The EGP group is used to
perform the following services:

- *egpInMsgs:*   This group records the total number of error-free EGP
  messages received at this module.

- *egpInErrors:*   This object records the number of messages received
  which were in error.

- *egpOutMsgs:*   This records the total number of messages generated
  by this EGP module.

- *egpOutErrors:*   This contains the value for those messages not sent
  because of problems.

- *egpNeighTable:*   This is the EGP table, the EGP neighbor table. It
  is used to contain information (logically enough) about this module's
  EGP neighbors. It contains the following objects:

  - *egpNeighState:*   This object describes the state of the specific
    neighbor, such as idle, acquisition, down, up, cease.

  - *egpNeighAddr:*   This value contains the IP address for this spe-
    cific neighbor.

egp(MIB - 2 8)

```
├─ egpInMsgs (1)
├─ egpInErrors (2)                    Note: These entries represent
├─ egpOutMsgs (3)                         Columns in a table
├─ egpOutErrors (4)
├─ egpNeighTable (5)  ── egpNeighEntry (1)
                                               (idle [1],
                          ├─ egpNeighState (1) ─ acquisition [2],
                          ├─ egpNeighAddr (2)   down [3],
                          ├─ egpNeighAs (3)     up [4],
                          ├─ egpNeighInMsgs (4) cease [5])
                          ├─ egpNeighInErrs (5)
                          ├─ egpNeighOutMsgs (6)
                          ├─ egpNeighOutErrs (7)
                          ├─ egpNeighInErrMsgs (8)
                          ├─ egpNeighOutErrMsgs (9)
                          ├─ egpNeighStateUps (10)
                          ├─ egpNeighStateDowns (11)
                          ├─ egpNeighIntervalHello (12)
                          ├─ egpNeighIntervalPoll (13)
                          ├─ egpNeighMode (14)
                          └─ egpNeighEventTrigger (15)
└─ egpAs (6)
```

Figure 5.14   The EGP group.

- *egpNeighAs:*   This value is the autonomous system number for this EGP neighbor.
- *egpNeighInMsgs:*   This object records the number of messages received without problems from this neighbor.
- *egpNeighInErrs:*   This records the number of messages received from this neighbor which were in error.
- *egpNeighOutMsgs:*   This value contains the number of EGP messages generated by the local EGP module to this neighbor.
- *egpNeighOutErrs:*   This object records the number of messages that were not sent to the neighbor because of problems.
- *egpNeighInErrMsgs:*   This object contains the number of messages received from this neighbor.
- *egpNeighOutErrMsgs:*   This value contains the number EGP messages that were defined to be in error and sent to the neighbor.
- *egpNeighStateUps:*   This records the number of EGP state transitions from this neighbor.
- *egpNeighStateDowns:*   This object records the number of state transitions for this neighbor.
- *egpNeighIntervalHello:*   This value contains the limit on when to send hello messages.
- *egpNeighIntervalPoll:*   This value determines the interval between successive EGP poll messages.
- *egpNeighMode:*   This value describes the polling mode of the neighbor. It is either passive or active.
- *egpNeighEventTrigger:*   This value is used to control operator-initiated start and stop events.
- *egpAs:*   This object contains the value of the autonomous system number for this EGP module.

The SNMP group.   The SNMP group (Fig. 5.15) provides information about SNMP objects, principally statistics relating to traffic and problems or error conditions. All these objects have a syntax of Counter with the exception of the last entry which is an integer (snmpEnableAuthenTraps).

- *snmpInPkts:*   Indicates the number of packets received from the layer below SNMP
- *snmpOutPkts:*   Identifies the number of packets delivered from SNMP to the layer below
- *snmpInBadVersions:*   Indicates the number of PDUs received with an erroneous version
- *snmpInBadCommunityNames:*   Indicates the number of PDUs received with unidentifiable or unauthenticated community names

snmp (MIB - 2 11)
├─ snmpInPkts (1)
├─ snmpOutPkts (2)
├─ snmpInBadVersions (3)
├─ snmpInBadCommunityNames (4)
├─ snmpInBadCommunityUses (5)
├─ snmpInASNParseErrs (6)
├─ snmpInBadTypes (7) -- not used
├─ snmpInTooBigs (8)
├─ snmpInNoSuchNames (9)
├─ snmpInBadValues (10)
├─ snmpInReadOnlys (11)
├─ snmpInGenErrs (12)
├─ snmpInTotalReqVars (13)
├─ snmpTotalSetVars (14)
├─ snmpInGetRequests (15)
├─ snmpInGetNexts (16)
├─ snmpInSetRequests (17)
├─ snmpInGetResponses (18)
├─ snmpInTraps (19)
├─ snmpOutTooBigs (20)
├─ snmpOutNoSuchNames (21)
├─ snmpOutBadValues (22)
├─ snmpOutReadOnlys (23) -- not used
├─ snmpOutGenErrs (24)
├─ snmpOutGetRequests (25)
├─ snmpOutGetNexts (26)
├─ snmpOutSetRequests (27)
├─ snmpOutGetResponses (28)
├─ snmpOutTraps (29)
└─ snmpEnableAuthenTraps (30)

Figure 5.15   The SNMP group.

- *snmpInBadCommunityUses:*   Indicates the number of bad community uses
- *snmpInASNParseErrs:*   Indicates the number of PDUs that could not be parsed to ASN.1 objects and vice versa
- *snmpInBadTypes:*   Not used
- *snmpInTooBigs:*   Indicates the number of PDUs received with the tooBig error status field
- *snmpInNoSuchNames:*   Indicates the number of PDUs received with the error status field NoSuchName field
- *snmpInBadValues:*   Indicates the number of PDUs received with the error status badValue field
- *snmpInReadOnlys:*   Not used

- *snmpInGenErrs:* Indicates the number of PDUs received with the genErr field

- *snmpInTotalReqVars:* Indicates the number of MIB objects that have been retrieved

- *snmpInTotalSetVars:* Indicates the number of MIB objects that have been changed/altered

- *snmpInGetRequests:*
  snmpInGetNexts: These values are used to indicate the
  snmpInSetRequests: number of the respective PDUs that
  snmpInGetResponses: were received.
  snmpInTraps:

- *snmpOutTooBigs:* Indicates the number of PDUs sent with the tooBig Field

- *snmpOutNoSuchNames:* Indicates the number of PDUs sent with the nosuchName field

- *snmpOutBadValues:* Indicates the number of PDUs sent with the badValue field

- *snmpOutReadOnlys:* Indicates the number of PDUs sent with the readOnly field (not used at the present time)

- *snmpOutGenErrs:* Indicates the number of PDUs sent with the genErr field

- *snmpEnableAuthenTraps:* Describes if traps are enabled or disabled; can be read or written

- *snmpOutGetRequests:*
  snmpOutGetNexts: These values are used to indicate the
  snmpOutSetRequests: number of the respective PDUs that
  snmpOutGetResponses: were sent.
  snmpOutTraps:

The NIST OSI Management Information Library

The NIST has been a sponsor of the OIW for the past several years. The purpose of this workshop is to refine the OSI standards as well as supplement them. These efforts represent input to the OSI network management specifications. The OSI MIB working group (which is part of the network management special interest group, or NMSIG) has developed a MIL that provides descriptions of managed objects, name bindings, attributes, actions, and notifications. In this section of the book we concentrate on the MOCs as well as the managed object attributes.

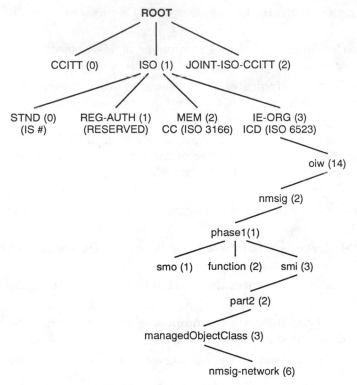

Figure 5.16   An NIST OSI registration hierarchy example.

Additionally, and as stated before, be aware that the OIW MIL represents a changing information repository. Nevertheless, it is hoped that the description in this section will give the reader an idea of the thrust of the OSI Network Management MIB.

Figure 5.16 shows an example of the NIST OSI registration hierarchy. As the reader might expect, the OIW is registered under the ISO organizational node (3). In turn, the NMSIG is registered under OIW. This example shows the leaf entry of the registration tree to be nmsig-network (6). This leaf entry contains the specific information on the OIW MIB.

The OIW MOCs

This section contains a description of the OIW MOCs. The structure for the MOCs is shown in Fig. 5.17.

As with the object groups for the Internet MIB, this section provides a general overview of each of the OIW MOCs.

- *nmsig-agent:*   This object class represents an agent system. This means that this MOC must support the management of one or more

Managed Object Classes (MOCs)

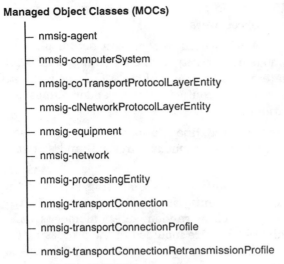

- nmsig-agent

- nmsig-computerSystem

- nmsig-coTransportProtocolLayerEntity

- nmsig-clNetworkProtocolLayerEntity

- nmsig-equipment

- nmsig-network

- nmsig-processingEntity

- nmsig-transportConnection

- nmsig-transportConnectionProfile

- nmsig-transportConnectionRetransmissionProfile

Figure 5.17 The OIW MOCs.

managed objects which must be made visible to other open systems that support the OSI standards. As of this writing, the agent MOC serves only to identify managed objects.

- *nmsig-computerSystem:* This MOC has been created to define a high-level view of an organization's computer system. It can be used to define hardware, software, and other components. It should be emphasized that this MOC is not an inheritance tree but rather a containment tree. Its intent is to allow MOCs to be added within a computer system without affecting other object classes.

  Although not defined in the standards, managed objects included in the computer system MOC are operating systems, hardware units (such as disk drives, tape units, printers), software (such as various types of applications), as well as OSI layer entities.

- *nmsig-coTransportProtocolLayerEntity:* This MOC is intended to describe any type of connection-oriented transport protocol. This includes both the OSI transport protocol as well as the Internet TCP. It defines all permissible values in the OSI definition of administrative and operational states as well as other attributes pertaining to addresses, maximum connections, counters, etc.

- *nmsig-clNetworkProtocolLayerEntity:* This MOC also does not represent any specific connectionless network protocol. Rather, it is intended to define a high-level view of any connectionless network layer protocol. Therefore, it could support the ISO connectionless network protocol (CLNP) or the IP.

  This MOC is defined through the use of the operational states contained in the OSI specification as well as attributes pertaining to local addressing, time to live, counters, etc.

- *nmsig-equipment:* This MOC is used to represent actual physical components, such as modems, private branch exchanges (PBXs), packet switches, repeaters, bridges, etc. This MOC includes attributes such as location names, contact names, vendor names, administrative and operational states, etc.

- *nmsig-network:* This is used to define the sources that comprise a network. The resources may be equipment (physical) and software (logical).

- *nmsig-processingEntity:* This defines the computing aspect of the computer system. Although this entry is somewhat abstract, it can be inferred that components such as random access memory (RAM) and arithmetic logic units (ALUs) are included in the processing entity. It is not intended to include peripherals such as disk drives, tape drives, printers, etc.

- *nmsig-transportConnection:* This MOC does not represent any specific transport-oriented protocol. It is used to define characteristics that are common across any type of connection-oriented transport layer entity. Specifically, it is used to record the events of an active transport connection.

- *nmsig-transportConnectionProfile:* This MOC is used to define default and overriding attribute values for each instance of a transport connection.

- *nmsig-transportConnectionRetransmissionProfile:* This MOC is used to define default and nondefault values relating to transport layer retransmissions.

The attributes

Figure 5.18 shows the structure for the attributes in the MOCs. This section provides a brief summary of each of these attributes.

- *nmsig-agentID:* This attribute is defined as the distinguishing attribute for the MOC agent.

- *nmsig-cause:* This attribute records the reason a transport connection was deleted.

- *nmisg-checksumTPDUsDiscardedCounter:* This attribute contains a value recording the number of transport PDUs that were discarded because the check sum revealed an error.

- *nmisg-coTransportProtocolLayerEntityId:* This attribute describes

MOC Attributes
- nmsig-agentId
- nmsig-cause
- nmsig-checksumTPDUsDiscardedCounter
- nmsig-coTransportProtocolLayerEntityId
- nmsig-clNetworkProtocolLayerEntityId
- nmsig-contactNames
- nmsig-cPU-Type
- nmsig-entityUpTime
- nmsig-equipmentId
- nmsig-equipmentPurpose
- nmsig-inactivityTimeout
- nmsig-localNetworkAddress
- nmsig-localNetworkAddresses
- nmsig-localTransportAddresses
- nmsig-localTransportConnectionEndpoint
- nmsig-locationName
- nmsig-manufacturerInfo
- nmsig-maxConnections
- nmsig-maxPDUSize
- nmsig-maxRetransmissions
- nmsig-memorySize
- nmsig-networkEntityType
- nmsig-networkId
- nmsig-networkPurpose
- nmsig-nPDUTimeToLive
- nmsig-octetsRetransmittedErrorCounter
- nmsig-osInfo
- nmsig-openConnections
- nmsig-pDUsDiscardedCounter
- nmsig-pDUsForwardedCounter
- nmsig-pDUsReasmblFailCounter
- nmsig-pDUsReasmblOKCounter
- nmsig-peripheralNames
- nmsig-productLabel
- nmsig-release
- nmsig-remoteNetworkAddress
- nmsig-remoteTransportConnectionEndpoint
- nmsig-retransmissionTimerInitialValue
- nmsig-serialNumber
- nmsig-systemId
- nmsig-systemTime
- nmsig-transportConnectionId
- nmsig-transportConnectionProfileId
- nmsig-transportConnectionReference
- nmsig-transportEntityType
- nmsig-userFriendlyLabel
- nmsig-vendorName
- nmsig-wrappedCounter

Figure 5.18 The OIW MIL attributes.

the disguising attribute for the MOC connection-oriented protocol entity.

- *nmisg-clNetworkProtocolLayerEntityId:*   This identifies the disguising attribute for the MOC connectionless network protocol layer entity.

- *nmsig-contactNames:*   This identifies the names of one or more contacts associated with this class.

- *nmsig-cPU-type:*   This is used to identify the type of central processing unit (CPU) relating to this entity.

- *nmsig-entityUpTime:*   This attribute records the time interval elapsed since the entity's operational state changed from disabled to some other value.

- *nmsig-equipmentID:*   This records the distinguishing attribute for the MOC equipment.

- *nmsig-equipmentPurpose:*   This describes the purpose of the equipment. For example, the equipment is used for concentrating, modulation, switching, etc.

- *nmsig-inactivityTimeout:*   This records the value in 1/100s of a second in which the transport connection can remain up, even though there is no activity.

- *nmsig-localNetworkAddress:*   This contains the local network address of the transport connection. For example, the IP address for TCP or a network service access point (NSAP) address for an OSI transport protocol.

- *nmsig-localNetworkAddresses:*   This is used to record the number of local network addresses that is supported by the network protocol entity.

- *nmsig-localTransportAddresses:*   This value identifies the set of transport address that the transport protocol entity can provide to its users. It must consist of a network address and a transport connection endpoint.

- *nmsig-localTransportConnectionEndpoint:*   This identifies the local transport connection endpoint. Its actual value would represent a TCP source port or an OSI transport protocol t-selector.

- *nmsig-locationName:*   This provides a location identifier for the entity, typically a geographical name.

- *nmsig-manufacturerInfo:*   This attribute is used to identify the manufacturer of the product.

- *nmsig-MaxConnections:*   This attribute places a limit on the maximum number of concurrent transport connections that can be supported by the transport entity.

- *nmsig-maxPDUSize:* This attribute specifies the maximum length of the PDU that can be supported by the underlying layer of the transport connection.

- *nmsig-maxRetransmissions:* This value places a boundary on the maximum number of times a transport PDU can be transmitted before the connection is aborted.

- *nmsig-memorySize:* This identifies the amount of RAM that is available to the processing entity.

- *nmsig-networkEntityType:* This identifies the specific type of network layer protocol.

- *nmsig-networkID:* This attribute is a distinguishing attribute of the network MOC.

- *nmsig-networkPurpose:* This identifies the purpose of the network: accounting, electronic funds transfer, reservations systems, etc.

- *nmsig-nPDUTimeToLive:* In a connectionless network, this places a boundary on the amount of time the network PDU can exist in the network.

- *nmsig-octetsRetransmittedErrorCounter:* This is used to record the value of the number of octets that had to be retransmitted from this entity.

- *nmsig-osInfo:* This attribute is used to record operating systems, names, and other related features that are supported by the entity.

- *nmsig-openConnections:* This value identifies the current number of established transport connections.

- *nmsig-pDUsDiscardedCounter:* This identifies the number of PDUs that have been discarded at the network protocol entity.

- *nmsig-pDUsForwardedCounter:* This identifies the number of PDUs that were forward by the network protocol entity.

- *nmsig-pDUsReasmblFailCounter:* This identifies the number of PDUs that could not be reassembled by the network protocol.

- *nmsig-pDUsReasmblOKCounter:* This value records the number of PDUs that were successfully reassembled by the network protocol.

- *nmsig-peripheralNames:* This attribute is used to list the auxiliary devices and their names that pertain to a processing entity.

- *nmsig-productLabel:* This identifies the brand name or label relating to a product at the entity.

- *nmsig-release:* This attribute identifies the release number of a product.

- *nmsig-remoteNetworkAddress:* This is used to record the remote network address relating to a local transport connection. For example, it is an NSAP for OSI transport protocol or a remote IP address for TCP.

- *nmsig-remoteTransportConnectionEndpoint:* This identifies the remote transport connection endpoint. For example, it is the t-selector for OSI transport protocol or the destination port for TCP.

- *nmsig-retransmissionTimerInitialValue:* This attribute is the initial value set up for the transport connection retransmissions.

- *nmsig-serialNumber:* This contains the serial number of the product relating to the resource.

- *nmsig-systemID:* This is the distinguishing attribute for the MOC computer system.

- *nmsig-systemTime:* This attribute contains a current time that is being clocked in a computer system.

- *nmsig-transportConnectionID:* This value contains a distinguishing attribute for the transport connection MOC.

- *nmsig-transportConnectionProfileID:* This is the distinguishing attribute for the transport connection profile MOC.

- *nmsig-transportConnectionReference:* This attribute identifies the local transport connection reference that is established when two transport connection endpoints are mapped together. As an example, it would be a local socket number in TCP or the local connection reference for an OSI protocol.

- *nmsig-transportEntityType:* This is used to specify the type of transport protocol, for example, a class of protocol in the OSI Model.

- *nmsig-userFriendlyLabel:* This attribute simply allows a friendly name to be attached to the entity.

- *nmsig-vendorName:* Likewise, this attribute allows a name to be attached to the entity.

- *nmsig-wrappedCounter:* This contains an attribute ID as a value for a counter that uses wraparound operations.

OSI Network Management Forum, Managed Objects, and Libraries

Several discussions in this book have focused on the work of the OSI Network Management Forum. The purpose of this section is to provide an introduction to the Forum object classes and object class libraries. As discussed before, the reader should be aware that the OSI Network Management Forum operations are dynamic and the entries in the library are undergoing change. Also be aware that this explanation does not include all the attributes in the Forum library.

OSI Network Management Forum MOCs

Figure 5.19 shows the structure of the OSI Network Management Forum MOCs which reside in the Forum object class library. This section provides a brief description of each of these object classes.

- The *agentCME* (agent conformant managed entity) is defined as an open system that supports the forum interoperable interface. This simply means that an agentCME makes available one or more managed objects across the interoperable interface. The agentCME, at this time, supports the naming of these managed objects: logs and sieves.

Managed Object Classes (MOCs)

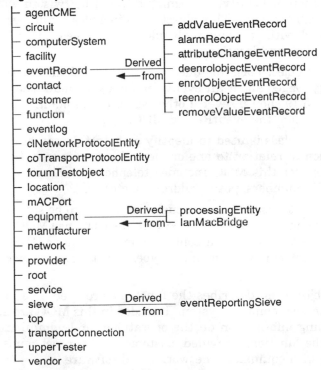

Figure 5.19   OSI/Network Management Forum MOCs.

- The *circuit* object class is used to describe a media that carries information on a point-to-point basis. A circuit can be a composite circuit consisting of more than one circuit. In turn these circuits are called component circuits of the composite circuit. A component circuit will determine the operational state of the composite circuit. The administrative states permitted are locked, shutting down, and unlocked. The operational states supported are disabled, enabled, active, and busy. As part of the object class definition, the circuit also has other attributes defined in the library, such as endpoint name, circuit bandwidth, circuit ID, type of circuit, component names, transmission direction, etc.

- The *computerSystem* object class includes components which comprise the data processing function, including CPUs, peripheral storage, file functions, etc. The computerSystem MOC consists of attributes such as administrative state, operational state, system identifier, peripheral names, processing entity names, up-time, etc.

- The *facility* object class includes any physical means of carrying signals. Indeed, a facility includes the definition of a circuit because facilities are used to carry circuits. Additionally, a facility can be contained within another facility. An example would be twisted wire pairs within a cable system. This object class includes a number of names associated with it: principally identifier names, manufacturer identification, and locations.

- The *eventRecord* object class includes commonly used information that is typically logged about all events in a network management system. As Fig. 5.19 shows, several other subordinate managed objects are derived from the eventRecord MOC.

- The *contact* object class is used to identify a contact person or contact organization in relation to one or more object instances. Common information for this MOC includes telephone numbers, electronic mail, FAX numbers, postal addresses, etc.

- The *customer* object class refers to a customer who is to be satisfied by the service being defined. Associated with the customer MOC are several attributes that deal with contact names, customer IDs, the types of services given to the customer (types of networks for example), etc.

- The *function* object class describes the functions provided by a network, equipment, or computer system. Included in this MOC are attributes providing information on the operational and administrative states of the functions provided, customer and contact names, names dealing with equipment, networks, and software.

- The *eventlog* is a managed object defined for storing of event records.

Its attributes contain information on permissible log size and what happens when a log reaches its maximum log size. The attributes also contain sieve constructs which define the criteria required before something is logged into the event log. Also included are log identifiers and operational and administrative states for the log.

- The *clNetworkProtocolEntity* (connectionless network protocol entity) managed class defines the attributes associated with the connectionless network protocol layer. As the reader may know, this type of managed object is typically implemented with the IP or CLNP. The attributes for this object class are similar to any network MIB for this type of protocol. For example, attributes stored as part of this MOC include a local network address, time-to-live value, number of PDUs sent and received, number PDUs reassembled or reassembly failed, and number of PDUs discarded. Also included in this MOC, as optional attributes, are identifiers dealing with products and manufacturers, releases, serial numbers, etc.

- The *coTransportProtocolEntity* (connection-oriented transport protocol entity) describes an object class for a connection-oriented transport protocol layer such as the ISO/CCITT transport protocol or the Internet TCP. The attributes included in this MOC describe the operational and administrative states, the number of connects, the number of disconnects (both locally and remotely), the maximum transport protocol data unit (TPDU) size supported, the maximum number of connections ongoing, local transport service access point (TSAP) identifiers, etc. Also included as optional attributes are labels that describe the manufacturer, release, serial number, and other administrative matters.

- The *forumTestobject* identifier relates specifically to the OSI Network Management Forum. Its intent is to establish procedures for performance testing in response to a common management information protocol (CMIP) M-ACTION request primitive.

- The *location* object class identifies a physical location of one or more objects or persons. As might be expected with such an object class, the attributes include geographic coordinates, location identifiers, addresses (a postal address for example), contact names, and other location details.

- The mACPort object class defines a LAN MAC port. The attributes within this class describe the administrative and operational state of the port, the specific MAC port identifier, number of packets transmitted (both in a unicast and broadcast mode), the data rate in octets for the port, etc. The purpose of this object class is to define a MAC port within a bridge, although the object class could certainly be used to describe any MAC port.

- The *equipment* object class defines, as to be expected, equipment within the network. The attributes for this object class deal principally with identifiers, associated customers, types of equipment, manufacturers' names, names dealing with service, software associated names, and other product related information.

- The *manufacturer* object class is used to identify and describe any organization which manufactures a physical resource. The attributes deal with the contact names, the manufacturer identifier, and other useful labels.

- The *network* object class describes a collection of physical or logical objects that work together to support the transmission of information. The principal attributes associated with this managed object are a network identifier and other labels to further define the services.

- The *provider* object class is used to describe an organization that is responsible for performing a service related to management. The services may be tariffed or nontariffed and the attributes in this object class describe the type service provided, a specific provider identifier, associated network, and service names.

- The *root* is the uppermost part of the MIB tree.

- The *service* object class includes attributes dealing with the types of network service provided to a client(s). The attributes for this object class include the identifier of the service, a provider name, names of clients, contact names, and types of service provided.

- The *sieve* object class defines the structure for provisioning a sieve to support some type of network management service. Its attributes include values describing the administrative or operational state of the object class, destination address, and the sieve construct and sieve ID.

- The *top* MOC is simply the object class from which every other object class is a subordinate class. It has no instantiations; it has no behavior.

- The *transportConnection* object class describes the attributes which form an active transport connection, either an OSI or TCP connection. It contains attributes dealing with times, time-out values, amount of traffic received, number of transport PDUs discarded because of problems, the maximum transport PDU size supported, and identifiers of the connections. Other values are associated with statistics normally associated with doing traffic analysis of any connection-oriented protocol.

- The *upperTester* object class defines the upper-layer CMIP tester. The purpose of this is to provide guidance on passing traffic between the CMIP upper tester and CMIP. The intent is to use C data structures which contain user data in the Abstract Syntax Notation 1 (ASN.1) notation.

■ The *vendor* object class contains attributes to identify a vendor as well as contact names.

Other MIBs

The Internet is quite active in the development of other MIBs. For example, MIBs are available for the definition of managed objects pertaining to DS1 and DS3 interfaces.

MIBs for LANs

As of this writing, the IEEE had not developed any definitions of MIB for its LANs or MANs. However the Internet has taken upon itself to define MIBs for the IEEE 802.5 token ring and IEEE 802.4 token bus.

Space limitations preclude any more examples of MIBs in this book. Perhaps a book solely devoted to MIBs and MILs is in order.

Summary

The MIB/MIL serves as the foundation for network management. It contains information about the network elements by describing a set of managed objects (the network resources) and their attributes. The Internet MIB and the OSI MIB are emerging as the most prevalent MIB standards. The OSI Network Management Forum has also published a comprehensive MIL.

CMISE and CMIP

Introduction

This chapter examines two OSI network management standards, the common management information service element (CMISE) and the common management information protocol (CMIP). The first part of the chapter provides a general introduction to the standards. The second part focuses on each one in more detail.

These standards are used by network management to (1) define the network management services to be provided between a network management function and CMIP (with CMISE) and (2) transport the network management information between agents and managing processes (with CMIP). Figure 6.1 shows these relationships.

To gain a better understanding of these standards, we return to Fig. 6.2, which we have been using throughout the book. Gateway A has sent network control an alarm message, which is contained in a CMIP protocol data unit (PDU; or message to some people). Its rather cryptic contents are simply shorthand notations used by CMIP/CMISE to de-

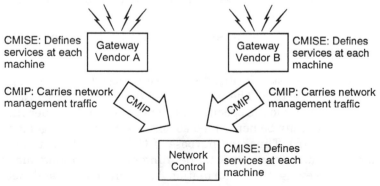

Figure 6.1 Relationships of CMISE and CMIP.

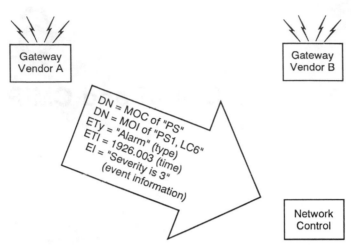

Figure 6.2   Example of a CMIP message.

note the following (the reader may wish to review Chap. 1, which introduced all the terms used in this introductory section, object class, object instance, etc.):

- *DN = MOC of "PS."*   The gateway reports that it is reporting on a packet switch (PS) managed object class (MOC). The DN is CMIP/CMISE shorthand for distinguished name.

- *DN = MOI of "PS1, LC6."*   The actual object being reported is an instance of the MOC, which is called a managed object instance (MOI). Its DN is "PS1, LC6".

- *ETy = "Alarm."*   The ETy is a shorthand notation for type of message (or simply type, for people who relate to plain English).

- *ETI = 1926.003.*   The ETI is a shorthand notation for the time that the alarm message was generated (which is further annotated in the figure with the term *time*).

- *EI = "Severity is 3."*   EI means event information. In this example, it deals with the severity level of the alarm.

Network control uses standardized software to decode the message and take appropriate action. The action is not defined in the CMISE/CMIP standards. The action is specific to the network and the permissible operations that may be performed as defined in the management information base (MIB). Thus, the purpose of CMISE/CMIP is to provide a general, common framework for defining network management operations for conveying this information between agents and network control.

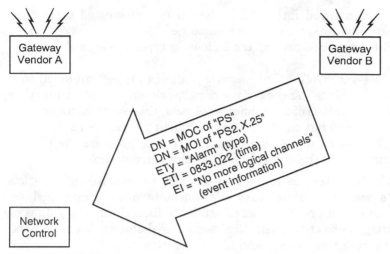

Figure 6.3   An alarm message from gateway B.

It may be difficult to see how these standards can be of any real value if they are not specific enough to define detailed management operations. Figure 6.3 provides the answer. Gateway B has sent an alarm message to network control using CMIP. Notice that the structure of the message is identical to the alarm message generated by gateway A in Fig. 6.2. However, this message is reporting on a problem with the X.25 operations at the gateway. Therefore, the MOI is "PS2, X.25" and the event information and time are different. Nonetheless, the same network control software is used to handle traffic from both gateways. It does not matter if gateway A is a Northern Telecom switch and gateway B is a Cisco router. All must use a standard CMIP message.

With this background information in mind, we now turn our attention to the specific operations of CMISE and CMIP.

9595   Common Management Information Service Element (CMISE)

Introduction

The CMISE is defined in ISO 9595. As the title suggests, it identifies the service elements used in management operations as well as their arguments (parameters). It also provides a framework for common management procedures that can be invoked from remote locations.

The reader should remember that the OSI service element standards contain the rules for the creation and use of primitives between adjacent layers in the same machine. These primitives and their parameters are mapped into a PDU, which is transmitted across the communications link(s) to another machine.

CMISE is organized around the following types of services:

- *M-EVENT-REPORT:* This service is used to report an event to a service user. Since the operations of network entities are a function of the specifications of the managed objects, this event is not defined by the standard but can be any event about a managed object that the CMISE user chooses to report. The service provides the time of the occurrence of the event as well as the current time.

- *M-GET:* This service is used by CMISE to retrieve information from its peer. The service uses information about the managed object to obtain and return a set of attribute identifiers and values of the managed object or a selection of managed objects. It can only be used in a confirmed mode, and a reply is expected.

- *M-CANCEL-GET:* This service is invoked by the CMISE user to request a peer to cancel a previously requested M-GET service. It can only be used in a confirmed mode, and a reply is expected.

- *M-SET:* A CMISE user can use this service to request the modification of attribute values (the properties) of a managed object. It can be requested in a confirmed or nonconfirmed mode. If confirmed, a reply is expected.

- *M-ACTION:* This service is used by the user to request that another user perform some type of action on a management object. It can be requested in a confirmed or nonconfirmed mode. If confirmed, a reply is expected.

- *M-CREATE:* This service is used to create a representation of another instance of a managed object, along with its associated management information values. It can only be used in a confirmed mode, and a reply is expected.

- *M-DELETE:* This service performs the reverse operation of the M-CREATE. It deletes an instance of a managed object. It can only be used in a confirmed mode, and a reply is expected.

Use of underlaying services and layers

The ISO 9595 standard uses the following remote operations service element (ROSE) services: (1) RO-INVOKE, (2) RO-RESULT, (3) RO-ERROR, and (4) RO-REJECT. In turn, ROSE uses the P-DATA service of the presentation layer. Figure 6.4 shows the relationship of CMIP and CMISE to association control service element (ACSE), ROSE, and the presentation layer.

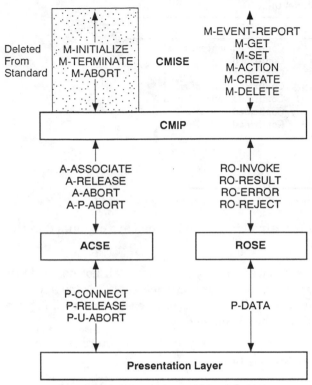

Figure 6.4 CMISE service elements with ACSE and ROSE.

Earlier versions of CMIP/CMISE defined services for the establishment of an application association. The services shown in the shaded box in Fig. 6.4 are no longer defined. An association is obtained by the CMISE service user invoking the ACSE primitives directly. The appendix to this chapter discusses this change in more detail.

Functional units

Like many OSI standards, the CMISE services are organized around the concept of *functional units* (see Table 6.1). The idea of functional units is really quite simple; a functional unit is associated with a service, which in turn is associated with a CMISE service primitive or primitives. Functional units are an efficient and readily available mechanism to describe and define the operations between the communicating entities.

Functional units in CMISE are categorized as kernel functional units and additional functional units. These definitions are provided

TABLE 6.1   CMISE Functional Units

Functional unit	Type
M-EVENT-REPORT	Confirmed/nonconfirmed
M-GET	Confirmed
M-CANCEL-GET	Confirmed
M-SET	Confirmed/nonconfirmed
M-ACTION	Confirmed/nonconfirmed
M-CREATE	Confirmed
M-DELETE	Confirmed
Multiple Object Selection	
Filter	
Multiple Reply	
Extended Service	

Note: First six services are part of the kernel functional unit

below, and the terms contained in the definitions are explained in the subsequent material.

■ *Kernel:*   (1) A linked identification parameter shall not be used unless the multiple reply functional unit is selected. (2) Scope and synchronization parameters shall not be used unless the multiple object selection functional unit has been selected.

■ *Additional:*   This option makes the use of parameters not permitted in the kernel functional unit.

The kernel functional units are described above; the other functional units are used in the following manner:

■ *Multiple Object Selection:*   This service makes available the scope and synchronization parameters for use in the kernel functional unit. It is not available in the M-EVENT-REPORT and M-CREATE operations.

■ *Filter:*   This service makes available the filter parameter in the kernel functional unit. It is not available in the M-EVENT-REPORT and M-CREATE operations.

■ *Multiple Reply:*   This service makes available the linked identification parameter in the kernel functional unit. It is not available in the M-EVENT-REPORT and M-CREATE operations.

■ *Extended Service:*   This service makes available presentation services other than the P-DATA service.

Establishing the association

ACSE must be invoked before any operations can take place (see Chap. 3). The A-ASSOCIATE user data field contains the following information:

- *Functional units:* The initiating CMISE user must supply the additional functional units that will be used during the operations.

- *Access control:* This parameter is not defined but is available if the CMISE user wants to establish access rules during the operation.

- *User information:* Any other information that the user wishes to include is placed in this parameter. Its value depends upon the application context.

CMISE services

This section examines each of the CMISE services. A time sequence diagram is provided for each service to show the relationships of the primitive operations. The parameters (arguments) contained in the service definition primitives are also examined.

Be aware that some of the parameters are used in more than one service and are described in each service. While this approach creates some redundancy in the text, it should prove helpful because the reader will not have to turn back repeatedly to previous pages to read about a parameter. Moreover, some of the parameters' use varies with each service, and these variances are also explained. Also, the term *CMIPM* refers to a CMIP "machine," a term used to connote a protocol entity.

M-EVENT-REPORT service. This service is likely to be of considerable interest to the reader. It is used by CMISE users to report events to each other. It can be used as both a confirmed and a nonconfirmed service.

Figure 6.5 shows the service definition primitives involved in this operation. Several parameters are used with these primitives. The reader is encouraged to compare the parameters in the M-EVENT-REPORT primitive with the CMIP messages in Figs. 6.2 and 6.3. It will be obvious that these parameters are used to create the fields in the CMIP message. Thus, the M-EVENT-REPORT service is used to support (in the examples in Figs. 6.5 and 6.7) the alarm reporting function between the gateways and network control by using the information in the CMISE primitives. The parameters are as follows:

- *Invoke identifier:* This parameter serves as the identifier that is used during the reporting operation. Its value is not defined in the standard. It should be unambiguous and distinct from the other identifiers that are being used at the current time. The invoke identifier is a required parameter in all the primitives for this service.

- *Mode:* This parameter is used to identify if the reporting operation is to be confirmed or nonconfirmed. It is a required parameter in the request and indication primitives.

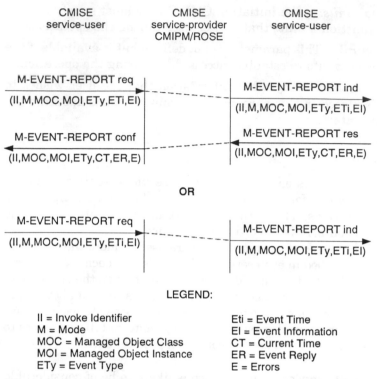

CMISE
service-user

CMISE
service-provider
CMIPM/ROSE

CMISE
service-user

M-EVENT-REPORT req

(II,M,MOC,MOI,ETy,ETi,EI)

M-EVENT-REPORT ind

(II,M,MOC,MOI,ETy,ETi,EI)

M-EVENT-REPORT conf

(II,MOC,MOI,ETy,CT,ER,E)

M-EVENT-REPORT res

(II,MOC,MOI,ETy,CT,ER,E)

OR

M-EVENT-REPORT req

(II,M,MOC,MOI,ETy,ETi,EI)

M-EVENT-REPORT ind

(II,M,MOC,MOI,ETy,ETi,EI)

LEGEND:

II = Invoke Identifier
M = Mode
MOC = Managed Object Class
MOI = Managed Object Instance
ETy = Event Type

Eti = Event Time
EI = Event Information
CT = Current Time
ER = Event Reply
E = Errors

Figure 6.5   The **M-EVENT-REPORT** service.

- *Managed object class:*   This specifies the class of the managed object on which the event is being reported. It is a required parameter in the request and indication primitives and is optional in the response and confirmation primitives.

- *Managed object instance:*   This parameter specifies the instance of the managed object during the event. It is required for the request and indication primitives and is optional for the response and confirmation primitives.

- *Event type:*   This parameter identifies the type of event that is being reported. However, its identification depends on the context of the managed object. It is required in the request and indication primitives and may exist in the response and confirmation primitives if the event reply parameter is included.

- *Event time:*   This parameter contains the time the event was generated. It is an optional parameter in the request and indication primitives. It does not reside in the response and confirmation primitives.

- *Event information:*   This parameter contains any information that the service user chooses to supply about the event being reported. It is not defined in the standard; it is application-specific. It is optional in the request and indication primitives. It does not reside in the response and confirmation primitives.

■ *Current time:* This parameter contains the time of the response generation. Of course, it is not included in the request and indication primitives. It is optional in the response and confirmation primitives.

■ *Event reply:* This parameter contains the reply to the event report, whether it is successful or not. It is not allowed in the request and indication primitives. It is a conditional parameter within the response and confirmation primitives depending on the user's choice of what to place in the parameter.

■ *Errors:* This parameter contains diagnostic information about the operation in the event an error occurred. The CMISE standard allows the errors to be reported as shown in Table 6.2.

Relationship of alarms, CMISE, CMIP, and ROSE. Figure 6.6 presents a summary of a number of concepts we have been discussing in this and previous chapters. It will be used to tie together several ideas. Alarm management uses CMISE to pass a primitive to CMIP. It contains the arguments used by CMIP to form the PDU. CMIP forms the PDU, takes appropriate actions, depending upon the primitive, and passes a ROSE primitive to ROSE. ROSE then invokes its services and passes the PDU to the presentation layer, etc.

The "A" (argument) field in the CMIP to ROSE primitive contains the information passed from the alarm management module to CMIP. Therefore, MOC, MOI, ETy, ETI, and EI are encapsulated into the ROSE argument field.

M-GET service. This service is used by a CMISE service user to obtain information from a peer service user. Typically this service is used to retrieve status indicators on managed objects in the network or information about the prior removal or adding of objects. This service is a confirmed service, as illustrated in Fig. 6.7.

The primitives for the M-GET service carry the following parameters:

■ *Invoke identifier:* This parameter serves as the identifier that is used during the M-GET operation. Its value is not defined in the standard. It should be unambiguous and distinct from the other identifiers that are being used at the current time. The invoke identifier is a required parameter in all the primitives.

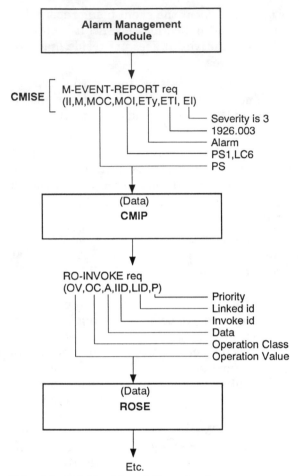

Figure 6.6 Relationships of the network management layers.

- *Linked identifier:*   The linked identifier is used only if multiple replies are to be transmitted for this particular operation (for example in a scoped operation). Its value is the same as the invoke identifier parameter in the indication primitive.

- *Base object class:*   This parameter specifies the class of the managed object. It also can specify the class of a managed object whose attribute values are to be retrieved during the M-GET operation. In the former case, the values are used as a starting point for managed object selections for the application of the filter.

- *Base object instance:*   This parameter specifies the instance of the managed object, again to be used as a starting point on which the filter is applied.

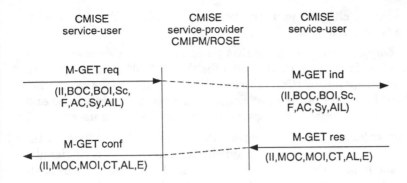

OR
For Linked Operations

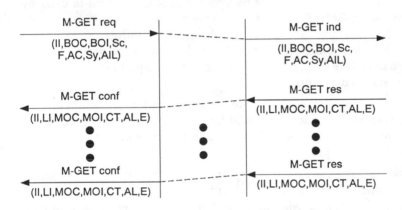

LEGEND:

II = Invoke Identifier	Sy = Synchonization
LI = Linked Identifier	AIL = Attribute ID List
BOC = Base Object Class	MOC = Managed Object Class
BOI = Base Object Instance	MOI = Managed Object Instance
Sc = Scope	CT = Current Time
F = Filter	AL = Attribute List
AC = Access Control	E = Errors

Figure 6.7 The M-GET service.

- *Scope:* This parameter is used to identify the subtree for the search and retrieval. Three levels of search are permitted: (1) base object alone, (2) the nth level subordinates of the base object, or (3) the base object and all its subordinates. The default for this value is base object alone.

- *Filter:* This parameter specifies the test conditions for the search. It is applied to the scoped managed objects. As discussed earlier, the filter uses boolean operators (AND, OR, NOT). The filter works on test conditions chained with the boolean operators. The test evaluates the true condition.

- *Access control:* The value for this parameter is not defined in the standard but is intended to be used for the CMISE service users to agree upon control functions during the association. Notice the access control parameter does not reside in the returning response and confirm primitives from the responding CMISE service user.

- *Synchronization:* This parameter allows the invoking user to inform the performing user how to synchronize information retrievals. Two methods of synchronization are available: atomic and best effort. The reader may wish to refer to Chap. 1 for a description of the synchronization services in CMISE.

- *Attribute identifier list:* This parameter is optional and is used by the requesting CMISE service user. This responding service user examines these IDs to determine which attribute values to return. If the parameter is omitted, all attribute identifiers are assumed. The actual use of this list is dependent upon the implementation specification selected by the MOC.

- *Managed object class:* This parameter specifies the class of the managed object in which the event has occurred. It is not used in the request and indication primitives and is conditional in the response and confirmation primitives.

- *Managed object instance:* This parameter specifies the instance of the managed object during the event. It is not used in the request and indication primitives and is optional for the response and confirmation primitives.

- *Current time:* This parameter contains the time of the response generation. It is not included in the request and indication primitives. It is optional in the response and confirmation primitives.

- *Attribute list:* This parameter contains the attribute identifiers and their values that are to be returned by the performing CMISE user. It may or may not be included depending on the success or failure of the operation.

- *Errors:* The M-GET services provide for several error reporting conditions for diagnostic purposes. These errors are listed and described briefly in Table 6.2.

M-CANCEL-GET service. The GET service is the only service that has a cancel option. One might question why the other services, such as set, create, and delete, do not have the a cancellation feature. The answer is that these other operations entail changing either the attributes of a managed object or its deletion. Therefore, other cancels are not allowed because it is not prudent to cancel an operation on an object before the operation is complete. A premature cancel might leave the object in an incomplete or incorrect state. With a simple GET, the invoker is only asking for the return of information, not the alteration of it. Nonetheless, even a GET operation should not be allowed to retrieve information about an object unless the object is in a stable state.

As another example, because of poor filtering and scoping, a GET operation may consume too much time and too many resources. Therefore, a user could cancel the operation if it is determined that such a problem is occurring.

Figure 6.8 illustrates the M-CANCEL-GET operations. The parameters associated with the M-CANCEL-GET are as follows:

- *Invoke identifier:* This parameter serves as the identifier that is used during the M-CANCEL-GET operation. Its value is not defined in the standard. It should be unambiguous and distinct from the other identifiers that are being used at the current time. The invoke identifier is a required parameter in all the primitives.

- *GET invoke identifier:* This parameter identifies the outstanding M-GET operation that is to be canceled.

- *Errors:* The M-CANCEL-GET services provide for several error reporting conditions for diagnostic purposes. These errors are listed and described briefly in Table 6.2.

M-SET Service. This service is used by an invoking-CMISE user to request the change of attribute values by a performing-CMISE service

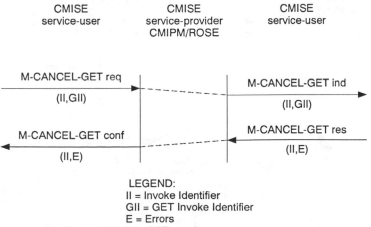

Figure 6.8   The M-CANCEL-GET service.

user. It can be used as a confirmed or nonconfirmed service as shown in Figs. 6.9 and 6.10. The information could be any type of information deemed appropriate for the network administrators. CMISE does not become involved in the information content of the change.

The parameters for the M-SET service are as follows:

■ *Invoke identifier:* This parameter serves as the identifier that is used during the operation. Its value is not defined in the standard. It

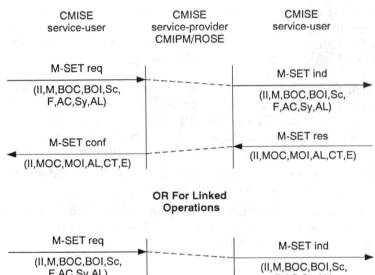

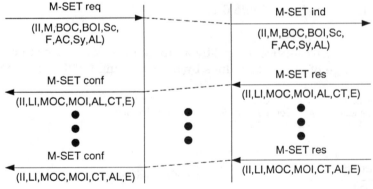

LEGEND:

II = Invoke Identifier	AC = Access Control
LI = Linked Identifier	Sy = Synchronization
M = MODE	MOC = Managed Object Class
BOC = Base Object Class	MOI = Managed Object Instance
BOI = Base Object Instance	AL = Attribute List
Sc = Scope	CT = Current Time
F = Filter	E = Errors

Figure 6.9   M-SET service.

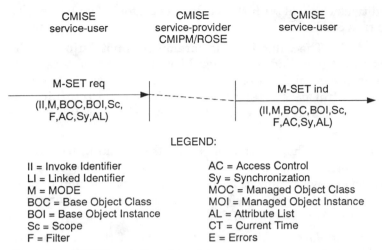

LEGEND:

II = Invoke Identifier   AC = Access Control
LI = Linked Identifier   Sy = Synchronization
M = MODE   MOC = Managed Object Class
BOC = Base Object Class   MOI = Managed Object Instance
BOI = Base Object Instance   AL = Attribute List
Sc = Scope   CT = Current Time
F = Filter   E = Errors

Figure 6.10   M-SET unconfirmed service.

should be unambiguous and distinct from the other identifiers that are being used at the current time. The invoke identifier is a required parameter in all the primitives.

■ *Linked identifier:*   The linked identifier is used only if multiple replies are to be transmitted for this particular operation.

■ *Mode:*   This parameter is used to identify whether the operation is to be confirmed or nonconfirmed. It is a required parameter in the request and indication primitives.

■ *Base object class:*   This specifies the class of the managed object in which the event has occurred. It is a required parameter in the request and indication primitives and is not used in the response and confirmation primitives.

■ *Base object instance:*   This parameter specifies the instance of the managed object during the event. It is required for the request and indication primitives and is not used in the response and confirmation primitives.

■ *Scope:*   This parameter is used to identify the subtree for the search. Three levels of search are permitted: (1) base object alone, (2) the nth level subordinates of the base object, and (3) the base object and all its subordinates. The default for this value is base object alone.

■ *Filter:*   This parameter specifies the test conditions for the search. It is applied to the scoped managed objects. As discussed earlier, the filter uses boolean operators (AND, OR, NOT). The filter works on test conditions chained with the boolean operators. The test evaluates the true condition.

- *Access control:* The value for this parameter is not defined in the standard, but it is intended to be used for the CMISE service users to agree upon control functions during the association. Notice that the access control parameter does not reside in the returning response and confirm primitives from the responding CMISE service user.

- *Synchronization:* This parameter allows the invoking user to inform the performing user how to synchronize information retrievals. Two methods of synchronization are available: atomic and best effort. The reader may wish to refer to Chap. 1 for a description of the synchronization services in CMISE.

- *Managed object class:* This specifies the class of the managed object in which the event has occurred. It is not used in the request and indication primitives and is a conditional parameter in the response and confirmation primitives.

- *Managed object instance:* This parameter specifies the instance of the managed object during the event. It is required for the request and indication primitives and is optional for the response and confirmation primitives.

- *Attribute list:* This is a required parameter. The service user returns these values based on the values of the attribute identifiers.

- *Current time:* This parameter contains the time of the response generation. It is not included in the request and indication primitives. It is optional in the response and confirmation primitives.

- *Errors:* The M-SET service provides several errors for diagnostic purposes. They are listed and briefly described in Table 6.2.

M-ACTION service. As the name implies, this service is used by the invoking service user to request the performing CMISE service user to operate on a managed object, that is to say, to perform an action on a managed object. It can be used as a confirmed and/or a nonconfirmed service. The parameters shown in Figs. 6.11 and 6.12 are as follows:

- *Invoke identifier:* This parameter serves as the identifier that is used during the operation. Its value is not defined in the standard. It should be unambiguous and distinct from the other identifiers that are being used at the current time. The invoke identifier is a required parameter in all the primitives.

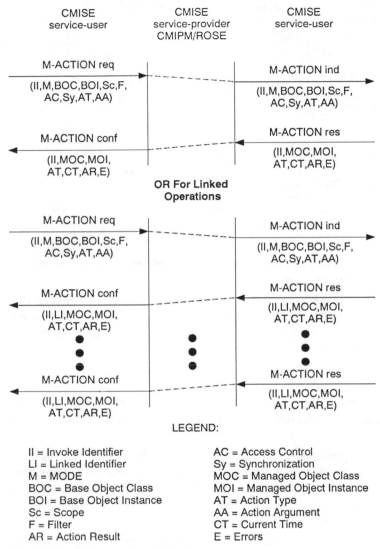

CMISE
service-user

CMISE
service-provider
CMIPM/ROSE

CMISE
service-user

M-ACTION req

(II,M,BOC,BOI,Sc,F,
AC,Sy,AT,AA)

M-ACTION ind

(II,M,BOC,BOI,Sc,F,
AC,Sy,AT,AA)

M-ACTION conf

(II,MOC,MOI,
AT,CT,AR,E)

M-ACTION res

(II,MOC,MOI,
AT,CT,AR,E)

**OR For Linked
Operations**

M-ACTION req

(II,M,BOC,BOI,Sc,F,
AC,Sy,AT,AA)

M-ACTION ind

(II,M,BOC,BOI,Sc,F,
AC,Sy,AT,AA)

M-ACTION conf

(II,LI,MOC,MOI,
AT,CT,AR,E)

M-ACTION res

(II,LI,MOC,MOI,
AT,CT,AR,E)

M-ACTION conf

(II,LI,MOC,MOI,
AT,CT,AR,E)

M-ACTION res

(II,LI,MOC,MOI,
AT,CT,AR,E)

LEGEND:

II = Invoke Identifier
LI = Linked Identifier
M = MODE
BOC = Base Object Class
BOI = Base Object Instance
Sc = Scope
F = Filter
AR = Action Result

AC = Access Control
Sy = Synchronization
MOC = Managed Object Class
MOI = Managed Object Instance
AT = Action Type
AA = Action Argument
CT = Current Time
E = Errors

Figure 6.11 The M-ACTION service.

- *Linked identifier:* The linked identifier is used only if multiple replies are to be transmitted for this particular operation.

- *Mode:* This parameter is used to identify whether the operation is to be confirmed or nonconfirmed. It is a required parameter in the request and indication primitives.

- *Base object class:* This specifies the class of the managed object in which the event has occurred. It is a required parameter in the re-

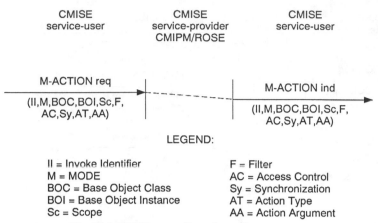

Figure 6.12   The M-ACTION unconfirmed service.

quest and indication primitives and does not exist in the response and confirmation primitives.

- *Base object instance:*   This parameter specifies the instance of the managed object during the event. It is required for the request and indication primitives and does not exist in the response and confirmation primitives.

- *Scope:*   This parameter is used to identify the subtree for the search. Three levels of search are permitted: (1) base object alone, (2) the nth level subordinates of the base object, and (3) the base object and all its subordinates. The default for this value is base object alone.

- *Filter:*   This parameter specifies the test conditions for the search. It is applied to the scoped managed objects. As discussed earlier, the filter uses boolean operators (AND, OR, NOT). The filter works on test conditions chained with the boolean operators. The test evaluates the true condition.

- *Managed object class:*   This specifies the class of the managed object in which the event has occurred. It is not used in the request and indication primitives. It is a conditional parameter in the other primitives.

- *Managed object instance:*   This parameter specifies the instance of the managed object during the event. It is optional for the response and confirmation primitives.

- *Access control:*   This parameter is not defined in the standard but is intended to be used for the CMISE service users to agree upon control functions during the association. Notice that the access control parameter does not reside in the returning response and confirm primitives from the responding CMISE service user.

- *Synchronization:* This parameter allows the invoking user to inform the performing user how to synchronize information retrievals. Two methods of synchronization are available: atomic and best effort. The reader may wish to refer to the introductory part of this book for a description of the synchronization services in CMISE.

- *Action type:* This parameter describes the type of action that is to be performed on the managed object.

- *Action argument:* This parameter provides extra information about the action. It is optional for the request and indication primitives and does not exist in the response and confirm primitives.

- *Current time:* This parameter contains the time of the response generation. It is not included in the request and indication primitives. It is optional in the response and confirmation primitives.

- *Action result:* This parameter contains the result of the action.

- *Errors:* The errors supported with the M-ACTION service are listed and described briefly in Table 6.2.

M-CREATE service. This service is requested by the invoking CMISE user to request a performing CMISE user to create the representation of a new object instance. In so doing, it must complete its identification and the values associated with the needed management information. It is used only as a confirmed service. The operations for the M-CREATE service are shown in Fig. 6.13. The parameters used for these primitives are as follows:

- *Invoke identifier:* This parameter serves as the identifier that is used during the operation. Its value is not defined in the standard. It should be unambiguous and distinct from the other identifiers that are being used at the current time. The invoke identifier is a required parameter in all the primitives.

- *Managed object class:* This specifies the class of the managed object in which the event has occurred. It is a required parameter in the request and indication primitives and is conditional in the response and confirmation primitives.

- *Managed object instance:* This parameter specifies the instance of the managed object during the event. It is required for the request and indication primitives and is conditional for the response and confirmation primitives.

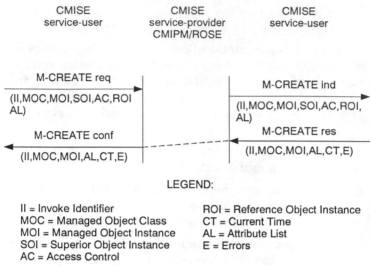

LEGEND:

II = Invoke Identifier   ROI = Reference Object Instance
MOC = Managed Object Class   CT = Current Time
MOI = Managed Object Instance   AL = Attribute List
SOI = Superior Object Instance   E = Errors
AC = Access Control

Figure 6.13   The M-CREATE service.

- *Superior object instance:*   This parameter specifies an existing MOI which is designated as the superior of the new object instance.

- *Access control:*   The values in this parameter are not defined in the standard but it is intended to be used by the CMISE service users to agree upon control functions during the association. The access control parameter does not reside in the returning response and confirm primitives from the responding CMISE service user.

- *Reference object instance:*   This parameter specifies the instance of the managed object during the event. It is required for the request and indication primitives and does not exist in the response and confirmation primitives.

- *Attribute list:*   This parameter is used by the performing CMISE service user. This service user returns these values based on the values of the attribute identifiers. If the parameter is omitted, all attribute identifiers are assumed. The actual use of this list is dependent upon the implementation specification selected by the MOC.

- *Current time:*   This parameter contains the time of the response generation. It is not included in the request and indication primitives. It is optional in the response and confirmation primitives.

- *Errors:*   The errors provided with this service are listed and briefly described in Table 6.2.

M-DELETE service.   This service is used to delete a representation of a MOI. It is also used to deregister its identification. It is only used as a

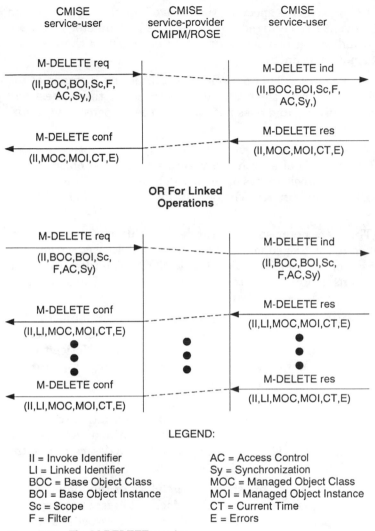

Figure 6.14 The M-DELETE service.

confirmed service. The parameters shown in Fig. 6.14 that are used with this service are as follows:

- *Invoke identifier:* This parameter serves as the identifier that is used during the operation. Its value is not defined in the standard. It should be unambiguous and distinct from the other identifiers that are being used at the current time. The invoke identifier is a required parameter in all the primitives.

- *Linked identifier:* The linked identifier is used only if multiple replies are to be transmitted for this particular operation.

- *Base object class:* This specifies the class of the managed object in which the event has occurred. It is a required parameter in the request and indication primitives and does not exist in the response and confirmation primitives.

- *Base object instance:* This parameter specifies the instance of the managed object during the event. It is required for the request and indication primitives and does not exist for the response and confirmation primitives.

- *Scope:* This parameter is used to identify the subtree for the search. Three levels of search are permitted: (1) base object alone, (2) the nth level subordinates of the base object, and (3) the base object and all its subordinates. The default for this value is base object alone.

- *Filter:* This parameter specifies the test conditions for the search. It is applied to the scoped managed objects. As discussed earlier, the filter uses boolean operators (AND, OR, NOT). The filter works on test conditions chained with the boolean operators. The test evaluates the true condition.

- *Access control:* The value for this parameter is not defined in the standard but it is intended to be used by the CMISE service users to agree upon control functions during the association. Notice the access control parameter does not reside in the returning response and confirm primitives from the responding CMISE service user.

- *Synchronization:* This parameter allows the invoking user to inform the performing user how to synchronize information retrievals. Two methods of synchronization are available: atomic and best effort. The reader may wish to refer to Chap. 1 for a description of the synchronization services in CMISE.

- *Managed object class:* This specifies the class of the managed object in which the event has occurred. It does not exist in the request and indication primitives and is conditional in the response and confirmation primitives.

- *Managed object instance:* This parameter specifies the instance of the managed object during the event. It does not exist in the request and indication primitives and is conditional for the response and confirmation primitives.

- *Current time:* This parameter contains the time of the response generation. It is not included in the request and indication primitives. It is optional in the response and confirmation primitives.

- *Errors:* The errors supportive of this service are listed and briefly described in Table 6.2.

TABLE 6.2   CMISE Errors

Error	Event report	Get	Set	Action	Create	Delete	Cancel Get
Access denied		x	x	x	x	x	
Class instance conflict		x	x	x	x	x	
Complexity limitation		x	x	x		x	
Duplicate invocation	x	x	x	x	x	x	x
Duplicate managed object instance					x		
Get list error		x					
Invalid argument value	x			x			
Invalid attribute value					x		
Invalid filter		x	x	x		x	
Invalid object instance					x		
Missing attribute value					x		
Invalid scope		x	x	x		x	
Mistyped argument		x	x	x	x		x
No such action				x			
No such argument	x			x			
No such attribute					x		
No such event type	x						
No such invoke identifier							x
No such object class	x	x	x	x	x	x	
No such object instance	x	x	x	x	x	x	
No such reference object					x		
Processing failure	x	x	x	x	x	x	x
Resource limitation	x	x	x	x	x	x	x
Set list error			x				
Sync not supported		x	x	x		x	
Unrecognized operation	x	x	x	x	x	x	

Summary of error codes for CMISE

Table 6.2 contains a list of the errors used by the CMISE. They are described in this section.

Access denied

Because of security problems, the requested operation is not performed.

Class instance conflict

The specified MOI is not a member of the specified class.

Complexity limitation

A parameter in the requested operation is too complex, so the operation is not performed.

Duplicate invocation

The invoke identifier is already specified; therefore, it cannot be used again.

Duplicate managed object instance

The invoking CMISE user has a new MOI value that is not allowed because it is already registered for a managed object of the specified class.

Get list error	One or more of the attribute values are not read because of access problems, or the attributes do not exist. Any attribute values that cannot be read are returned.
Invalid argument value	The argument specified in the primitive is unrecognizable, out of range, or otherwise unacceptable.
Invalid attribute value	The value is not permitted. It could be out of a threshold range or simply not allowed.
Invalid filter	The filter parameter is not supported, or it contains unknown values.
Invalid object instance	The name of the object instance violates naming rules.
Missing attribute value	A required attribute value is not supplied or a default value is not available.
Invalid scope	The scope parameter value is in error.
Mistyped argument	An argument (parameter) is not agreed upon for use on the association.
No such action	The action type is not supported.
No such argument	The argument is not recognized.
No such attribute	The attribute is not recognized.
No such event type	The receiver does not know about the event; it is not logged in as an event type.
No such invoke identifier	The receiver does not recognize the invoke identifier.
No such object class	The specified managed object parameter is not recognized.
No such object instance	The specified MOI cannot be found.
No such reference object	The parameter of a reference object instance is not recognized.
Processing failure	Any type of error occurrence which creates a failure; the type of failure is not defined in the standard.
Resource limitation	The performing service user is not able to perform the requested operation because of constraints on its resources.
Set list error	The attribute values that can be modified are modified, but one or more at-

	tribute values have not been modified for the reasons given.
Synchronization not supported	The requested type of synchronization is not supported.
Unrecognized operation	The operation requested is not agreed upon by the CMISE service users.

9596 Common Management Information Protocol (CMIP)

The ISO 9595 establishes the protocol specification for CMIP. CMIP supports the services listed in Table 6.3. These services were explained in the previous section. Notice that some of the services are confirmed, nonconfirmed, or have an option of using either confirmed or nonconfirmed operation. These services allow two OSI management service users to set up actions to be performed on managed objects, to change attributes of the objects, and to report the status of the managed objects.

Like the other OSI protocols, CMIP must follow rules on the composition and exchange of PDUs. All the CMIP PDUs are defined by ASN.1. The operations are defined in ISO 9072-1 (ROSE) with the OPERATION and ERROR external macros. Because of its dependence on ROSE, CMIP does not contain state tables, event lists, predicates, or action tables.

CMIP user information for A-ASSOCIATE

The CMISE user is responsible for setting up an association before any management operations can begin. This procedure is governed by the ACSE and is discussed in Chap. 4.

The user information field in the A-ASSOCIATE service contains the information to identify the additional functional units, the version of the protocol, access control mechanisms, and specific user information. They have been described earlier in this chapter. Figure 6.15

TABLE 6.3 CMIP Services

Service	Type of confirmation
M-EVENT-REPORT	Confirmed/nonconfirmed
M-GET	Confirmed
M-CANCEL-GET	Confirmed
M-SET	Confirmed/nonconfirmed
M-ACTION	Confirmed/nonconfirmed
M-CREATE	Confirmed
M-DELETE	Confirmed

```
--Example of CMIP user information in the
--A-ASSOCIATE service (simplified)

CMIPUserInfo :: = SEQUENCE
                { protocolVersion     [0] IMPLICIT ProtocolVersion
                  functionUnits       [1] IMPLICIT FunctionalUnits
                  accessControl       [2] EXTERNAL OPTIONAL
                  userInfo            [3] EXTERNAL OPTIONAL
                }

   FunctionalUnits :: = BIT STRING
                { multipleObjectSelection    (0),
                  filter                     (1),
                  multipleReply              (2),
                  extendedService            (3),
                }
```

Figure 6.15   CMIP information for A-ASSOCIATE.

shows the ASN.1 coding for this information (code is abbreviated for purposes of simplicity).

Example of a CMIP protocol data unit

Figure 6.16 is the ASN.1 coding for an M-CREATE PDU. The examination in this section will focus on an analysis of the line entries of the code. We will also use Figs. 6.17 and 6.18 during this discussion. These figures are more detailed definitions of the attributes in the full PDU that is shown in Fig. 6.16. The reader may wish to refer to Chap. 4 for a refresher on the presentation layer and ASN.1 coding.

```
--Example of a CMIP protocol data unit (simplified)
m-Create OPERATION
ARGUMENT      CreateArgument
RESULT        CreateResult
ERRORS        {accessDenied, classInstanceConflict,
               duplicateManagedObjectInstance,
               invalidAttributeValue, invalidObjectInstance,
               missingAttributeValue, noSuchAttribute,
               nosuchObjectClass, noSuchObjectInstance,
               soSuchReferenceObject, processingFailure}
```

Figure 6.16   The M-CREATE PDU coded in ASN.1.

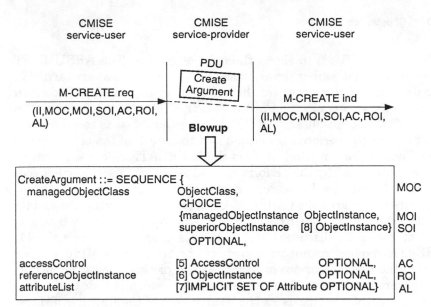

Figure 6.17 Definition statements and importing information.

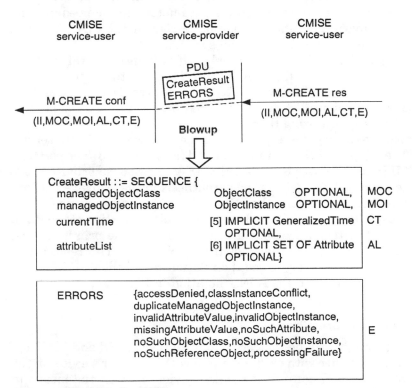

Figure 6.18 Defining the PDU.

The code in Fig. 6.16 shows three major entries. The ARGUMENT CreateArgument defines the arguments (parameters) that are carried in the data unit. Later examples show that these arguments are derived from the parameters in the CMISE M-CREATE request primitive. The RESULT CreateResult and ERRORS (accessDenied, etc.) contain information from the performing entity about the result of the create operation. These values are derived from the M-CREATE response primitive parameters issued by the performing CMISE service user. Further coding must be examined to understand how these values are used.

Figure 6.17 shows the CMISE M-CREATE request primitive and its relationship to the M-CREATE PDU. The top part of this figure is part of Fig. 6.13, discussed earlier in this chapter. It shows the M-CREATE request primitive issued by the invoking CMISE service user to the CMISE service provider. As the picture shows, the primitive parameters are used to create the PDU, which is sent to the performing CMISE service user. The bottom part of the figure is a "blow up" of a portion of the contents of the PDU. The ASN.1 code defines the type of the fields in the PDU. To the right of this shaded box are the initials used to represent the parameters in the CMISE primitive. With one exception, all the primitive parameters are mapped into the PDU. The invoke identifier (II) is not carried in the PDU, but it is used by ROSE for the identification support.

It is hoped the ASN.1 code is largely self-descriptive at this point in the book. The reader will notice that the MOI and the superior object instance (SOI) are defined with CHOICE. The access control, object instance, and attribute list are all optional parameters, although most networks today are using them.

Figure 6.18 shows the response from the performing CMISE service user. The top part of this figure is derived from Fig. 6.13. The performing CMISE service user issues an M-CREATE response primitive, the parameters are shown within the parenthesis in the figure. As before, primitives are mapped into the PDU and sent to the initiating CMISE service user. The blow up reveals the contents of a portion of the PDU. To the right of the shaded box are the initials of the primitives and their relationship to the types in the ASN.1 code. The reader may wish to refer to Table 6.2 to see the relationship of the CMISE errors to the ERRORS code in the ASN.1 notation in Fig. 6.18.

Example of CMIP operations

The reader might still be wondering how all the CMISE and CMIP operations fit together with each other and with the other services of the application layer. Figure 6.19 should provide us with the means to piece the puzzle together. It shows one of the principal operations of the CMIP-event reporting.

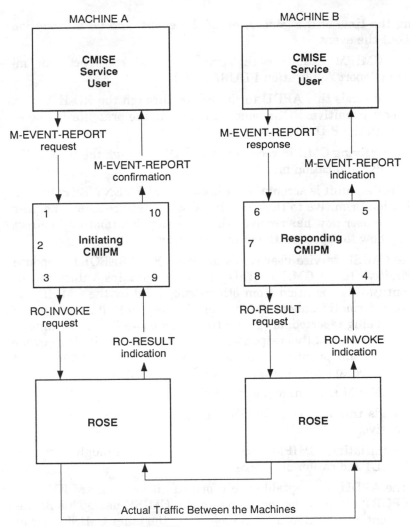

Figure 6.19   An example of CMIP operations.

The operation between the two CMIP entities are known as *machines* (CMIPMs). The figure shows the operations between the CMISE service user, the CMIP machine (the protocol), and the underlying ROSE service element. The CMISE service users and the underlying ROSE follow the steps numbered in the figure and described here.

1. The CMIPM receives an M-EVENT-REPORT request primitive from a CMISE service user. The parameters in the primitive contain values (*a*) to identify this operation from other operations supported by the CMISE, (*b*) information about the managed object, (*c*) the type of event being reported, (*d*) a time stamp specify-

ing the time of the generation of the event, and (e) information about the event.

2. The CMIPM examines the primitive and constructs an m-EventReport Application PDU (APDU).

3. It then sends this APDU to the ROSE through the RO-INVOKE request primitive. ROSE sends this unit to the presentation layer through the P-DATA primitive.

4. The receiving CMIPM receives the APDU through the ROSE RO-INVOKE indication primitive.

5. If the data unit is acceptable, it issues an M-EVENT-REPORT indication primitive to the receiving CMISE service user. The peer service user now has received the necessary information to direct it on how to report on the managed object.

6. The CMISE service user sends an M-EVENT-REPORT response primitive to its CMIPM. This primitive contains values to: (a) identify this operation from others supported by the CMISE, (b) give information about the managed object, (c) give the type of event being reported, (d) give a time stamp specifying the time of the generation of this response, and (e) give the result of the event report. If this primitive is a failure response, an error parameter is included to describe the nature of the error.

7. The CMIPM uses these parameters to construct a new ADPU.

8. It sends this ADPU to ROSE through an RO-RESULT request primitive.

9. The initiating CMIPM receives the ADPU through the RO-RESULT indication primitive.

10. If the APDU is acceptable (well formed), it issues an M-EVENT-REPORT confirmation primitive to the CMISE user. This primitive contains the information created by the other CMISE user in event 6.

The reporting procedure is complete.

Parameters associated with the CMIP services

It should prove instructive to examine the parameters associated with these services because (1) their examination further clarifies the use of CMIP and (2) it provides an opportunity to examine some important issues that must be addressed by an organization. Table 6.4 lists these parameters and this section explains their use.

TABLE 6.4   The CMIP Parameters

Invoke identifier
Superior object instance
Managed object class
Access control
Reference object instance
Attribute list
Current time
Errors
Functional units
User information
M-Abort-Source
Mode
Event type, time, argument, and result
Linked identifier
Base object class and instance
Scope
Filter
Synchronization
Action type and argument

- *Invoke identifier:*   This field is used to uniquely identify a specific create or delete operation from other operations that the managing process would have in progress. The invoke identifier value also is used to identify the other data units associated with this network control operation. That is, the field is used in the M-SET, M-GET, and other operations. OSI network management does not specify the specific syntax and format of the identifier, so the network manager is free to develop any scheme it chooses. Notwithstanding, any type of network identification and naming convention must be given careful consideration.

- *Superior object instance:*   This parameter specifies an existing MOI which is designated as the superior of the new object instance.

- *Managed object class:*   The identifier of a managed object is placed in the MIB along with a set of attributes which describe the characteristics of the managed object. For example, a communications circuit may be described by attributes such as its line speed, whether it is switched or dedicated, half-duplex or full-duplex, etc. This set of attributes is identified by the *class* of a managed object. A managed object that belongs to the same class contains the same list of attributes (although the value of the attributes could differ). The field is used by the network client or the network control center to identify the attributes of the resource that is being created. Again, values such as line speed, dedicated access, full-duplex, etc. are stored in the MIB for informational and control purposes.

- *Access control:* This parameter is not defined concisely in OSI, but it allows access control functions to be invoked between network clients and network control.

- *Reference object instance:* A reference object instance is the reference to an existing managed object. For example, an existing and active communications circuit already has its attributes defined to the MIB. Consequently, if a client wishes to create an instance of another circuit (that is to say, make the circuit known to the network management system), it is not necessary for its attributes to be defined from scratch. Rather, an existing object (a communications link) can be referenced, and its values are then the default values for the new circuit.

- *Attribute list:* Let us assume two network users (for example, a network client and a network control center) are to create an instance of a managed object. In OSI terms, the party that wishes to create the object is the invoking user, and the party that receives the M-CREATE data unit is the performing party. The attribute list parameter is used by the invoking party to assign the attributes to the object. (These values override any previous default values as well as the values in the referenced object instance parameter.) In turn, the performing user returns an M-CREATE confirm, which also contains a list of parameters. These parameters may or may not be the same as those issued by the invoking user. In essence, OSI gives CMISE users the opportunity to negotiate the parameters (and therefore the characteristics) of a managed object. Most likely this will be an important feature for an OSI-based network control center because it gives the network and its clients considerable flexibility in setting up the network resources.

- *Current time:* This parameter is simply the time that an event occurs in the network.

- *Errors:* This parameter may contain no values or many. Its use requires that a network and its clients set up standards (based on OSI) on error-reporting mechanisms.

- *Functional units:* As stated earlier, functional units provide the network manager a convenient means of categorizing the services that are established between the network and its users.

- *User information:* The values of this field are not defined in any of the OSI network management standards. They are said to be application-context-specific, which, in OSI terms, means the value depends on the agreements reached between the communicating parties. This distinction is important because it emphasizes that the OSI standards are interface and interworking standards and do not dictate the values of the user information carried within the user data field. However, it should also be remembered that the user data field might contain values from an upper-layer protocol.

- *M-Abort-Source:* This parameter is used if a CMISE/CMIP abort data unit is issued. A network may use this as a service provider, or a network customer may use it as a service user.

- *Mode:* This parameter is used to indicate if the operation between the two devices is to be (1) confirmed or (2) nonconfirmed.

- *Event type:* The standards permit an operation between devices to be classified by its type. The actual type depends upon the nature (or context, in OSI terms) of the network resource (the managed object). It may be used by a network to standardize names and identifiers for all network operations.

- *Event time:* This parameter contains the time of the generation of the reporting of an event.

- *Event argument:* The device, which issues a data unit that reports an event, uses this parameter to provide information about the event on which it is reporting.

- *Event result:* Typically, an organization uses this parameter to report on the success or failure of an operation.

- *Linked identifier:* Some network operations require that a managed object or the managing process send more than one PDU in response to a query about its status. This parameter allows the communicating parties to "chain" these related data units together.

- *Base object class:* Reference was made earlier to the concept of class. This parameter is used to specify the starting point for identifying the attribute values (the class) of a managed class or for filter operations (see below).

- *Base object instance:* This parameter is used to determine the instance of the base object class.

- *Scope:* This parameter is used to identify the subtree for the search. Three levels of search are permitted: (1) base object alone, (2) the nth level subordinates of the base object, and (3) the base object and all its subordinates. The default for this value is base object alone.

- *Filter:* Many network control systems use the concept of filters. Some organizations use this term to describe the removal of extraneous information in a data unit before display to an operator. OSI uses the term in a slightly different context. An ISO 9595 filter is an assertion or a set of assertions about the attributes of a managed object. In its simplest terms, it is a way to select tests for the selection of operations. The filter operations can be coded into C, ASN.1, etc., to select operating parameters from the MIB. Filters use the conventional boolean operators of AND, NOT, and OR.

- *Synchronization:* The synchronization parameter is used by the invoking user to notify the performing user how it is to synchronize changes to the instances of objects. The standard defines two modes of operations:

  - *Atomic:* All proposed changes are first checked to determine if they can be performed. All must be performed; otherwise, none are performed.
  - *Best effort:* Modifications are made in any order. If modifications cannot be made, this will not affect the changes that can be made.

- *Action type:* This parameter is used to describe the specific action that a managed object is to perform. The type is dependent upon the context of the managed object.

- *Action argument:* If necessary, this parameter is used to further define the nature of the action.

Conformance requirements

Section 8 of ISO 9596 establishes a number of requirements that must be met by anyone developing this protocol. They are classified as either static, dynamic, or Protocol Implementation Conformance Statement (PICS) requirements. The section is rather terse at this stage of its development.

Relationship of CMISE Primitives and CMIP Operations

To conclude this chapter, Table 6.5 lists the CMISE primitives and their corresponding CMIP operations and the associated mode and linked-ID services.

Summary

The ISO 9595 (CMISE) and 9596 (CMIP) Standards are the foundations for the OSI network management standards. They are used by all the functional protocols, such as fault management, performance management, etc. Thus, they are truly common application service elements, because they provide services to many other applications entities.

The standards are designed to interact gracefully with ACSE, ROSE, and the presentation layer. Indeed, ACSE, ROSE, and the pre-

TABLE 6.5   CMISE Primitives and CMIP Operations

CMISE Primitive	Mode	Linked ID	CMIP Operation
M-EVENT-REPORT req/ind	NC	NA	m-EventReport
M-EVENT-REPORT req/ind	C	NA	m-EventReport-Confirmed
M-EVENT-REPORT rsp/conf	NA	NA	m-EventReport-Confirmed
M-GET req/ind	C	NA	m-Get
M-GET rsp/conf	NA	A	m-Get
M-GET rsp/conf	NA	P	m-Linked-Reply
M-SET req/ind	NC	NA	m-Set
M-SET req/ind	C	NA	m-Set-Confirmed
M-SET rsp/conf	NA	A	m-Set-Confirmed
M-SET rsp/conf	NA	P	m-Linked-Reply
M-ACTION req/ind	NC	NA	m-Action
M-ACTION req/ind	C	NA	m-Action-Confirmed
M-ACTION rsp/conf	NA	A	m-Action-Confirmed
M-ACTION rsp/conf	NA	P	m-Linked-Reply
M-CREATE req/ind	C	NA	m-Create
M-CREATE rsp/conf	NA	NA	m-Create
M-DELETE req/ind	C	NA	m-Delete
M-DELETE rsp/conf	NA	A	m-Delete
M-DELETE rsp/conf	NA	P	m-Linked-Reply

A = Absent
NA = Not applicable
C = Confirmed
NC = Not confirmed
P = Present

sentation layer are required if CMISE and CMIP are to execute their tasks properly.

Appendix. Older Release of CMISE/CMIP

Introduction

The earlier work on the CMISE/CMIP standards included three other services that are described in this appendix. They were deleted because the ISO and CCITT concluded that comparable functions can be obtained by invoking ACSE. This appendix is useful for those organizations that have implemented earlier versions of CMISE/CMIP because it describes these earlier features, which may be in your system.

The revised ISO 9595 eliminated the following direct services with the ACSE:

- *M-INITIALIZE:* This service is used to establish an association with a peer CMISE service user for the purpose of exchanging information. In so doing, it must use the underlying ACSE. It passes the necessary control information to establish the association. A reply is expected with this service.

- *M-TERMINATE:*   This service is used to obtain a normal, orderly termination of the association between the CMISE service users. A reply is expected with this service.

- *M-ABORT:*   The service user can obtain an abrupt release of the association with the use of this service.

Earlier versions of CMISE/CMIP defined services based on the organization depicted in Figure 6A.1. The new releases do not use this nomenclature.

Overview of defunct services

M-INITIALIZE service.   This service is invoked by a CMISE service user to establish an association with a peer user. It is the required initiating phase for any subsequent activity between the two entities. It is used only to create a connection. It may not be used with an established association. Figure 6A.2 shows the operations between the CMISE service users and the CMISE service provider. With this service, the service provider must be the ACSE.

Three parameters are used with the request and indication primitives. These parameters are mapped into A-ASSOCIATE PDUs. The parameters are as follows:

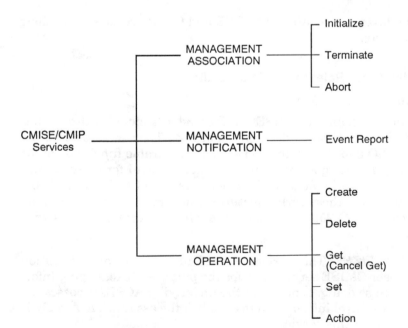

Figure 6A.1   Earlier CMISE and CMIP service structure.

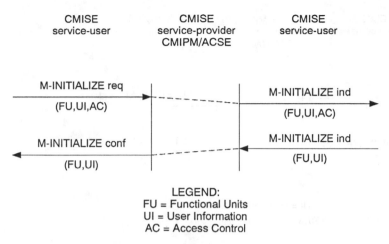

Figure 6A.2   CMISE M-INITIALIZE service.

- *Functional units:* The initiating CMISE service user employs this parameter to define the set of functional units it wishes to invoke during its association with its peer CMISE service user. The returning response primitive contains the functional units that the responding service user is able to support. They may be different from the values in the request primitive.

  If the functional unit parameter is not supplied, it is assumed that both users have a prior knowledge of the set of functional units that are going to be used during this communications process.

  The extended service functional unit, if successfully negotiated between the two users, allows the use of the P-DATA service in the presentation layer. It also makes other presentation layer services available during this association. However, CMISE does not define the presentation layer services; they are established with ACSE through the application context parameter during the association set up.

- *User information:* This parameter contains user data. It is not defined within the standard. Its meaning rests on the application context.

- *Access control:* This parameter is not defined in the standard but is intended to be used for the CMISE service users to agree upon control functions during the association. Notice that the access control parameter does not reside in the returning response and confirm primitives from the responding CMISE service user.

M-TERMINATE service.   The M-TERMINATE service is used by either CMISE service user to execute an orderly and normal release of the association. It is a confirmed service.

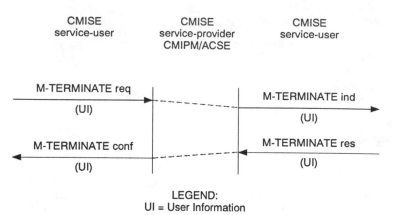

LEGEND:
UI = User Information

Figure 6A.3   CMISE M-TERMINATE service.

The M-TERMINATE service is provided by the use of the lower-layer ACSE release service. Consequently, the CMISE standard only stipulates that the parameters in this primitive be relevant to the CMISE operations. As indicated in Fig. 6A.3, only one parameter is provided—the *user information* field, which, as the reader probably expects, is not defined in the standard because it is application-context-specific.

M-ABORT service.   The M-ABORT service is used by either the CMISE service user or the CMISE service provider to cause an abrupt release of the association. It is a nonconfirmed service.

Since this service is provided by the use of the ACSE A-ABORT service, the CMISE standard does not define parameters associated with the ABORT, although it does define two parameters that are relevant to the ABORT services at the CMISE level. These parameters are:

- *M-ABORT source:*   This parameter indicates which entity caused the ABORT. It may identify (1) the ACSE service provider, (2) the CMISE service provider, or (3) the CMISE service user.

- *User information:*   User information is not defined in the CMISE standard because it is application-context-specific.

Figure 6A.4 shows scenarios for the M-ABORT service. Notice that the invocation can occur from the service user side or from the service provider side.

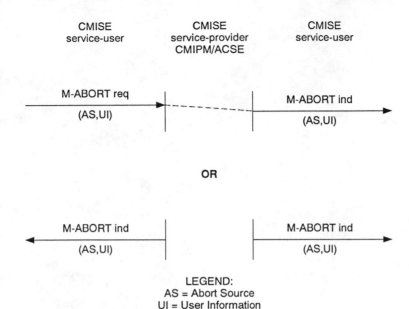

LEGEND:
AS = Abort Source
UI = User Information

Figure 6A.4 CMISE M-ABORT service.

The Functional Areas of OSI Network Management

Introduction

OSI network management is grouped into the five functional areas. They were introduced in Chap. 1. This chapter provides a general overview of these areas and Chap. 8 explains other documents that are considered part of the framework of the five functional areas and contain more detail about the areas. The functional areas are:

- Configuration management
- Fault management
- Performance management
- Security management
- Accounting management

These functional areas make reference to specific management functional areas (SMFAs). Each SMFA identifies the following:

- A defined set of functions
- A defined set of procedures that are associated with each function
- The service to support the procedures
- The underlying services that are needed to support the SMFA
- The class of managed objects that will be affected by the SMFA operations

Since the five functional standards are not yet complete, it is impossible to present the reader with a complete description of OSI network management. Nonetheless, enough detail exists in many of the documents to permit their use in planning activities.

This chapter examines each of the functional areas and provides examples of how they are used in a typical network management operations center. Several examples are provided to give the reader an idea of how these standards are used in a network. The examples are far from exhaustive and the reader should refer to the original standard for a complete description of all operations.

SMFAs and SMFs

The material in this chapter is very closely related to the material in Chap. 8, which deals with the systems management functions (SMFs; under the ISO 10164 documents). Indeed, the reader should understand that the descriptions of the five SMFAs in this chapter are derived from *all* the OSI network management standards specifications and especially the ISO 10164 documents. The SMFAs and the SMFs were split apart because it was recoginized that the five SMFAs overlap. In addition, the SMFs are considered to be generic capabilities that can be applied to any management application.

Filters

The functional area protocols make extensive use of filters. As explained in Chap. 1, filters are used to determine which events in a network are to be acted upon or reported.

Filters are defined with Abstract Syntax Notation 1 (ASN.1) to contain a set of assertions about (1) the presence of attributes, or (2) the values of attributes in a managed object. If the filter operation is to test more than one assertion, the boolean operators AND, OR, and NOT can be employed to group the assertions together. The network management protocols use a distinguished name with a filter to identify the managed object. As Fig. 7.1 indicates, an attribute can be

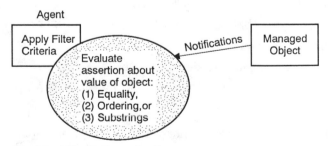

Figure 7.1 Evaluating assertions.

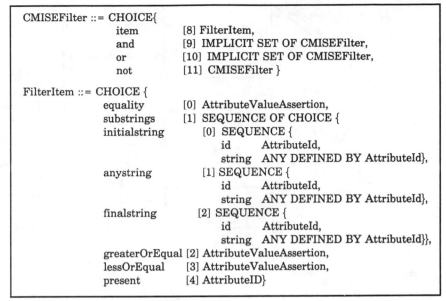

```
CMISEFilter ::= CHOICE{
          item          [8] FilterItem,
          and           [9] IMPLICIT SET OF CMISEFilter,
          or            [10] IMPLICIT SET OF CMISEFilter,
          not           [11] CMISEFilter }

FilterItem ::= CHOICE {
          equality      [0] AttributeValueAssertion,
          substrings    [1] SEQUENCE OF CHOICE {
          initialstring     [0] SEQUENCE {
                              id      AttributeId,
                              string  ANY DEFINED BY AttributeId},
          anystring         [1] SEQUENCE {
                              id      AttributeId,
                              string  ANY DEFINED BY AttributeId},
          finalstring       [2] SEQUENCE {
                              id      AttributeId,
                              string  ANY DEFINED BY AttributeId}},
          greaterOrEqual [2] AttributeValueAssertion,
          lessOrEqual   [3] AttributeValueAssertion,
          present       [4] AttributeID}
```

Figure 7.2   ASN.1 filter definitions.

evaluated by equality, greater than or equal to or less than or equal to assertion, or substrings assertions.

The ASN.1 coding for a filter is shown in Fig. 7.2 [the example is from the Common Management Information Protocol (CMIP) definition]. A filter operation may involve more than one assertion. If so, the logical operators can be used to group the assertions (with nested operations, if necessary).

CMISEFilter is a CHOICE type which allows choosing a filter item or any of the three boolean operators. In turn, FilterItem is also a CHOICE type, which allows choosing one of five types for matching: (1) equality, (2) a substring of objects, bits, etc., (3) greater than or equal to, (4) less than or equal to, or (5) the presence of a value.

Reporting with sieves

An event-reporting mechanism called a *sieve* is used to support the functional areas. The concept of a sieve is shown in Fig. 7.3 (this example is used by the Network Management Forum implementation). It is derived from the use of filters. Its function is to determine which network management events are to be filtered and reported to a managing entity. It works in conjunction with the event log activity. Indeed, the sieve is used to filter data to be placed in the event log.

As Fig. 7.3 illustrates, data of an unsieved event is filtered in one of

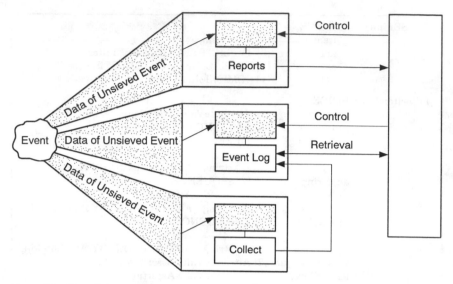

Figure 7.3 Use of sieves.

three ways. The top of the picture is an illustration of the data sieved to produce a report directly to a network management center or some other managing entity. In the middle of the figure is the application of the sieve function to determine which events are recorded on the log. This log can be used by the managing entity for retrieval and evaluation purposes. The bottom of the picture illustrates yet another function of the sieve. It uses additional software for refinement, summarization, and categorization of event data. In this figure, the software is called the collection module.

Be aware that this figure is quite simple; it is not meant to imply that data must be reported three times. Rather, the data of an unsieved event is reported once and then applied to the reports, event log, or collection modules for further use.

Configuration Management

A communications system, by its very nature, must support a dynamic environment. Changes within the system occur constantly. Switches, multiplexers, and modems function at various levels of operability and performance, and their relationships with each other vary. For example, a packet switch may be removed as a node in the network because of hardware or software failures. If the problem is transient, it may be necessary only to logically remove the switch by routing traffic around the node. In such a case, a part of the network would be reconfigured to handle this problem.

The ISO configuration management standard establishes facilities to report on logical or physical configurations in an OSI environment. Configuration management is responsible for the following services [by operating on the management information base (MIB)]:

- Identifies any managed object and the assignment of names to the object
- Defines any new managed object
- Sets the initial values for the attributes of objects
- Manages the relationships of managed objects
- Changes the operational characteristics of managed objects and reports on any changes in the state of the objects
- Deletes managed objects

The ISO configuration management specification relies on several other ISO management standards for the definition of its functions. For example, the concepts of locked states, active states, etc., in 10164-2 are integral to this standard.

As noted earlier, the five major functional standards of OSI's network management standards are users of the common management information service element (CMISE). Configuration management uses the CMISE services shown in Fig. 7.4. The services in this figure must use a number of the CMISE parameters discussed in Chap. 8.

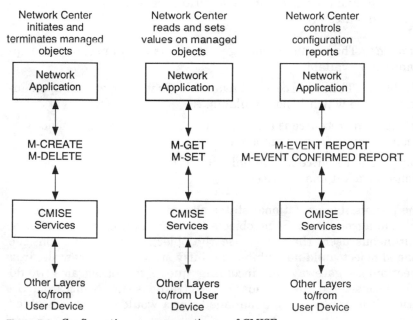

Figure 7.4 Configuration management's use of CMISE.

The M-CREATE and M-DELETE services are used to create and delete an instance of a managed object, such as designation of a backup
circuit, the patching to an alternate modem, etc. The M-GET and M-
SET services are used to retrieve and modify network management information. The M-EVENT-REPORT services are used to report an
event such as a configuration status message at a client private
branch exchange (PBX).

The "network application" shown in Fig. 7.4 is software that is written to conform to the configuration management standard. Although
not shown in this figure, the actions of configuration management are
invoked by yet another layer of software sending transactions (primitives to the network application, i.e., configuration management).
This relationship is explained in more detail later in this section (the
curious reader may wish to review Fig. 7.8).

Operational states of managed objects

The configuration management standard defines the operational
states of managed objects. Configuration management relies on ISO
10064-2 for the definitions of states (see Chap. 8).

Four operational status states are defined. If an organization uses
the OSI network management standards, it is required to use these
status indicators. Figure 7.5 shows the relationships of the operational states and the permissible transitions between these states. The
operational states are:

- *Enabled:*   The resource (managed object) is not in use, but it is operable and available.

- *Disabled:*   The resource is not available, or it is dependent upon another source which is not available.

- *Active:*   The resource is available for use, and it has the capacity to
  accept services from another source.

- *Busy:*   The resource is available, but it does not have the spare capacity for additional services.

The permissible operational states shown in Fig. 7.5 are not found
in all managed objects. Some objects have no limit on the number of
simultaneous users that could use the object. In this situation, the
managed object could not exhibit the busy state. As an example, in a
connectionless gateway, an incoming queue for datagrams would
never be considered busy because excess traffic is simply discarded. In
addition, it is unlikely that a managed object would exhibit a disabled

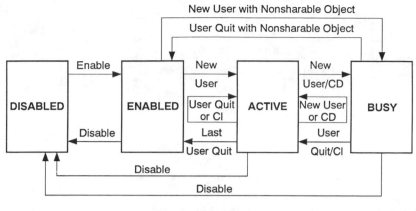

Figure 7.5 Configuration management operation status states.

state if it has no dependencies on other managed objects since the state of "disabled" is irrelevant.

Certain rules are evident from an examination of Fig. 7.5. For example, the transition to the enable state means the taking of actions which make the managed object operable. Actions, such as replacing a faulty line card, making a change to a software bug, etc., may permit the object to be declared operable. Notice that the transition to enable can only occur if the object's operational state is disabled. However, certain other activities allow an object to move to the enabled state. For example, a user may quit using a nonsharable object, which could move the object from a busy to an enable state.

The disabled state occurs when a managed object is declared inoperable. For example, a network component might exhibit some defect that is beyond a permissible threshold and unacceptable to network control. A managed object can be declared disabled from any operational state. For example, it could even be declared disabled again because a second problem is noted. This could occur in many network components. One that comes to mind is a number of software bugs that manifest themselves as a program is diagnosed.

Figure 7.5 also shows the action of user quit, which allows the managed object to move from a busy to an inactive state or from an active to an enable state. Just because a user quits does not mean the managed object need become disabled or inactive.

The notations CI and CD mean capacity increase and capacity decrease, respectively. These events can cause the managed object to move from active to busy state, from busy to active state or remain in the busy state.

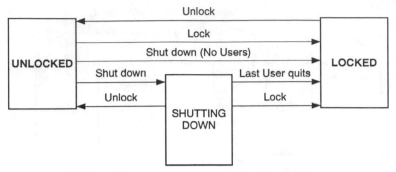

Figure 7.6   Configuration management administrative states.

Administrative states of managed objects

Configuration management also relies on ISO 10064-2 to describe three administrative states (see Fig. 7.6):

- *Unlocked:*   The managed object can be used.
- *Locked:*   The managed object cannot be used.
- *Shutting down:*   The managed object can be used by current users but cannot be used by new users.

As the reader might expect, managed objects need not exhibit all three possible administrative states. That is, some resources may not be locked; therefore, they could not exhibit the locked state. As an example, and as a general rule, a local area network (LAN) read-only file server would not be allowed to exist in a locked state except for subsets of the file that might have security and access restrictions. In addition, certain resources may not be allowed to be shut down gracefully; and, there would be no such thing as a shutting-down state. An example of this situation would be an administrative logical channel on a packet switch card which must exist in an perpetually unlocked state. The 0 Channel on an X.25 interface comes to mind. Any graceful shutting down might create havoc on the dependent logical channels.

Table 7.1 provides a summary of the permissible combinations of operational and administrative states. The notation NP means the combination of the administrative and operational state is not possible. A brief summary of this table follows.

The *disabled lock state* defines a managed object that is prohibited from use administratively. It is also disabled because it has exhibited some type of problem. In order to make the managed object op-

TABLE 7.1   Operational and Administrative States

Admin.	Operational			
	Disabled	Enabled	Active	Busy
Locked	Disabled Locked	Enabled Locked	NP	NP
Shutting down	Disabled Locked*	Enabled Locked*	Active Shutting down	Busy Shutting down
Unlocked	Disabled Unlocked	Enabled Unlocked	Active Unlocked	Busy Unlocked

*Automatic transition to these states.

erable, diagnostics must be performed, and some action must be taken on the object to unlock and enable it.

The *enabled lock* managed object is prohibited from use administratively, but it is exhibiting no defects. This state could certainly occur with resources that are placed in standby to assume functions in the event that problems occur with other enabled units.

A *busy shutting down* managed object is operable, but, for whatever reason, network control is shutting the resource down. This situation could occur when a network resource must be taken off-line or have fewer users accessing the object. Typically, the lack of spare capacity would precipitate actions that would move a managed object to this state.

The *disabled unlocked* state is not prohibited administratively from use; however, it has exhibited a problem and has been disabled. This typically occurs with software or hardware problems in network components.

The *enabled unlocked* state simply means that the managed object is operable. Next the active unlocked state defines a managed object that is operable and is in use and has extra capacity for additional users.

The *busy unlocked* managed object is one in which an object is busy or is operating at full capacity. Of course, with this state other users are not permitted to access the managed object until an existing user relinquishes the use of part or all of the resource.

The *active shutting down* state means the object is currently available and has capacity to accept new services, but it is not accepting any.

The *active unlocked* state is one in which the managed object has capacity and can be used.

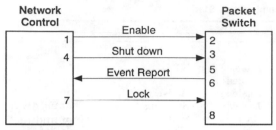

LEGEND:
1. Send enable signal
2. Trunk is enabled and unlocked
3. Trunk accepts traffic
4. Control Center issues shutdown
5. Switch accepts traffic from ongoing users,
   but refuses traffic on this trunk from new users
6. Traffic is cleared on this trunk and Center notified
7. Center locks out resource for trouble-shooting
8. Resource is locked

Figure 7.7   A scenario for configuration management.

One possible operation (among many) for an organization's use of configuration management is shown in Fig. 7.7. First, a network control center enables a packet switch trunk by the use of a configuration management *enable* signal. Next, assuming the packet switch trunk is active and accepting traffic, it notifies the network center in the event the trunk becomes too busy (buffer problems, etc.) and states the reason for the problem. In this hypothetical scenario, network control could issue a shut down. This command would force the packet switch to remain active on this trunk until all users that are mapped to the trunk have terminated their network session (or until the switch issues a CMISE/CMIP abort because of severe problems). Network control would then issue a lock command to prevent any more traffic from using the problem trunk.

Again, it is emphasized that the operations in Fig. 7.7 represent only one possibility among many for the use of configuration management. It is hoped this section gives the reader a general idea of how the standard could be used.

It is important to emphasize once again that the OSI standards are *not* intended to define how a network resource is actually configured. This operation is vendor-specific. The standards establish common protocols and MIBs for *reporting* on the network resources.

Configuration management facilities

ISO configuration management is organized around five facilities:

- *Object configuration:* Manages the addition, deletion, enrolling, deenrolling, and naming of instances of managed objects. The term *enroll* refers to how one CMISE service user announces to another that an instance of a managed object has arrived at the announcer's MIB.

- *State management:* Manages the examination, setting, and notification of changes to the management state of the managed objects.

- *Attribute management:* Manages the examination, setting, and notification of changes of the general attributes of the managed objects.

- *Relationship management:* Manages the examination, setting, and notification of changes in the relationships of managed objects.

- *Software distribution:* Manages the distribution of software and the notification of version changes, as well as the triggering of boot procedures within a managed object.

Examples of configuration management operations

Figure 7.8 provides an example of the use of configuration management to modify attributes about a managed object. The configuration manage-

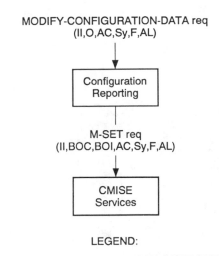

MODIFY-CONFIGURATION-DATA req
(II,O,AC,Sy,F,AL)

Configuration
Reporting

M-SET req
(II,BOC,BOI,AC,Sy,F,AL)

CMISE
Services

LEGEND:

FOR CMISE:

II = Invoke ID
BOC = Base Object Class
BOI = Base Object Instance
AC = Access Control
Sy = Synchronization
F = Filter
AL = Attribute List

FOR CONFIGURATION:

II = Invoke ID
O = Object
Ac = Access Control
Sy = Synchronization
F = Filter
AL = Attribute List

Figure 7.8   Configuration management operations.

ment protocol uses CMISE as a supporting service provider. Be aware that the primitives named *MODIFY-CONFIGURATION-DATA* in these examples are not part of the OSI network management standard. This example is derived from AT&T's Network Management Protocol (NMP) and its *Configuration Management Message Set Specification*.

The parameters used in the configuration management primitive are mapped to the CMISE parameters; in turn, some of these parameters are mapped directly to the remote operations service element (ROSE) primitive. The *invoke identifier (II)* is the identifier used in ROSE to uniquely identify the transaction between the two entities. The *object (O)* parameter maps to the CMISE base object class and base object instance. It identifies the class and instance from which the data is to be modified. Classes could include software, network types, services, equipment, facilities, etc.

The *access control (AC)* parameter defines what type of control would be used during the operation. The remainder of the parameters in these primitives have been defined in previous discussions in this chapter and in preceding chapters.

Figure 7.9 shows the results of the configuration management operations. The principal difference is that fewer primitive parameters

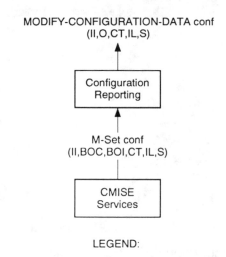

MODIFY-CONFIGURATION-DATA conf
(II,O,CT,IL,S)

Configuration
Reporting

M-Set conf
(II,BOC,BOI,CT,IL,S)

CMISE
Services

LEGEND:

FOR CMISE: FOR CONFIGURATION:

II = Invoke ID   II = Invoke ID
BOC = Base Object Class   O = Object
BOI = Base Object Instance CT = Current Time
CT = Current Time   IL = Item List
IL = Item List   S = Status
S = Status

Figure 7.9 The results of the configuration management operations.

are included in the service definitions and the *current time, item list,* and *status* parameters are used to provide information about the results of the operation.

Examples of ASN.1 definitions for configuration management

This section takes a somewhat different approach than the other examples in this chapter in that it shows some examples of template notations. As before, these examples are taken from several implementations and the author's own work with clients.

Figure 7.10 is an example of a blank template for the circuit OBJECT CLASS. The first line of the template contains the name of the object class, which is circuit. The entires below this line deal with definitions on the inheritance of the object class and its behavior definitions. Next, a relative distinguished name (RDN) may be defined for the object class. The MUST CONTAIN and MAY CONTAIN statements include the attributes that are required and that are optional for the object class. Typically, an enterprise includes only the ASN.1 name for each attribute and assumes the interested reader will delve into other documentation for further information on the attributes. The permissible operations are defined in the next part of the template. Again, only ASN.1 names are included here. Finally, the unique registered name is coded in the last entry of the template.

The template in Fig. 7.11 is from the Network Management Forum object class library. Even though these examples are included in the configuration management section, they are applicable to other functional areas as well. Figure 7.11 shows an actual template to define an

---

circuit OBJECT-CLASS
--Statements dealing with superior and
--behavior characteristics
RDN--May be included
MUST CONTAIN
--ASN.1 name(s) of required attribute(s)
MAY CONTAIN
--Optional attribute(s)
OPERATIONS
--ASN.1 Name(s) for permitted operations
--such as changing an attribute, enrolling
--an object, etc.
::= {......} --Unique Name for the object class

--Template format varies between enterprises

Figure 7.10 A blank template for a circuit object class.

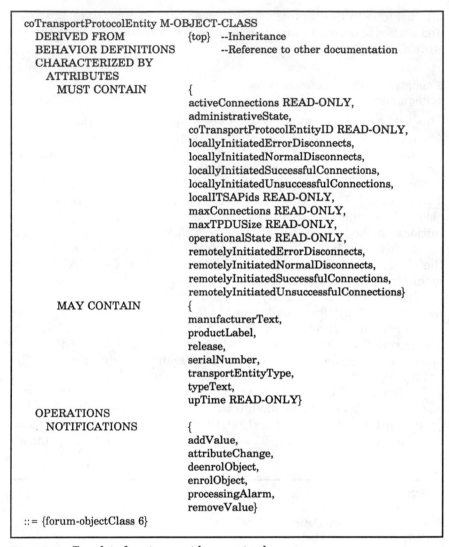

```
coTransportProtocolEntity M-OBJECT-CLASS
    DERIVED FROM              {top}  --Inheritance
    BEHAVIOR DEFINITIONS             --Reference to other documentation
    CHARACTERIZED BY
    ATTRIBUTES
        MUST CONTAIN         {
                             activeConnections READ-ONLY,
                             administrativeState,
                             coTransportProtocolEntityID READ-ONLY,
                             locallyInitiatedErrorDisconnects,
                             locallyInitiatedNormalDisconnects,
                             locallyInitiatedSuccessfulConnections,
                             locallyInitiatedUnsuccessfulConnections,
                             localITSAPids READ-ONLY,
                             maxConnections READ-ONLY,
                             maxTPDUSize READ-ONLY,
                             operationalState READ-ONLY,
                             remotelyInitiatedErrorDisconnects,
                             remotelyInitiatedNormalDisconnects,
                             remotelyInitiatedSuccessfulConnections,
                             remotelyInitiatedUnsuccessfulConnections}
        MAY CONTAIN          {
                             manufacturerText,
                             productLabel,
                             release,
                             serialNumber,
                             transportEntityType,
                             typeText,
                             upTime READ-ONLY}
    OPERATIONS
     . NOTIFICATIONS         {
                             addValue,
                             attributeChange,
                             deenrolObject,
                             enrolObject,
                             processingAlarm,
                             removeValue}
    ::= {forum-objectClass 6}
```

Figure 7.11   Template for a transport layer protocol.

object class for a transport layer protocol, such as the Internet Transmission Control Protocol (TCP) or the CCITT/ISO transport layer (CCITT X.224/ISO 8073). The analysis concentrates on the ATTRIBUTES and OPERATIONS notations. The entries are explained in relation to the rationale for their inclusion in a network management system.

For any connection-oriented protocol, it is important to know how many connections are active. As shown in the figure under the *MUST*

CONTAIN clause, *activeConnections* provides this statistic. The network control center typically uses such a statistic to determine the amount of traffic passing through the transport layer. As the reader will notice, the value for the activeConnections may not be changed as indicated by the *READ-ONLY* clause associated with it.

Likewise, the *administrativeState* of a protocol layer is an important statistic for the network control center. Under OSI network management, the administrativeState reflects the ability of the transport protocol to support user services. This statistic is relatively easy to gather in a connection-oriented protocol such as TCP or TP4. As discussed earlier in this chapter, the administrativeState values that are permitted in OSI network management are unlocked, locked, and shutting down.

The next entry, labeled *coTransportProtocolEntityID*, provides an unambiguous identifier for each transport layer connection. Although OSI network management does not define the specific values that are placed in such a field, the most likely candidates are a TCP socket number and/or ISO/CCITT source and destination reference-values (SRC-REF and DST-REF).

The next four attributes in the MUST CONTAIN clause, *(locallyInitiatedErrorDisconnects, locallyInitiatedNormalDisconnects, locallyInitiatedSuccessfulConnections,* and *locallyInitiatedUnsuccessfulConnections)*, are also important components for the network management center. As their names suggest, they are used to determine the performance of the transport layer regarding successful connections and unsuccessful connections (and associated errors). Although these attributes provide useful information on transport layer connections, they do not necessarily describe the problems at the transport layer. In many networks, some of the statistics for these attributes would be determined by lower layers. An example that comes to mind is the connection-oriented network layer that issues restarts and resets or clears with errors because of lower-layer problems. Those operations would also affect the statistics generated by these attributes.

This template also provides the same statistics for the remote connection (a remote TCP socket or the destination-reference value in the CCITT/ISO suite). These are listed further down on the template *(remotelyInitiatedErrorDisconnects, remotelyInitiatedNormalDisconnects, remotelyInitiatedSuccessfulConnections,   remotelyInitiatedUnsuccessful Connections)*.

Between the local and remote values is the entry labeled *localTSAPids*. This contains the transport service access point (TSAP) identifiers for each connection. The TSAP is an OSI term that is used to uniquely identify the local connection. Typically it is mapped to a remote TSAP. Conceptually, it plays the same role as a TCP socket.

Practically all connection-oriented protocols (regardless of the layer in which they reside) are designed to support a finite number of connections. This approach is necessary because attempting to support an unlimited number of connections could lead to degraded performance because of excessive loading on the machine. Therefore, the *maxConnections* value is a threshold specifying the number of simultaneous connections that can be supported through the transport layer.

The *maxTPDUSize* specifies the maximum size of the transport protocol data units (TPDUs) in octets that the transport layer entity can accommodate.

The operational state of the protocol is equally important to that of the administrative state. This value is defined with *operationalState*. As we learned earlier, OSI network management permits operationalStates to be one of four values: enabled, disabled, active, and busy.

The *MAY CONTAIN* clause allows for optional information to be provided for the transport layer object class. Most of the entries are largely self-descriptive, but we will provide a brief description of each. The *manufacturerText* entry provides the name of the manufacturer or other information that might be relevant regarding the manufacturer of the managed object. The value is a printable string in text which allows any type of value to be placed in this field.

The *productLabel* attribute is used to specifically identify the manufacturer's product number. One could see this used as a model number to identify the product.

The *release* attribute is used to identify a specific release of the managed object. For example, with a piece of software such as a transport layer entity, version 1 typically would be coded to identify the initial release of the software. As the reader might expect, this is a very useful feature when two transport protocol entities initially establish a connection. By furnishing the release number, it can be ascertained if any compatibility problems might occur.

The *serialNumber* contains the serial number of entity. One is hard pressed to figure out why the serial number would be an important component for the transport layer protocol; perhaps that is why it is in the MAY CONTAIN clause. Typically, a serial number is used at lower-layer protocols to identify a number for a physical entity (such as an Ethernet station).

Transport layers may have a number of entities associated with them. The entity could translate into different services available with the transport layer. The *transportEntityType* is used to indicate the specific type of transport layer entity available.

The *typeText* field is used to provide additional information about the transport layer which is not contained in the other attributes. It provides supplemental information about the object class.

The *upTime* attribute specifies the time interval since the transport layer changed its state. This value might capture the time (in seconds) that the protocol changed administrative or operational states.

The last part of the template, labeled *OPERATIONS NOTIFICA-TIONS,* is used to define the permissible operations on the object class. The ASN.1 codes in this part of the template show the reader what actions can take place on the object class. As the entries show, the object class can have values added to it (*addValue*), attributes may be changed (*attributeChange*), objects may be enrolled and deenrolled (*enrolObject and deenrolObject*), processing may occur on this object (*processingAlarm*), and a value may be removed in the object class (*removeValue*).

This example should be sufficient to show the value of templates. Keep in mind that a network management system typically defines scores or hundreds of templates and each of the entries in the templates, discussed here in a very general way, are defined in considerable detail in an MIB.

Fault Management

Introduction

Fault management is defined to include (1) the maintenance of error logs, (2) performing actions upon error detections, (3) performing diagnostic tests to trace and identify faults, and (4) correcting faults.

Fault management makes use of the OSI CMISE service element to provide for three primary activities:

- *Fault detection:*   Faults can be detected by either monitoring or error report generation.

- *Fault diagnosis:*   Faults are diagnosed by implementing diagnostics on a component (an OSI managed object) by (1) reproducing the error, (2) analyzing the error, or (3) receiving reports from the managed objects.

- *Fault correction:*   Fault correction is accomplished through the use of other facilities, such as the configuration management facility.

Fault management relies on several other services (functions) defined in other OSI network management standards (see Chap. 8):

- *Event reporting:*   Supports the transfer of event and error reports

- *Confidence and diagnostic testing:*   Supports the means to determine if a managed object is able to perform its function

- *Log control:*   A common function which supports activities such as managing event logs, restricting access to managed objects, and so forth

- *Alarm reporting:*   Supports the use of alarm reporting in the system

Example of alarm reporting

Figure 7.12 provides an example of the OSI network management alarm reporting services. (This example is AT&T's Network Management Protocol's Fault Management specification.)

As illustrated in the figure, the alarm reporting entity passes an INITIATE request primitive to CMISE. CMISE recognizes a priori that the INITIATE service requires the CMISE confirmed action service. Therefore, the INITIATE signal is mapped into the CMISE actiontype (AT) parameter. The INITIATE signal also maps to the CMISE mode (M) parameter. In this operation the mode parameter must be set to a confirmed service.

The *invoke identifier (II)* maps directly to the CMISE invoke identifier, which (as we learned in Chap. 4) maps to the ROSE invoke identifier.

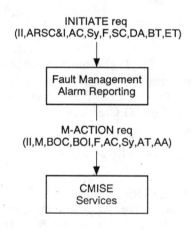

INITIATE req
(II,ARSC&I,AC,Sy,F,SC,DA,BT,ET)

Fault Management
Alarm Reporting

M-ACTION req
(II,M,BOC,BOI,F,AC,Sy,AT,AA)

CMISE
Services

LEGEND:

FOR CMISE:

II = Invoke Identifier
M = Mode
BOC = Base Object Class
BOI = Base Object Instance
Sc = Scope
F = Filter
AC = Access Control
Sy = Synchronization
MOC = Managed Object Class
AT = Action Type
AA = Action Argument

FOR ALARM REPORTING:

II = Invoke Identifier
ARSC&I = Alarm Report
    Sieve Class & Instance
Ac = Access Control
Sy = Synchronization
F = Filter
SC = Sieve Construct
DA = Destination Address
BT = Begin Time
ET = End Time

Figure 7.12 Relationship of fault management and alarm reporting to CMISE.

The *alarm report sieve class* and *instance* parameter (ARSC&I) is used to identify the report sieve. This parameter maps to the CMISE object class and object instance parameters.

The *access control, synchronization,* and *filter* parameters in the INITIATE primitive map directly to their counterparts, respectively, in CMISE.

The next four parameters in the INITIATE primitive are labeled *sieve construct (SC), destination address (DA), begin time (BT),* and *end time (ET)*. These parameters map to the CMISE action argument (AA) parameter. A brief description of each of these parameters follows:

The sieve construct parameter identifies the source of the alarm and any alarm attributes that are to be reported.

The destination address identifies the application entity that is to receive the alarm report. If an address is not present, the default address is the application entity requesting the initiation.

The begin time and end time parameters specify when the reporting function is to begin and when it is to end.

Figure 7.13 shows the operations for the confirm primitive. The parameters in the confirm and response primitives are not as numerous

INITIATE conf
(II,ARSC&I,CT,S)

Fault Management
Alarm Reporting

M-ACTION conf
(II,BOC,BOI,CT,S)

CMISE
Services

LEGEND:

FOR CMISE:

II = Invoke Identifier
BOC = Base Object Class
BOI = Base Object Instance
CT = Current Time
S = Status

FOR ALARM REPORTING:

II = Invoke Identifier
ARSC&I = Alarm Report
  Sieve Class & Instance
CT = Current Time
S = Status

Figure 7.13   The confirm primitive for the alarm report.

as those in the request indication primitives. As seen in Fig. 7.13 the invoke identifier is still present, as is the alarm report, sieve, class, and instance parameters. Two additional parameters are the *current time* (CT) and *status* (S) parameters. The current time and the alarm report, sieve, class, and instance parameters apply only to the return result. The status parameter applies only to the primitive in the event of a problem; therefore, it applies to a return error or a reject.

Examples of ASN.1 definitions for fault reporting

Figures 7.14 through 7.17 provide illustrations of how ASN.1 is used to define the types of equipment problems that can be reported through fault management. This example is not contained in any of the OSI network management standards, but it represents an amalgamation of current efforts of different groups as well as the author's own views (although several items are derived from the OSI Network Management Forum's, British Telecom's and AT&T's fault management constructs).

The explanations of the code cites either (1) names that are inserted for readability (that begin with a lowercase letter) or (2) names that must have a type appended (that begin with an uppercase letter); the choice of the citation depends on the nature of the code.

The service in this example is for an equipment alarm. The event consists of reporting on four types of information: (1) an alarm head (AlarmHead), (2) the type of equipment problem (Equipment ProblemType), (3) the ID of the problem (EquipmentProblemID), and (4) an alarm tail (AlarmTail). The types code (see Fig. 7.14) defines the EVENTINFO with SEQUENCE. The types labeled EquipmentProblemType and EquipmentProblemID are assigned private tags of 4 and 5, respectively. AlarmHead and AlarmTail are defined as COMPONENTS OF. In all four types, additional code must be read to determine the nature of the alarm.

```
—Example excludes preliminary statements such as IMPORTS, etc.

equipmentAlarm EVENT
      EVENTINFO       SEQUENCE{
                      COMPONENTS OF AlarmHead,
                      equipmentProblemType    [4]EquipmentProblemType,
                      equipmentProblemID      [5]EquipmentProblemID,
                      COMPONENTS OF AlarmTail}
      ::= 1
```

Figure 7.14   ASN.1 code for an equipment alarm.

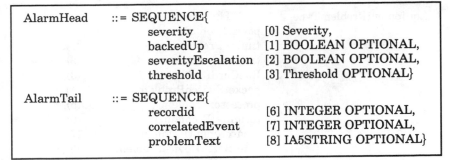

```
AlarmHead     ::= SEQUENCE{
                  severity            [0] Severity,
                  backedUp            [1] BOOLEAN OPTIONAL,
                  severityEscalation  [2] BOOLEAN OPTIONAL,
                  threshold           [3] Threshold OPTIONAL}

AlarmTail     ::= SEQUENCE{
                  recordid            [6] INTEGER OPTIONAL,
                  correlatedEvent     [7] INTEGER OPTIONAL,
                  problemText         [8] IA5STRING OPTIONAL}
```

Figure 7.15 Next level of detail of the alarm report.

```
Severity          ::= INTEGER{
                      cleared                     (0),
                      informational               (1),
                      warning                     (2),
                      minor                       (3),
                      major                       (4),
                      critical                    (5)}

Threshold         ::= CHOICE{
                      absoluteCount               [0] INTEGER,
                      countOverFixedTimeInterval  [1] CountInterval,
                      countOverSlidingWindow      [2] CountWindow,
                      valueAndDuration            [3] ValueDuration,
                      absoluteValue               [4] REAL}

CountInterval     ::= SEQUENCE{
                      count                       INTEGER,
                      startTime                   GeneralizedTime,
                      endTime                     GeneralizedTime}

CountWindow       ::= SEQUENCE{
                      count                       INTEGER,
                      window                      Printable String
                                                  --hh:mm:ss:ms}

ValueDuration     ::= SEQUENCE{
                      value                       INTEGER,
                      duration                    Printable String
                                                  --hh,mm,ss,ms}
```

Figure 7.16 Coding the remainder of AlarmHead and AlarmTail.

Figure 7.15 shows more detailed coding for the equipment alarm. AlarmHead is a SEQUENCE of four types (with private tags) that describe: (1) the severity of the alarm (Severity), (2) information on a backup (notice the usefulness of the user-supplied word *backedUp*; without it, the reader would be left to ponder the significance of [1]

EquipmentProblemType	::= INTEGER {	
	powerProblem	(0),
	timingProblem	(1),
	trunkCardProblem	(2),
	lineCardProblem	(3),
	packetSwitchProblem	(4),
	processorProblem	(5),
	terminalProblem	(6),
	environmentProblem	(7),
	externalIFDeviceProblem	(8),
	dataSetProblem	(9),
	multiplexerProblem	(10),
	receiverProblem	(11),
	transmitterProblem	(12)}
EquipmentProblemID	::= CHOICE {	
	Printable String,	
	INTEGER}	

Figure 7.17 Possible types for equipment problem reporting.

BOOLEAN OPTIONAL), (3) if the severity can be escalated (severityEscalation), and (4) a threshold value for reporting of the alarm condition (Threshold).

AlarmTail is also defined as SEQUENCE of the three other types which contain other optional information about the alarm.

Additional coding is needed to define the Severity and Threshold types in Fig. 7.15. Notice that these entries have not yet been assigned a type. Since they begin in uppercase letters, code must be examined that defines their types. Figure 7.16 shows the ASN.1 coding in which they are defined as INTEGER and CHOICE, respectively. The Severity coding reveals that this alarm report can be coded with values ranging from a cleared severity (0) to a critical severity (5).

The Threshold attribute may take on one of five types:

1. *absoluteCount:* An absolute count value (number of occurrences) that exceeds a threshold. Typically, this count does not decrease and is reset if it is to be reused.

2. *CountInterval:* A count (number of occurrences) that is recorded between a startTime and an endTime. Typically, this count is set at startTime and is incremented with each occurrence of an event. When endTime is reached, the counter is reinitialized.

3. *CountWindow:* A count (number of occurrences) about an event during a specified time. It is different from CountInterval in that the time interval ends at the present time and spans any defined period (e.g., 1 week, 24 hours, etc.).

4. *ValueDuration:*   An indication that the behavior of the managed object has been beyond a threshold for a specified duration of time. Typically this tool is used to analyze intermittent conditions.

5. *absoluteValue:*   A fixed absolute value to represent a threshold for an associated parameter.

Figure 7.17 shows the remainder of code for the alarm report, the EquipmentProblemType and the EquipmentProblemID. The code is self-descriptive.

The value of protocols

It is a good idea to pause here and consider the value of the information pertaining to Figs. 7.14 through 7.16. These definitions enable an organization to use standard network management protocols (in this example, alarm reporting protocols) regardless of the type of equipment, software, or vendor. Perhaps the illustrations in Figs. 6.2 and 6.3 can be more fully appreciated now.

As stated in the preface of this book, it is also important to understand that the major task in network management is not just the acceptance and use of a standard protocol but *what* to define in an MIB, because the MIB represents the network resources. Simply stated, if the information about a managed resource is not in an MIB, the network management protocol [CMIP, Simple Network Management Protocol (SNMP), etc.] has nothing on which to operate or report. The next discussion reinforces these points.

The decision as to what types of problems to report is quite important. The definitions in Fig. 7.17 can create some confusion at the network management center. For example the alarm report would return a type 10 to identify a multiplexer problem, but, what type of multiplexer problem would it be? It could also be a line card problem in a multiplexer, in which case type 3 should be used. Certainly it is possible to report multiple messages, first identifying a multiplexer and then the line card problem within the multiplexer. In order for these events to be interpreted correctly at network control, the software must be set up to receive recursive messages about a particular problem.

Figure 7.18 shows another definition for reporting problems. This example is ASN.1 coding (again, taken from a number of sources and the author's imagination) for reporting transmission problems. When used with the other definitions in this example, there is less ambiguity about the nature of the problem.

The coding for *signalLoss* simply represents an alarm event in which the carrier is lost on a channel (or the sync signal is lost in a digital circuit). The *excessiveIdle* condition coded as 1 is used in some networks when idle bits or characters are detected. Likewise, *abortSignals* are

TransmissionProblemType	::= INTEGER{	
	signalLoss	(0),
	excessiveIdle	(1),
	abortSignal	(2),
	framingError	(3),
	transmissionError	(4),
	callSetUpFailure	(5) }

Figure 7.18 Possible types of transmission problem reporting.

used in some systems to denote the sudden stopping of the sending of data and the substitution of a special abort signal. The *framingError* is coded in the event that the signal on the line (the frame) cannot be aligned properly and therefore cannot be interpreted.

The *transmissionError* is a more general notation to describe other types of problems. Typically in a modern digital transmission system or a conventional data communication system, this error would be coded when a cyclic redundancy check/frame check/sequence check error is detected. The *callSetUpFailure* error indication could describe the inability to establish a connection between two end devices. This problem typically occurs at the link layer or the network layer of a seven-layer protocol suite.

Performance Management

The performance management standard uses ISO 10064-11 to define the requirements and criteria for measuring performance. It also defines a number of parameters relating to workload, throughput, resource waiting time, response time, propagation delay, availability, and any QOS changes. The performance activity is modeled as a monitoring and tuning protocol in that it continuously monitors OSI resources to (1) measure system performance, (2) adjust measurement criteria, and (3) determine if performance is satisfactory.

The performance management standard could be used by an organization to measure several critical characteristics and operations of the network. Presently, the OSI standard defines the following measurements:

1. Throughput

2. Workload

3. Propagation delay

4. Wait time

5. Response time

6. Quality of service (QOS)

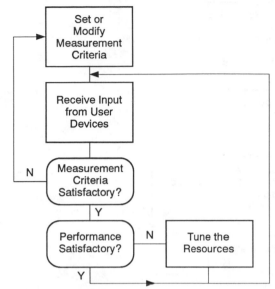

Figure 7.19 Performance management monitoring and tuning model.

An enterprise would use performance management based on the monitoring and tuning model shown in Figure 7.19.

One of the important features of any network management system is alarm reporting. The performance management standard could serve as a model for developing this service based on OSI standards. The reader should be aware that a typical network's alarm functions traverse across OSI's fault and performance standards.

Performance management functions

At the broadest level, performance management is organized around monitoring, analysis, and tuning functions. Figure 7.20 shows the organization of the performance management functions. The *workload monitoring* function will be described shortly.

The *throughput* monitoring function is used to measure the throughput on a communications circuit or a network node. It is defined for each direction of transfer as follows: The sending throughput is the ratio of successfully transferred PDUs, within a sequence of data units provided at the maximum rate to the time between the first and last request for the unit transfers. This assumes that all units measured are transmitted without errors.

The receiving throughput is the ratio of successfully transferred PDUs, in the sequence of service data units, provided at the maximum

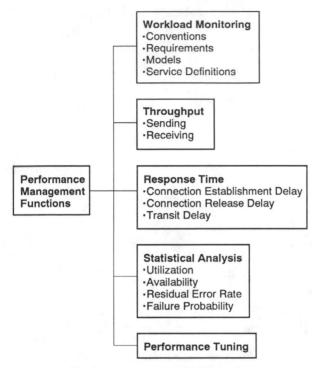

Figure 7.20   Performance management.

rate to the time between the first and last requests. Again, the units must be delivered without errors.

The *response time* monitoring function is used to evaluate the response time of a communications node or a network. Response time is defined as the time between the issuance of a request and the receipt of an indication (one-way) or the receipt of a confirm (two-way).

The *connection release delay* defines the time required to release the connection and the *transit delay* measures the delay from the sending to the receiving end users.

The *connection establishment delay* defines the time required to establish a connection starting at the time a connection request is sent to the time a corresponding connection request is received.

The *statistical analysis* function is a broad group of activities used to monitor records and determine performance of entities within an OSI managed network. The use of performance management logs and the performance model are important components of the statistical analysis function. Within this function are other QOS operations, notably: utilization, availability, residual error rate, and failure probability.

The *performance tuning* function, as the name implies, is used to measure the performance of queue lengths and queue waiting times. The model measures the waiting time (time spent in waiting for a service), the service time (the time in processing the activity), and the interarrival time (the time between the arrival of events at a queue).

Workload monitoring

The standard describes a model for monitoring the performance and measuring the workload of a managed object. On a broad basis, the monitoring model is organized around (1) requirements, (2) models for monitoring, and (3) service definitions. The requirements specifications are organized further around:

- Early warning workload
- Early warning workload clear
- Overload
- Warning rejection
- Warning rejection clear

The monitoring function specifications are organized around the following:

- Workload model
- Workload threshold
- Workload clear threshold
- Overload threshold
- Overload model
- Load threshold
- Loss threshold
- Loss clear threshold

Finally the service definition specifications are organized around:

- Report workload alarm service
- Report loss alarm service
- Set PM threshold service

The *early warning workload* function is used to measure and notify the network control of a possible overload condition or an approaching overload condition. As the reader might expect, the early warning workload is organized around a value exceeding some other threshold value.

The *early warning clear* function is used to clear some condition after the workload level has moved below a major threshold value. This service is intended to be used after an early warning workload notification has been sent.

The *overload* function is used to report an overload situation for a managed object. Typically, it is used to notify the managing process that a managed object has reached the maximum capacity and cannot service future requests.

The *warning rejection* service is used when a managed object is rejecting services beyond a permitted threshold value. In turn, the *warning rejection clear* clears the warning rejection from a previous threshold violation.

The workload monitoring function (as we discussed earlier) is organized around seven principal activities. The fundamental activity is the *workload model*. Figure 7.21 shows the foundations for the workload model. It is based on the measurement of the activity on a resource from the standpoint of actual demand and anticipated demand vis-à-vis an early warning and overload alarm.

Security Management

The security management standard relies on ISO 10164-7, 10164-8, and 10164-9 to establish the requirements for security audit trails, including alarm deliver, selection analysis, event detection, and journaling of these operations. In addition, it defines the nature of services to control audit trail logs and alarm distribution.

The reader may wish to review the ISO 7498-2 (the part on secu-

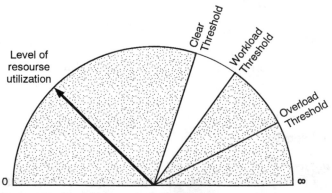

Figure 7.21   Use of gauges in performance management.

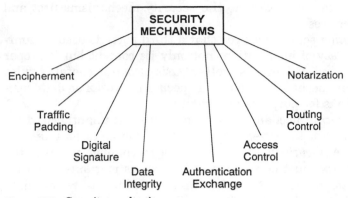

Figure 7.22   Security mechanisms.

rity); many of the features in OSI network management will use the material in the 7498-2 document (but they are not yet defined).

As shown in Figs. 7.22 and 7.23, OSI network management is obtained with 14 "services" and 8 "mechanisms" (as defined in ISO 7498-2). This section will provide a brief explanation of each of the mecha-

Figure 7.23   Security services.

nisms and services. We examine the security mechanisms first and the security services next.

The *notarization* service ensures that a third party is used to guarantee the accuracy of information, not only its content but it proper origin, timing, and delivery as well. *Routing control* contains rules that allow relay mechanisms to avoid specific networks or data communications links for purposes of security.

The *access control* mechanism is used to prevent unauthorized access to a resource or to prevent the use of a resource in an unauthorized manner. *Authentication exchange* is a mechanism wherein the identity of a party must be verified before access is granted to a resource. *Data integrity* is a mechanism that is used to ensure that data has not been destroyed or altered in an unauthorized manner. *Digital signature* is used to ensure that the recipient of data is the proper recipient and also to ensure that the data unit has not been changed. This is done by applying cryptographic information to a PDU. *Traffic padding* is a mechanism wherein spurious bits, octets, or other blocks of data are appended to PDUs. *Encipherment* uses cryptographic techniques to encrypt data.

We now take a brief look at the security services that are likely to be found in some parts of OSI network management. We will begin the discussion in relation to Fig. 7.23 with the left-most service peer entity authentication and work around the figure in a clockwise fashion.

The *peer entity authentication* service is used to ensure that the association with a peer entity is the one that it is supposed to be. *Data origin authentication* is a service to ensure that the source of the data is as it is claimed. *Access control service* ensures that an unauthorized user is not allowed to gain access to a resource. The *connection confidentiality* service ensures that (N)-user data on an (N)-connection is secure. *Connectionless confidentiality* ensures the confidentiality of all end user data for an individual (N)-service data units (SDU). The *selective field confidentiality* is used to provide for confidentiality of certain data elements within a larger array of data. *Traffic flow confidentiality* ensures that a service is provided to prevent any potential adversary from analyzing a user's traffic.

Connection integrity with recovery ensures that all end user data on the respective (N)-connection is protected from modification, deletion, or insertion. It also attempts recovery in the case of problems. The *connection integrity without recovery* forms the same functions as the previously described, but there is not recovery attempted with this service. *Selective field connection integrity* ensures the integrity of selected fields within SDUs in relation to protection against modification, deletion, insertion, or replaying. *Connectionless integrity* provides the integrity of a single SDU in relation to modification and replaying. *Selective field connectionless integrity* is a service that ensures selective fields within a connectionless PDU are not altered. *Non-repudiation with proof of origin* requires that a sender be unambiguously identified and not allowed to deny the sending of data. *Non-repudiation with proof of delivery* allows the sender of data to be provided with a service that guarantees the data has been delivered to prevent a recipient from denying receipt of the data. The other two entries in Fig. 7.23 are specific to networks and not defined in the standard.

Unfortunately, the OSI network management standards have not progressed to the point of defining which of these services and mechanisms will be used.

Accounting Management

The accounting management standard in ISO 10164-10 identifies and defines the accounting management requirements for OSI. It also provides an accounting operations model. In addition, it provides guidance on the use of units of charge, accounting logs, records (such as, duration of calls), service provided, charge rate, source and destination id. This standard is the least complete of all the five functional areas. It is not due to be an IS status until mid-1992. Since this SMFA consists of one document (10164-10), we will defer discussion of it until Chap. 8.

Approaches to the Use of the Functional Areas

The OSI Network Management Forum (OSI/NMF) has developed a management matrix to provide a framework and frame of reference for the functional areas. Table 7.2 shows an example for the general planning stages of the implementation of an OSI network management system. The NMF approach is to identify and define four aspects of resources for the service provider as one dimension of the matrix and the five functional areas as the other dimension. The five functional areas have been defined previously. The definitions of the resources are:

- *Service:* The provision of a function for the functional area
- *System:* An identifiable collection of resources that provide a function

TABLE 7.2   Example of NMF Management Matrix for a Planning Stage AREA

Resource	Configuration	Fault	Performance	Security	Accounting
Service	Name service types and mix	Define software and hardware upgrade strategy	End to end requirements	Service and network security policy	Forecast revenue and ROI
System	Network topology and routing for specific services	Assess network availability	Network design for performance	Risk assessment of design	
Generic system source	Relate network element config. to element	Relate equipment to network availability	Relate equipment to network performance	Control of access on customer sites	
Specific managed resource	Physical equipment build level	Failure rates, maintenance action	Access physical performance		

- *Generic system resource:* A logical representation of the resource
- *Specific system resource:* A specific and identifiable instance of the generic system resource

Summary

The five functional areas of OSI network management are called *SMFAs*. They continue to evolve with refences to the SMFs. Several vendors (AT&T, British Telecom, the Network Management Forum) are using the SMFAs as a platform for their own SMFs.

The System Management Functions

Introduction

This chapter examines other aspects of the OSI network management standards. We will delve into as much detail as the particular SMF allows; some are not complete; others are complete or nearing completion.

In the early development of the OSI network management standards, the protocols were organized into the five specific management function areas (SMFAs). During the ISO Subcommittee 21/Working Group 4 (SC21/WG4) in Sydney, Australia, in December 1988, it was decided that certain services that were being developed in the functional areas were common to more than one function. These functions are called *system management functions (SMFs)*. As an example, a log control function (LCF) is applicable to more than one SMFA; it is used with fault management (FM) and security management (SM). As a result of the Syndey deliberations, the SMFs were created.

These standards are published in the ISO 10164 documents. Many of their services and requirements were examined in Chap. 7. This chapter continues the analysis. The SMFs are organized as shown in Table 8.1.

Figure 8.1 shows the relationship of the SMFAs, SMFs, and common management information service element (CMISE). As stated several times in this book, be aware that this structure is changing and as it evolves, other SMFs will probably be added to the standards.

As of this writing, seven SMFs are draft international standards (DIS). Three SMFs are committee drafts and two SMFs are working drafts.

One last point needs to be made before we review these standards.

TABLE 8.1   The SMF Standards

Systems Management-Configuration Management
   Part 1: Object Management Function (10164-1)
   Part 2: State Management Function (10164-2)
   Part 3: Relationship Management Function(10164-3)

Systems Management-Fault Management
   Part 4: Alarm Reporting Function (10164-4)
   Part 5: Event Report Management Function (10164-5)
   Part 6: Log Control Function (10164-6)

Systems Management-Security Management
   Part 7: Security Alarm Reporting Function (10164-7)
   Part 8: Security Audit Trail Function (10164-8)
   Part 9: Objects & Attributes for Access Control (10164-9)

Systems Management-Accounting Management
   Part 10: Accounting Metering Function (10164-10)

Systems Management-Performance Management
   Part 11: Workload Monitoring Function (10164-11)

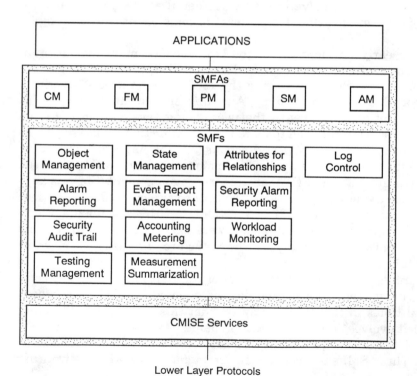

Figure 8.1   Relationship of SMFs and SMFAs.

The OSI network management standards provide for a pass-through service. This term means that a one-to-one mapping occurs between the services of an upper layer and a corresponding CMISE services.

Object Management Function (OMF) 10164-1

The network management application uses the OMF to describe the following services:

- Object creation reporting
- Object deletion reporting
- Object name changes reporting
- Attribute values changing

OMF also describes pass-through services for the following:

- Object creation
- Object deletion
- Performing actions on objects
- Changing attributes
- Reading attributes
- Reporting errors

The OMF defines the pass-through services for OSI network management. The operations for mapping the pass-through services are listed in Table 8.2.

The term *pass-through (PT)* refers to a description of a mapping that applies across a managed-object boundary and an underlying service. Currently in the OSI standards, this underlying service is a Common Management Information Service Element (CMISE) service.

TABLE 8.2   Pass-Through Services

SMI operation	Pass-through operations
Create	PT-CREATE
Delete	PT-DELETE
Action	PT-ACTION
Replace	PT-SET
Add	PT-SET
Remove	PT-SET
Replace-with-Default	PT-SET
Get	PT-GET
Notification	PT-EVENT

The OMF standard establishes the relationship of the services listed above and their parameters to the parameters associated with the Common Management Information Protocol (CMIP)/ CMISE. Each of the services contains one or more tables which describe the relationships of the parameters between the two services. For a PT service there is a one-to-one mapping between the PT services and the corresponding CMISE services. For the other services listed above, the reader should consult the OMF document to see the relationship of the non-pass-through services parameters to the CMISE parameters.

State Management Function (SMF) 10164-2

The SMF provides for the examination, setting, and notification of instantaneous changes in the state of network resources (managed objects). The state can be an operational state or an administrative state (defined in considerable detail in Chap. 7 in the configuration management section). In addition, SMF defines a usage state attribute. To provide for continuity in this discussion, Table 8.3 summarizes the OSI network management states.

The operations and services typically implemented with state management deal with reporting and reading state changes. The state reading operation is used by the managing system to request the managed system to retrieve values regarding the configuration state of one or more instances of the managed objects. The returning values include the operational and administrative states of these objects.

TABLE 8.3   Permissible States

Type	Description
Operational	
Disabled	Resource is completely unable to perform services.
Enabled	Resource is able to perform full or partial services.
Usage	
Idle	Resource is not being used.
Active	Resource is being used and has capacity for accepting services.
Busy	Resource is being used and has no spare capacity.
Unknown	Managed object has no knowledge on the resource's usage.
Administrative	
Locked	Resource is not allowed to perform services.
Unlocked	Resource is allowed to perform services.
Shutting down	Resource can service existing users, but not new users.

The state change reporting operation allows the managed system to report a change in a state attribute of one of its managed objects. It is allowed to report a change to an operational and/or administrative state.

In addition to the operational, administrative, and usage states described in this chapter and the previous chapter, the SMF standard provides a status attribute which is used to more fully qualify the operational, usage, and administrative state attributes. This attribute can have one or more of the following values. Be aware that all are not applicable to every managed object class (MOC).

The *repair status* attribute is used to identify if a managed resource is (1) under repair and/or (2) has an outstanding fault report.

The *installation status* attribute is used to report if a managed object is (1) not installed, installed improperly, or incompletely installed; (2) requires initialization before it can be made available (initialization has begun but is not yet complete); or (3) initialization has not yet begun.

The *availability status* attribute is used to determine if a managed object is (1) undergoing testing, (2) contains a fault which prevents it from being used, (3) requires power but is not powered, (4) requires some type of manual or automatic switching before it can be brought on-line, (5) has been made unavailable because of an ongoing time schedule (such as maintenance), (6) requires another resource and cannot operate because this source is disabled, and/or (7) the managed object has been degraded (for whatever reason) because of unacceptable performance.

The *control status* attribute is used to determine if (1) a managed object is currently under testing, (2) reserved for testing, (3) service has been administratively suspended to the users, and/or (4) part of the services for the managed resource are locked up.

Table 8.4 shows the relationship of this service in the state management standard parameters to that of the CMISE reporting parameters.

Relationship Management Function (RMF) 10164-3

The RMF defines relationships of network components and their effect on each other. The purpose of RMF is to enable a network control center to track the dependencies and interactions between all resources in the network. Several categories of relationships are defined in the RMF. They are shown in Fig. 8.2.

RMF defines the relationships of managed objects as (1) *direct* or (2)

TABLE 8.4   State Change Parameter Mapping

State change parameter	CMISE parameter
Invoke identifier	Invoke identifier
Mode	Mode
Managed object class	Managed object class
Managed object instance	Managed object instance
State change	Event type
Event time	Event time
State change information:	
OldOperationalState	Event information
NewOperationalState	Event information
OldUsageState	Event information
NewUsageState	Event information
OldAdministrativeState	Event information
NewAdministrativeState	Event information
OldRepairStatus	Event information
NewRepairStatus	Event information
OldInstallationStatus	Event information
NewInstallationStatus	Event information
OldAvailabilityStatus	Event information
NewAvailabilityStatus	Event information
OldControlStatus	Event information
NewControlStatus	Event information
Additional State Change Info	Event information
Current time	Current time
Event reply	Event reply
Errors	Errors

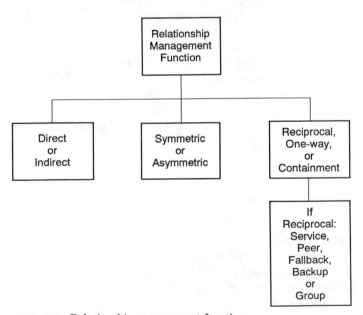

Figure 8.2   Relationship management functions.

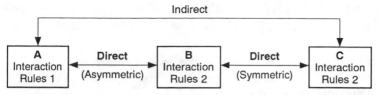

Figure 8.3 Direct, indirect, symmetric, and asymmetric relationships.

indirect (see Fig. 8.3). A direct relationship exists between two managed objects when some portion of the information about one object identifies the other object with which it has a relationship. An indirect relationship exists between two managed objects when the relationship can be deduced from the concatenation of two or more direct relationships.

Two managed objects may also exhibit (1) symmetric or (2) asymmetric relationships. A symmetric relationship exists between two managed objects when the rules governing their interaction with each other are the same; therefore, their roles are the same. An asymmetric relationship exists between two managed objects when the rules governing their interaction with each other are different; therefore, their roles are different.

The relationships between managed objects can also be described as (1) reciprocal, (2) one-way, or (3) containment.

A *reciprocal* relationship occurs when the name of a managed object is included as one of a set of values of an attribute of each of the managed objects. This relationship creates a binding between the two managed objects.

A *one-way* relationship is an asymmetric relationship in that the relationship between two managed objects is expressed in only one of the pair.

The idea of *containment* was introduced in Chap. 1. It describes a relationship in which one managed object is the owner or container of another managed object. It fits well with the notion of OSI naming hierarchies and domains because the identity of the "owning" managed object is implicit in the name of the owned or contained object. A containment relationship must be asymmetric because the roles of the containing and contained managed objects must be different with regard to each other. A containment relationship is created each time a new instance of an object is created.

Finally, RMF defines five types of relationships:

- *Service:* One managed object is a service provider to another managed object.

- *Peer:* The managed objects are similar (although their detailed parameters may be different) and their rules of communicating with each other are the same; therefore, a peer type relationship is symmetric.

- *Fall-back:* One managed object serves as a "preferred" fall back to a primary object. More than one fall-back managed object can exist. This relationship is asymmetric.

- *Backup:* One managed object serves as a backup to another managed object in the event the first object is in the disabled operational state. The first object is the primary object and the backup object is the secondary object. The backup relationship is asymmetric.

- *Group:* A relationship in which a member object belongs to a group represented by the owner object. This concept aids in grouping together similar member objects.

Table 8.5 shows the mapping of the relationship change parameters to the CMISE parameters. This standard uses the CMISE M-Event-Report-Service for its operations.

Alarm Reporting Function (ARF) 10164-4

This function allows the managed objects to send notifications to the managing process about a variety of problems encountered by a managed object. The services are defined by this function to assist in the analysis of faults, throughput, alarms, etc. This standard provides many definitions on alarm types, alarm causes, severity levels, and

TABLE 8.5   Relationship Change Parameter Mapping

Relationship change parameter	CMISE parameter
Invoke identifier	Invoke identifier
Mode	Mode
Managed object class	Managed object class
Managed object instance	Managed object instance
Relationship change	Event type
Event time	Event time
Relationship change info	Event information
Relationship change definition	Event information
Relationship attribute id	Event information
Old relationship value	Event information
New relationship value	Event information
Additional relationship	Event information; change information
Current time	Current time
Event reply	Event reply
Errors	Errors

other terms. Typically, an organization uses ARF to report the following problems:

- *Communication failure:* Includes call establishment problems, distortion of signal, cycle redundancy check (CRC) error, flag error, framing error, etc.

- *Processing failure:* Includes processing problems such as buffer overflow, software bugs, lack of memory, version mismatches, and database and file access errors

- *Quality of service failure:* Includes problems associated with throughput, response time, excessive transmissions, excessively long queues, and reduced transmission capacity

- *Equipment failure:* Includes failures such as cable problems, failed trunks, streaming printers, locked ports, etc.

- *Environmental failure:* Includes failures such as high or low temperatures exceeded, excessive humidity, smoke detection, etc.

Figure 8.4 shows an example of Abstract Syntax Notation 1 (ASN.1) code that is used in the alarm reporting function. This example is not defined as such in the standard but is shown to clarify some of these rather abstract concepts. The *ErrorInfo* is defined as a set of optional indicators coded as tagged types. The *[0] ProbableCause* entry (in this example) would convey a tag of 1 to identify a communication error. The *[6] ThresholdInfo* entry must be present when the error is a result of a threshold violation. The *[7] StateChange* entry must be present when a state change is associated with the error. The SET clause al-

```
--Example is for a communication type error
communication-Error EVENT
            EVENTINFO Errorinfo
            ::= {errorfunction 1}

 Errorinfo ::= SET {
            [0] ProbableCause OPTIONAL,
            [1] Severity OPTIONAL,
            [2] TrendIndication OPTIONAL,
            [3] BackedUpStatus OPTIONAL,
            [4] DiagnosticInfo OPTIONAL,
            [5] ProposedRepairAction OPTIONAL,
            [6] ThresholdInfo OPTIONAL,
            [7] StateChange OPTIONAL,
            [8] OtherInfor OPTIONAL}
```

Figure 8.4   Example of alarm reporting ASN.1 code.

Errorinfo : := SET {

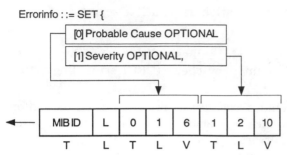

Figure 8.5   Relationship of ASN.1 code to transfer syntax.

lows the entries to be used in any order, and through the use of the tag, they are uniquely identified. We state once again that this approach gives a network manager considerable latitude in how to use ASN.1 code for network management. The entries in Fig. 8.4 are largely self-explanatory. The coding of the names is important. It is obvious that some thought has been given to them, because they are meaningful. Since programmers, engineers, and designers will probably read the ASN.1 code to get an idea what the network management system is doing, it is a very good idea to spend some time to compose meaningful names.

Figure 8.5 shows the relationship of the ASN.1 code in Fig. 8.4 to the transfer syntax, discussed in Chap. 4. For purposes of simplicity, only tags 0 and 1 are shown. The transfer syntax is illustrated at the bottom of the figure. The notation MIB ID is the author's indicator that the type value could be a context-specific or private-use tag identifying an entry in the management information base (MIB). The purpose of this field is to uniquely identify the data that is being transferred. Of course, the tags of 0 and 1 serve to identify what aspect of the error information is being reported. The shaded areas and pointers show how the probable cause and severity entries are coded in the transfer syntax.

Table 8.6 shows the relationship of the alarm reporting services parameters to that of the CMISE parameters. The alarm reporting service makes use of the CMISE M-Event-Report-Service.

Event Reporting Management Function (ERMF) 10164-5

This function is used for distributing and controlling event reports. The function allows a managing process to select the events that are to be reported within a selected period of time. ERMF is built on an

TABLE 8.6   Alarm Reporting Parameter Mapping

Alarm reporting parameter	CMISE parameter
Invoke identifier	Invoke identifier
Mode	Mode
Managed object class	Managed object class
Managed object instance	Managed object instance
Alarm type	Event type
Event time	Event time
Alarm information:	
Probable cause	Event information
Specific problems	Event information
Perceived severity	Event information
Backup object instance	Event information
Backed-up status	Event information
Trend indication	Event information
Threshold information	Event information
Notification identifier	Event information
Correlated notifications	Event information
Generic state change	Event information
Monitored attributes	Event information
Proposed repair actions	Event information
Problem text	Event information
Problem data	Event information
Current time	Current time
Event reply	Event reply
Errors	Errors

event management model which consists of an event forwarding control function and a service access control function (also called the management service control discriminator).

The ERMF can support the following services:

- Receive and analyze a notification from a managed object
- Initiate the event reporting service
- Terminate the event reporting service
- Suspend event reporting service
- Resume event reporting service
- Modify event forwarding criteria
- Retrieve event forwarding criteria

Figure 8.6 is an illustration of the ERMF model. It consists of two major functions: (1) the event detection and processing function and (2) the event forwarding discriminator processing function. The former function has the task of receiving and processing the notifications that come from the managed object. The latter is responsible for reporting the events to a specific destination with a specified time pe-

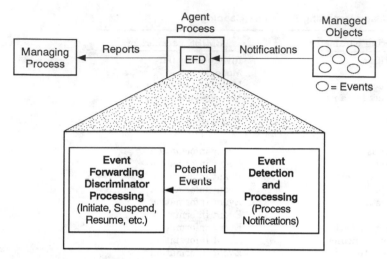

Figure 8.6   The ERMF model.

riod. The user (as one possibility) at the managing process may want a report to be generated and sent to some destination. For this to occur, the user must create event forwarding discriminator objects that contain a *DiscriminatorConstruct*. This construct is used to specify the filtering conditions under which the event is to be forwarded to the destination. The construct is shown in Fig. 8.7.

The relationship of the event report management services parameters and the parameters of CMISE are still being defined.

Log Control Function (LCF) 10164-6

ISO 10164-6 describes the operations for the network management log. Network management logs are used to record information about the managed objects in the network. The LCF establishes the rules for the operation of the log. These rules are known as log behavior. The behavior is determined by the log's status, state attributes, and the

---

--Example of discriminator construct

test-filter   CMISFilter ::=
        and {item equality {objectClass, M-Object-Class protocolEntity}
            item substring {type entityID, string {initial Printable String }}
            subfilter}

--next is the subfilter definition, not shown here

Figure 8.7   The discriminator construct.

discriminator construct. Each log class must support the following attributes:

- *Administrative state:* The log is allowed to assume either the locked or unlocked states.

- *Availability status:* This attribute describes the operational state of the log. It allows a user to determine which records can be retrieved, which records can be appended as add-ons, or if the log is full, etc.

- *Capacity alarm threshold:* This threshold is used to determine when the log is becoming full. Its value is determined as a percentage of the maximum log size.

- *Current log size:* This attribute specifies the size of the log (in octets).

- *Discriminator construct:* This attribute is used to perform filtering and scoping tests to determine which information is to be logged.

- *Log full action:* This attribute defines the action that is to be taken if the maximum size of the log has been reached. The standard requires that (1) no more records will be logged or (2) that a wrap-around operation occurs in which the earliest records are deleted to make room for new records.

- *Log ID:* This attribute is used to unambiguously identify the instance of a log.

- *Maximum log size:* As the name suggests, the maximum log size specifies the log storage capacity (in octets).

- *Operational state:* The log is allowed to represent an enabled or a disabled state.

- *Packages:* This attribute specifies the packages that have been instantiated for each log instance. The purpose of the package is to allow the log to switch (without manual intervention) between logging-on and logging-off conditions. The package determines periodicity regarding the logging; it could be in terms of hours, weeks, months, etc.

- *Usage log:* The log may be represented as active, idle, busy or unknown.

Security Alarm Reporting Function
(SARF) 10164-7

The SARF defines the security alarms that are used in OSI network management, the causes for the alarms, and the rules for the gen-

TABLE 8.7   Security Alarms

Type	Causes
Integrity violation	Duplicate information
	Information missing
	Information modification detected
	Information out of sequence
	Unexpected information
Operational violation	Denial of service
	Out of service
	Procedural error
	Other
Physical violation	Medium tamper
	Intrusion detection
	Other
Security service violation	Authentication failure
	Confidentiality breach
	Unauthorized access attempt
	Other
Time domain violation	Delayed information
	Authentication key obsolete
	Out of hours activity

eration of the alarms. The structure of the standard is shown in Table 8.7.

Table 8.8 shows the relationship of the security alarm parameters and the CMISE parameters. The security alarm function makes use of the CMISE M-Event Reporting Service.

Security Audit Trail Function (SATF) 10164-8

The SATF standard defines the operations of the OSI network management audit log. It is similar in concept to the log discussed earlier in this chapter, except this log contains information about security-related events. The standard is rather terse regarding the information to be stored and reported through the security log. Presently, the following reports are defined (although these reports are suggestions only):

- Number of connections to a managed object
- Number of disconnections to a managed object
- Information on types of management operations performed on the managed object
- Statistics relating to the usage of the managed object
- Security mechanisms applied to the managed object

TABLE 8.8   Security Alarm Parameter Mapping

Security alarm report parameter	CMISE parameter
Invoke identifier	Invoke identifier
Mode	Mode
Managed object class	Managed object class
Managed object instance	Managed object instance
Security alarm type	Event type
Event time	Event time
Security alarm information:	
Security alarm cause	Event information
Security alarm severity	Event information
Security alarm generator	Event information
Service user	Event information
Service provider	Event information
Notification identifier	Event information
Correlated notifications	Event information
Problem text	Event information
Problem data	Event information
Current time	Current time
Event reply	Event reply
Errors	Errors

Table 8.9 shows the relationship of the security audit trail function parameters to that of the CMISE parameters. This function uses the CMISE M-Event-Report-Service.

Objects and Attributes for Access Control (OAAC) 10164-9

The OAAC function is used to prevent unauthorized access to network elements. The standard provides for various levels of access control options, such as read only, write only, and read-write. In addition, it provides a model for accessing sets of managed objects.

Before examining this function, it might be useful to provide some definitions:

- *Access control information (ACI):*   Contains information pertaining to access control parameters

- *Access control decision function (ADEF):*   Examines information such as requestor name, data, time, and the target ACI (a managed system), and makes decisions regarding access control

- *Access control enforcement function (AEF):*   Receives decision from ADEF and acts upon the decision. The access control enforcement function (AEF) receives the initial management requests pertaining

TABLE 8.9 Security Audit Trail Parameter Mapping

Security audit trail report parameter	CMISE parameter
Invoke identifier	Invoke identifier
Mode	Mode
Managed object class	Managed object class
Managed object instance	Managed object instance
Security audit trail type	Event type
Event time	Event time
Security audit information:	
Service report cause	Event information
Notification identifier	Event information
Correlated notifications	Event information
Problem text	Event information
Problem data	Event information
Current time	Current time
Event reply	Event reply
Errors	Errors

to an object, and passes this request to the access control decision function (ADF), which passes the decision back to AEF.

These operations are shown in Fig. 8.8. Notice the CMIP request goes to an agent system management application entity (SMAE), which in turn sends an access request to AEF. AEF passes this request to ADF, which makes decisions regarding access rights. These decisions are passed back to AEF, which will provide for a denial to the SMAE or a permission to the managed object itself. In turn, the

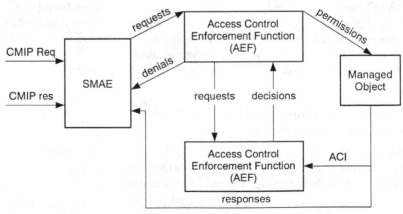

Figure 8.8 Objects and attributes for access control.

managed object will send a response to SMAE, if needed. All of these operations result in a CMIP response back to the requesting entity.

Accounting Meter Function (AMF) 10164-10

The AMF provides the rules for developing usage, accounting data, and other kinds of meters for managed objects. This standard is not complete, but it contains a number of templates which are used to show how the accounting standard behaves.

The accounting meter function is organized around *packages*, which are further defined by the attributes, actions, and notification pertaining to the packages. The function specifies four packages. The *meter-control-info package* is used for controlling the operation of accounting metering. It is required for all operations. The *accounting-Meter-Control-Action* is used to support the creation and deletion and other actions pertaining to an accounting operation. The resource-Name is a unique identifier with an instance of an accounting operation. The *data-object-reference-info* package is used to identify and control the operation if more than one instantiation is realized in a different managed object.

The attributes for the accounting meter control functions are:

- *Units of usage:*   Identifies the types of measurement pertaining to the accounting function. These units could be protocol data units (PDUs), time (such as minutes or seconds), number of bits, number of octets, number of characters, etc.

- *Recording trigger:*   This is used to specify an occurrence, which will cause data to be updated.

- *Reporting trigger:*   This is used to determine what will cause accounting information to be recorded. Both of the triggers could be controlled by periodic scheduling, some type of interrupt, or simply the resumption of an operation.

- *Data object reference attribute:*   This is used to identify some of the related instances of accounting meter data which may be of use.

- *Resource name attribute:*   This attribute simply identifies each metered OSI resource.

Perhaps of particular interest to the reader is the data that is associated with the accounting meter function. This section contains a brief description of the attributes for the accounting meter data. Part of the data area contains a *requestor ID* and a *responder ID*. These attributes are used to indicate who is the user and who is the provider of the service. The *subscriber ID* is used to indicate which subscriber is subject to the accounting meter operation. The requestor, responder, and subscriber IDs are mandatory and must be used by all metering operations.

The *meter info attribute* is used to provide accounting data pertaining to a specific metering function. It consists of a unit parameter, which defines the unit used in the measurement; a usage parameter, which contains a value on the number of units recorded; and an optional tariff identifier, which may be used to identify the tariff and accounting rules.

Two other attributes are used as options. The *service requested attribute* is used to identify some type of service needed by the user. And, the *service provided attribute* is used to identify what type of service is being provided.

Two other attributes used are called *usage start time* and *usage meter time*. These attributes are used for accounting purposes to define what time metering begins and the amount of time consumed for the operation.

The *data object state attribute* is used to describe the condition of the meter operation. It can be set to either running or suspended.

The *control object reference attribute* is used to uniquely identity the instance of an accounting meter control object operation.

Finally, the *resource name attribute* is used to identify each OSI metered resource.

Figure 8.9 shows a greatly simplified accounting metering function ASN.1 module. The coding includes only the high-level view of the accounting data. The reader should refer to Annex A of this standard for a complete explanation of the ASN.1 modules for this function.

Workload Monitoring Function (WMF) 10154-11

The WMF standard is introduced in Chap. 7. To briefly restate it, monitoring functions in the OSI network management standards provide for gauge models for workload monitoring. In addition, this standard has a number of very useful definitions on performance, thresholds, and other things related to workload monitoring. The standard also defines templates that govern its behavior. These templates are some very useful algorithms. The standard also has some informative annexes that explain calculations for rates, sampling, etc.

```
AccountingMeterFunction {joint-iso-ccitt ms(9) function(2)
part (10) asn1Modules(2) (1)}

DEFINITIONS IMPLICIT TAGS ::=
BEGIN
—EXPORTS everything
IMPORTS
  DistinguishedName FROM CMIP-1 {joint-iso-ccitt ms(9)
  cmip(1) version(1) protocol(3)}

  AccountingDataInfo ::= SEQUENCE {
    notationCause                       Trigger,
    requesterId        AccountingId,
    responderId        AccountingId,
    subscriberId       AccountingId,
    meterId            MeterInfo,
    serviceRequested   [1]  ServiceVariant OPTIONAL,
    serviceProvided    [2]  ServiceVariant OPTIONAL,
    usageStartTime     [3]  UsageStartTime OPTIONAL,
    usageMeterTime     [4]  UsageMeterTime OPTIONAL,
    resourceName       [5]  ResourceName OPTIONAL}
```

Figure 8.9   Accounting metering function.

Summary

The SMFs are applied across all OSI network management-specific management functional areas (SMFAs). The standards, published as ISO 10164, are generic services across any OSI network managed object. The SMFs operate above CMIP/CMISE in the OSI Model.

The Internet Management Protocols (SNMP and CMOT)

Introduction

A large number of installations use the Transmission Control Protocol/Internet Protocol (TCP/IP) in their local and wide area networks (LANs and WANs). These protocols were developed within the Internet framework and are used extensively throughout the world. Because of their wide use and their recognition as a de facto standard, and because many people believe Common Management Information Protocol/Common Management Information Service Element (CMIP/CMISE) and related protocols' widespread use to be some time in the future, the Internet network management standards are gaining increased attention.

The Internet network management standards are divided into two major protocol suites. One protocol was published to address short-term solutions; it is called the *Simple Network Management Protocol (SNMP)*. The other protocol (not used much) addresses long range solutions; it is called *Common Management Information Services and Protocol over TCP/IP (CMOT)*. Both protocols are designed to work with the *Internet Structure for Management Information (SMI)* and the *Internet Management Information Base (IMIB)*, which were explained in Chaps. 1 and 2.

The Internet Activities Board emphasized the need to keep SNMP as simple as possible and to develop the protocol quickly. The Internet Engineering Task Force (IETF) chairperson was given considerable leeway in resolving problems within the working group in order to get SNMP published in an expeditious manner. We shall see the effects of this approach in this chapter.

This chapter presents an overview of the SNMP operations. For the reader who wishes more information, obviously the Requests for Comments (RFCs), explained in Chap. 1, are the primary sources. Additionally, for an excellent tutorial as well as some examples of SNMP modules (in code) the reader should refer to *The Simple Book* written by Marshall T. Rose (Prentice-Hall, Inc.).

The Internet network management model

Internet uses the term *network element* to describe any object that is managed. This term is the same as an OSI managed object.

The Internet network management standards are designed to allow the communication of management information between agents located in the network elements and a network management station (typically, a network control center). From the context of Fig. 9.1, the network element consists of the *managed entity* and the managed entity's *agent*.

Figure 9.1 also shows the use of a proxy agent. This entity may be invoked for elements that are not reachable by using the conventional management protocol. The *proxy agent* can provide for convergence functions such as protocol conversion and filtering operations. Proxy management is performed on the behalf of network resources that cannot communicate with a managing element directly. For example, low-function devices such as bridges and modems typically are not able to support sophisticated management protocols. When a managing entity wishes to communicate with a managed device that cannot support the management protocols, it simply routes the traffic to the proxy agent. It is the responsibility of the proxy agent to understand the management protocol and perform the functions of communicating with the managed device.

This approach is attractive because it keeps operations transparent to network management, which only knows that it must have an additional instance of information to select the proxy instead of a specific

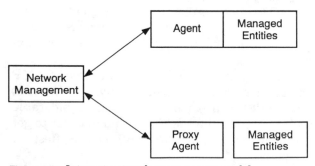

Figure 9.1 Internet network management model.

network resource. Consequently, a proxy agent is allowed to manage many devices using instances of information to tailor the operations.

The SNMP

SNMP architecture is organized around these concepts and goals:

- Keep management agent software as inexpensive as possible.
- Support remote management functions to the fullest extent possible in order to take advantage of an internet resource.
- Develop the architecture to accommodate additions in the future.
- Keep SNMP architecture independent of specific host computers and specific gateway types.

SNMP's development began with research and development efforts at several universities and laboratories in the United States. The first SNMP products were available in late 1988 from several internetworking firms (Cisco, Advanced Computer Corporation, and Proteon). Since then, almost all internetworking vendors have developed and are marketing SNMP products.

The protocol architecture is closely related to a predecessor, Simple Gateway Monitoring Protocol (SGMP), which was developed in 1987. As a side note, even though SGMP serves as the foundation for SNMP, it is different because SGMP was intended to monitor gateways only; therefore, it is more limited. Additionally, SGMP did not have a fully defined set protocol data unit (PDU) and had no community framework for authentication and security measures.

SNMP administrative relationships

The SNMP architecture uses a variety of terms that are explained in this section. Using Fig. 9.2 as a discussion point, entities that reside at

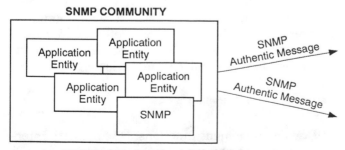

Figure 9.2 SNMP administrative relationships.

COMMUNITY PROFILE

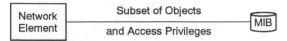

Figure 9.3   SNMP community profile.

management network stations and network elements that communicate with each other using using the SNMP standard are called *SNMP application entities*. The pairing of application entities with SNMP agents is called an *SNMP community*. Each community is identified by an Internet hierarchical name.

SNMP messages are originated by SNMP application entities. They are considered to belong to the SNMP community that contains the application entity. These messages are termed *authentic SNMP messages*. Authentication schemes are used to identify the message and verify its authenticity. This process is called an *authentication service*.

Figure 9.3 provides a view of other administrative relationships for SNMP. An SNMP element uses objects from the Internet management information base (IMIB). This subset of objects pertaining to this element is called SNMP *MIB view*. In turn, an SNMP access mode represents an element of the set (for example, read-only elements, write-only elements). Finally, a pairing of the SNMP access mode with the MIB view is called the *SNMP community profile*. In essence, the profile is used to specify access privileges for a MIB view. These relationships are determined by the SNMP community pairing by the development of profiles called *SNMP access policies*. These access policies then provide the directions on how SNMP agents and network elements can use the MIB.

Typically, the community information and other data is stored in a configuration file in the system. The file contains information about a user and agent's community. The file must contain a community name and the Internet Protocol (IP) address of the entity associated with the community. Access privileges such as write only, read-write, etc., are defined with the community name. In addition, a view is provided, which describes the subset of the MIB is available to this community name. Trap information is typically included as well; it defines the community to which traps are to be sent. Variable names are also included; they include system location and system contacts.

SNMP management strategy through polling and traps

SNMP operates with two management functions: (1) an entity interacts with a management agent to retrieve (get) variables, and/or (2) an entity interacts with a management agent to alter (set) variables. The idea behind this simple approach is that it significantly limits the functions that can be performed with SNMP, which, as a consequence, limits the complexity of the software.

These functions can be implemented through polling operations. An SNMP manager can be programmed to send periodic polling messages to the managed devices at certain intervals. These intervals can be established through the SNMP MIB.

This concept is important in an evaluation of SNMP for three reasons. First, the use of polling keeps the system relatively simple. Second, since polling is controlled by the SNMP manager, it can limit the amount of management information traffic that is created through the Internet. Third, a polling management protocol severely restricts the flexibility of the managed elements to react to conditions in an ad hoc manner; therefore it limits the number of devices that can be managed in the Internet.

SNMP is not a complete polling protocol. It does allow some unsolicited traffic, called *traps,* based on restricted parameters. The relationship of polling and traps is shown in Fig. 9.4.

Figure 9.4 shows a conventional interrupt process (Fig. 9.4*a*). In this situation the network control center (labeled control in this illustration) reacts to the managed object when the managed object sends an interrupt to it. The interrupt is a well-tried convention for managing communications between machines. The controlling device, upon receiving the message, "Be aware of the following" decides to take some actions and returns with the message, "Very well, do this...."

Interrupts are not favored by some designers because they are difficult to predict. Therefore, the workload on the network becomes even less predictable. Moreover, they may entail considerable overhead at the network computers' central processing units (CPUs) because each interrupt must be serviced with the use of CPU cycles.

In contrast, with pure polling systems, (in Fig. 9.4*b*) the control machine continuously sends messages (called *polling messages* or just *polls*) to the managed objects. In this example we see the message, "Respond to me, I wish to know your status," which forces a response from the managed object.

The polling operations can consume a substantial amount of overhead by introducing nonuser data traffic into the network. These operations are especially troublesome if the polls are issued frequently and nothing productive is reported in response to them. Media "bandwidth" and machine CPU cycles are consumed—without any positive discernible effect on network efficiency. Nonetheless, polling protocols are relatively simple to implement and they allow the network designer to compile a more predictable traffic profile.

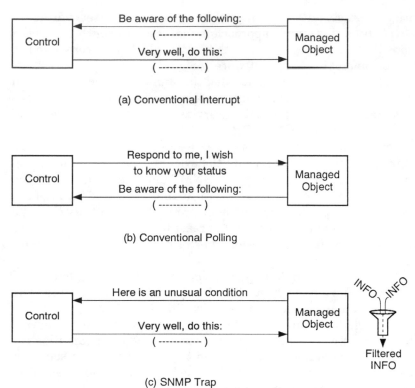

(a) Conventional Interrupt

(b) Conventional Polling

(c) SNMP Trap

Figure 9.4 Polling and interrupt operations.

SNMP approaches the situation with a modified interrupt called a *trap*. This operation is illustrated in Figure 9.4c. The managed object's agent is responsible for performing threshold checks (commonly called a *filter*) and only reporting conditions that meet certain threshold criteria. For example, a temperature gauge becomes too hot, queues become too large, etc. Upon receiving the message, "Here is an unusual condition," the control machine may decide to take certain actions.

Well yes, but a trap is still an interrupt. So what is the big deal, and what has been gained by this approach? The advantages are: (1) the trap (the interrupt) is performed on a very few and critical events, and (2) the interrupt message is simple and small. Therefore, precious media "bandwidth" and CPU cycles can be used in a more efficient manner.

However, regardless of one's view of these matters and as a practical matter, it is prudent to continue to use polling (at least periodically) to maintain an up-to-date awareness of the network resources.

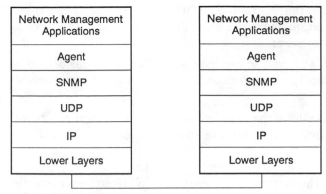

Figure 9.5 The SNMP layers.

The SNMP layers

SNMP was designed by the IETF for use on internets. Presently, it is designed to run on top of the User Datagram Protocol (UDP) as shown in Fig. 9.5, although no technical reason exists why it cannot operate over other protocols if the implementor is willing to develop some interface modules to the protocol.

Because it uses UDP, SNMP is a connectionless protocol. There is no guarantee that the management traffic is received at the other entity. As with all connectionless protocols, processing overhead is reduced, and simplicity is obtained. However, if reliability and accountability are needed, the network manager must build connection-oriented operations into upper-layer applications.

SNMP PDUs

This protocol uses relatively simple operations and a limited number of PDUs to perform its functions. Five protocol data units have been defined in the standard. They are as follows:

- *Get Request:*   This PDU is used to access the agent and obtain values from a list. It contains identifiers to distinguish it from multiple requests as well as values to provide information about the status of the network element.

- *Get-Next Request:*   This PDU is similar to the Get Request, except it permits the retrieving of the next logical identifier in a MIB tree.

- *Get Response:*   This PDU responds to the Get Request, Get-Next Request, and the Set Request data units. It contains an identifier that associates it with the previous PDU. It also contains identifiers to provide information about the status of the response (error codes, error status, and a list of additional information).

- *Set Request:*   This is used to describe an action to be performed on an element. Typically, it is used to change the values in a variable list.

- *Trap:*   This PDU allows the network management module to report on an event at a network element or to change the status of the network element.

Figure 9.6 shows the boundary between the SNMP software and the upper-layer software. The interface is achieved by passing PDUs between the two entities. The flow of the PDUs can proceed in either direction, although Fig. 9.6 shows that the management system has initiated most of the PDUs. The directions of the arrows at the managed system shows that the PDUs are passed from SNMP to the upper layer. Traps can be issued by either entity.

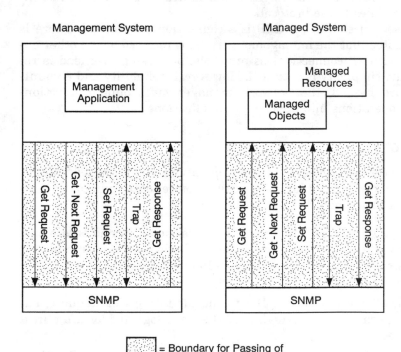

Figure 9.6   SNMP interface with upper layer.

Operations between SNMP agents and managers

Figures 9.7, 9.8, and 9.9 show some typical operations between the SNMP agents and the managing process. Each of the figures shows that the managing process software is located in the network control station (NCS). The master MIB is also stored at the NCS. However, nothing requires the managing software and the master MIB to reside in any station on the network. For example, this software and MIB could reside in a host computer.

Figure 9.7 shows a typical *get* and *get response* operation. The NCS issues a get to the WAN gateway. The contents of the get PDU contain an identifier (ID) to uniquely identify the PDU. Error fields are also contained in the get PDU (however they are blank for a get operation). The managed object (MO) names identify what information is to be retrieved at the gateway MIB. The MO names must be coded in conformance with the definitions in the MIB.

The gateway returns a get response. This PDU also contains the same ID that was in the get PDU. The error fields are filled in if any

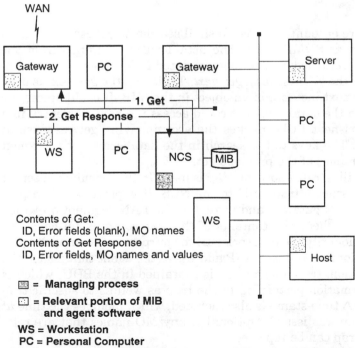

Contents of Get:
   ID, Error fields (blank), MO names
Contents of Get Response
   ID, Error fields, MO names and values

▨ = **Managing process**

▢ = **Relevant portion of MIB and agent software**

WS = Workstation
PC = Personal Computer

Figure 9.7 The get and get response operation.

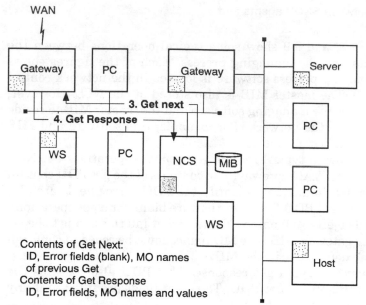

Contents of Get Next:
  ID, Error fields (blank), MO names
  of previous Get
Contents of Get Response
  ID, Error fields, MO names and values

Figure 9.8 The get-next and get response operations.

problems were encountered. As we shall see shortly, these error fields are coded under SNMP rules. The actual values obtained from the MIB are also returned, as are the associated MO names.

In Fig. 9.8, the NCS issues a *get-next*. Typically, the get-next is used to access the next instance of an object in the MIB. It could access the next object in the database, or it could access the next row entry in a table. The get-next PDU invokes the accompanying get response at the gateway. The keys to the search in the database for the get-next are the MO names of the previous get.

Figure 9.9 illustrates how the trap is used. In this example, a server on the LAN issues a trap PDU to the NCS. It is processed transparently at the LAN gateway and passed to the LAN segment on which the NCS is attached. The contents of the trap contains sufficient information to identify the enterprise ID for purposes of community profile information, as well as the IP address of the agent that issued the trap. In addition, trap information is contained in the PDU, which is general information pertaining to the trap as well as to specific trap information. A time-stamp is also included, which includes the time at which the trap was issued. Optionally, any MO names that are relevant to the trap can be reported.

In event 2 in Fig. 9.9, the NCS issues either a get or a set to (1) ob-

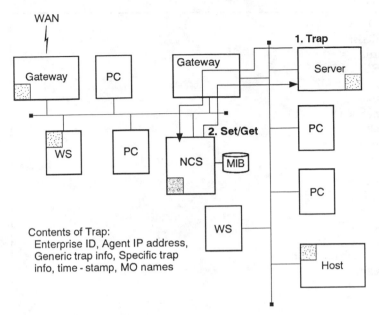

WAN

Figure 9.9   The trap operations.

tain more information about the nature of the problem or (2) change some parameters in the server's MIB.

Examples of ASN.1 Code for SNMP PDUs

All the SNMP PDUs have a common coding format based on Abstract Syntax Notation 1 (ASN.1). Figure 9.10 shows the encoding for the common format. The *Request ID* field is used to distinguish between the different requests in the PDUs. The *ErrorStatus* coding provides a list to describe the type of error that is being recorded. This list is accessed through the *ErrorIndex* field, which is listed below the *ErrorStatus* field. The *ErrorStatus* field provides values for reporting problems. The *noError* field simply reports that no error has occurred. The *tooBig* value is used to report that the results of an operation would not fit into an SNMP data unit. The *noSuchName* indicator is used to inform the controller that the variable name cannot be identified. The *badValue* is used if a variable cannot be identified or if its syntax makes no sense. The *readOnly* indicator is used to report that a variable has a profile of read only and it cannot be written. The *GenErr* is used to report anything else.

The *VarBind* sequence is used to identify the name of the managed element and any associated value. The *VarBindList* is a set of values

```
RequestID ::=
    INTEGER
ErrorStatus ::=
    INTEGER{
        noError (0),
        tooBig (1),
        noSuchName (2),
        badValue (3),
        read Only (4),
        genErr (5)}

ErrorIndex ::=
    INTEGER
VarBind ::=
    SEQUENCE {
        name
            Object Name,
        value
            Object Syntax
    }
VarBindList ::=
    SEQUENCE OF
        VarBind
```

Figure 9.10   The SNMP common ASN.1 code for PDUs.

to set the variable bindings. Be aware that SNMP uses the term *variable* to describe an instance of a MO, and the term *VarBind* simply describes the pairing of a variable to the variable's value. The VarBindList simply contains a list of the variable names and their corresponding values.

Figure 9.11 shows an actual example of ASN.1 coding of a Get Request. The parameters in this PDU were discussed earlier.

Figure 9.12 shows another way to view the PDUs (except the trap PDU). The reader may be more familiar with the illustration on the right side of the figure, which shows the conventional method for showing PDUs. This technique has been used in the industry for many years. The fields in a PDU are labeled with the assumption that the top-most field is transmitted first, with transmission moving on down to the bottom of the figure. These notations are no longer used in newer protocols. They rely on the notation on the left for describing the fields. Nonetheless, it is hoped that this illustration will be helpful to the readers who do not wish to burden themselves with reading ASN.1 code. The fields in the PDU were described previously in this chapter (in relation to Fig. 9.10).

```
Get Request-PDU :: =
    [0]
            IMPLICIT SEQUENCE {
                request ID,
                    Request ID,
                error-status          -always 0
                    Error Status,
                error-index           -always 0
                    Error-Index,
                variable-bindings
                    VarBindList
            }
```

Figure 9.11   The get request PDU.

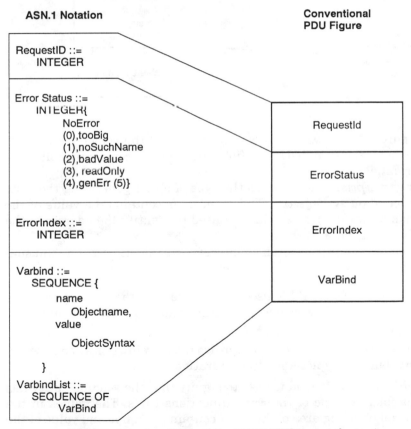

Figure 9.12   ASN.1 code and a picture of the SNMP PDU (except the trap).

ASN.1 Notation

**Conventional
PDU Figure**

```
Trap-PDU ::=
    [4] IMPLICIT SEQUENCE{
    enterprise
        OBJECT IDENTIFIER
    agent-addr
        NetworkAddress,
    generic-trap
        INTEGER{
            coldStart(0),
            warmStart(1),
            linkDown(2),
            linkUp(3),
            authenticationFailure(4),
            egpNeighborLoss(5),
            enterpriseSpecific(6)
        }
    specific-trap
        INTEGER,
    time-stamp
        TimeTicks,
    variable-bindings
        VarBindList
```

enterprise
agent-addr
generic-trap
specific-trap
time-stamp
variable-bindings

Figure 9.13   The trap PDU.

Figure 9.13 shows the ASN.1 notation and the conventional PDU graphic for the trap PDU. The fields in the PDU convey the following information.

The *enterprise* field contains the type of object generating the trap. It is based on sysObjectID. The *agent-addr* contains the value of the agent's network address, which is used to identify the address of the object that generates the trap.

The *generic-trap* contains information about certain unusual events:

- *coldStart:* This field is used to indicate that the sending entity is reinitializing. This means that states and configurations might be affected.

- *warmStart:* This field also signifies that a reinitialization is occurring, but it may not affect configurations.

- *linkDown:* This field is used to signify that the sending entity has a problem on one of the communications links. The values in the variable binding area of the PDU contain the name and value of the affected interface as defined through an instance of *ifIndex*.

- *linkUp:* Conversely, this trap is used to signify that one of the communications links is now operational. Again, the variable bindings indicator contains the name and value of the interface as defined by an instance of *ifIndex.*

- *authenticationFailure:* This trap value is used to indicate that an address in a protocol message cannot be authenticated properly.

- *egpNeighborLoss:* This value is used to indicate that an EGP neighbor has been declared down and the EGP peer relationship no longer exists. The variable bindings field contains the name and value of the instance for the egpNeighAddr instance for the neighbor.

- *enterpriseSpecific:* This value is used to indicate that the sending entity has recognized that an event has occurred; it affects something specific to the event. The very nature of the name of this trap depends on the value of the specific trap field (discussed next).

The *specific-trap* field is used to identify the enterpriseSpecific trap just discussed. This value is set to zero if enterprise-specific traps are not being used. The *time-stamp* field contains the value of sysUpTime. Finally, the *variable-bindings* field contains other information about the trap. This field was described earlier.

Mapping SNMP to transport layer services

As discussed earlier in this chapter, SNMP uses the services of the underlying transport layer. The most common approach is to place SNMP over a connectionless transport layer such as UDP or the OSI connectionless transport layer. This operation is shown in Fig. 9.14 with a time sequence diagram. The SNMP PDU is passed to the transport layer through the T-UNITDATA request primitive. The transport layer is responsible for conveying the SNMP data unit transparently to the other machine and passing it to the SNMP module through the T-UNITDATA indication primitive.

The connectionless approach is quite simple. It requires very few re-

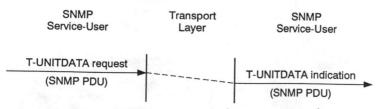

Figure 9.14 Mapping SNMP to a connectionless transport service.

sources and few machine cycles. Since it is connectionless, it does not concern itself with the reliable delivery of traffic.

Figure 9.15 shows the use of SNMP over a connection-oriented transport layer. Primitives are required to establish connections and disconnects and a connection must exist between the two entities before SNMP data units can be exchanged. Also, this type of protocol requires the disconnection operations to release any resources that were used during the session between the two entities. If SNMP wishes to send only one or a few transactions, it must go through the overhead and possible delay in obtaining some type of virtual relationship between the entities.

Notwithstanding, it is certainly possible to use a connection-oriented protocol. Nothing precludes the establishment of a transport layer connection between two entities and simply leaving it up indefinitely and allowing it to form a pipeline for the SNMP traffic. Although many connection-oriented supporters dislike this approach, it does have the advantage of allowing the network manager to obtain end-to-end integrity.

In a typical operation, an SNMP agent waits for an incoming trans-

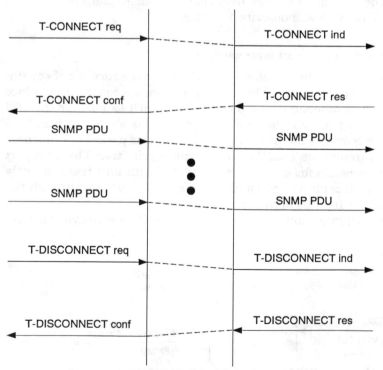

Figure 9.15 Mapping SNMP to a connection-oriented transport service.

mission from either UDP, TCP, or an OSI transport protocol. Upon receiving this PDU, it stores the address of the sending entity. Its next job is to decode the datagram according to ASN.1 rules and translate this to an SNMP message. Edit checks are made on version fields and authentication is determined by a community name analysis. If all goes well and the PDU is valid and well formed, the agent then uses the variables in the request to determine what part of the MIB to search. If the operation is a get, a get response is returned to the requestor through the use of UDP, TCP, or some other transport protocol entity.

SNMP operations in more detail

This section contains additional information on the SNMP operations. To begin this discussion, it is important to note that SNMP is not designed to access a complete table in the MIB. Some language and access packages allow the programmer to access all the rows and columns in a table with one iteration of a source code get/put/set command. SNMP accesses a table a row at a time if needed. If the next row is needed, a get-next request can be used to obtain the next row. The access to the entries of a row depend on how the arguments in the request are formulated.

Furthermore, SNMP is not designed to access anything except leaf object instances of the table. Therefore, the notion of accessing a node within the tree does not exist.

In order to use SNMP, the SNMP client must provide OBJECT TYPE names to an SNMP server. In turn, the SNMP server returns the first instance of this OBJECT TYPE name or names encountered in the database. For example, the command get (tcpConnState) would obtain the first instance of the variable tcpConnState in the MIB.

As we have mentioned before, the results of this value could be used in the next get-next operation to obtain the next entry in the MIB and so on.

SNMP permits multiple operands in the argument. For example, get-next (tcpConnState, tcpConnLocalAddress, etc.) can be used to obtain multiple entries within the database.

SNMP can be used to find the location in the MIB. For example, a get-next with an argument of say ipRouteNextHop.127 would retrieve the first entry beyond this value in the table. If, for example, the network identifier 122 was stored in the MIB and the next network ID was 127, SNMP would retrieve the first entry after 122, perhaps 127.1.3.6.

It is useful to know that SNMP is an *atomic* protocol in the sense that it performs actions successfully on all requests or it performs none of them.

Access is made to the MIB through the identification of object instances. As we have learned earlier, each object type defined in the

MIB is called by its variable name and is identified as an OBJECT
IDENTIFIER. To illustrate this point, Fig. 9.16 shows the MIB for the
IP group. If we wish to identify an instance of IPDefaultTTL, we could
use the hierarchical identifier scheme with the value of 1.3.6.1.2.1.4.2.
Furthermore, if we appended a 0 to this number, SNMP would under-
stand that this is a specific instance and the one-and-only instance of
IPDefaultTTL.

The bottom part of Fig. 9.16 shows two ways of identifying a variable.
The top part of the box in the lower part of this figure shows the concatenated names of the node in the Internet hierarchical tree with an

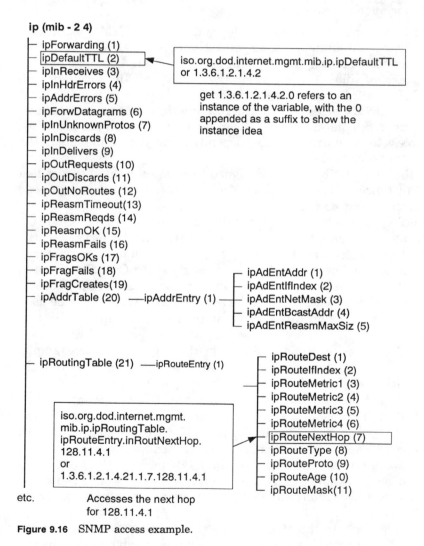

Figure 9.16   SNMP access example.

Internet number attached as the last concatenated number. This could be used to access the next hop (the IPRouteNextHop variable) for an Internet address 128.11.4.1. For both a get and a get-next, if an instance does not exist the get response returns a noSuchName message.

Remember that SNMP is an atomic protocol; if an error occurs in a request, the remainder of the parameters in the request are not processed. This can create some problems in the sense that a user might wish to obtain the information that was valid. One solution is to use some type of general argument to SNMP, as illustrated in Fig. 9.17. The get-next (sysObjectID, sysLocation) might search against, let us say, MIB 1. Since sysLocation was not defined in MIB 1, the operation

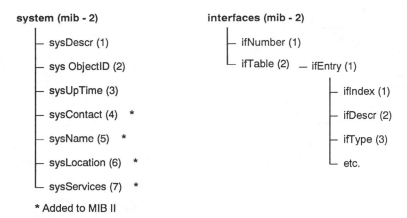

get: An instance is retrieved for each named object (variable), with the name and value returned.

get-next: Retrieves the next instance following the name instance.

For both: If an instance does not exist, a noSuch Name is returned with the get response.

Problem: If an error occurs in a request, the remainder of the parameters in the request are not processed. How to structure the requests in consideration of traffic?

Approach: Use a general argument:

get-next (sysObjectID,sysLocation)

system (mib - 2)
- sysDescr (1)
- sys ObjectID (2)
- sysUpTime (3)
- sysContact (4) *
- sysName (5) *
- sysLocation (6) *
- sysServices (7) *

* Added to MIB II

interfaces (mib - 2)
- ifNumber (1)
- ifTable (2) — ifEntry (1)
  - ifIndex (1)
  - ifDescr (2)
  - ifType (3)
  - etc.

If search is against MIB I, sysObjectID.0 and IfNumber.0 are returned, but operation is not aborted. It is easy to determine that sysLocation is not available.

Successful search: sysObjectID.0 and sysLocation.0

Figure 9.17 SNMP access examples.

is not aborted, but the search goes to the *next* entry in the library, which is ifNumber0. With a little checking by the software, it is quite easy to determine that sysLocation is not available. Obviously, a successful search would yield sysObjectID.0 and sysLocation.0.

CMOT

CMOT was also designed by IETF. It is based on the ISO network management standards and can be used to run on a connection-oriented transport layer (such as TCP), or on a connectionless layer (such as UDP). The principal purpose of CMOT is to describe the mapping rules to be used with the IMIB and the ISO MIB. CMOT never got off the blocks and is not considered a contender in the network management arena. We speak of CMOT in the present tense, since it still has some limited use.

The CMOT layers

The CMOT architecture is shown in Fig. 9.18. A reader familiar with OSI should be quite at ease with the information in this figure. Notice the OSI association control service element (ACSE) is used in the ap-

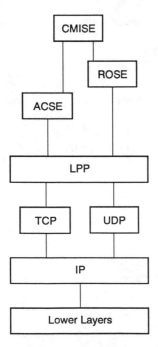

Figure 9.18   CMOT layers.

plication layer to provide services to the network management application service elements (ASEs).

The lightweight presentation protocol

Figure 9.18 also shows an additional layer, the lightweight presentation protocol (LPP). Since TCP and UDP have not been developed with OSI service definitions, the job of LPP is to map the OSI application service elements to the TCP/UDP modules. With the layering shown in Fig. 9.18, LPP must map ROSE and ACSE onto the transport layer (TCP or UDP). In the spirit of OSI, the next lower level, which is the IP, is transparent to the CMOT applications in the upper layers.

An easy way to determine which transport layer protocol is used at a remote machine is to simply send a PDU to the remote machine requesting a specific quality of service (QOS). If the transport entity at the remote machine cannot support the QOS, it will return the P-CONNECT confirm primitive with a negative connotation. Additionally, four port numbers have been defined for interfacing CMOT with TCP or UDP. They are as follows:

- CMOT Manager: 163/TCP
- CMOT Manager: 163/UDP
- CMOT Agent: 164/TCP
- CMOT Agent: 164/UDP

The LPP is designed to provide a minimum level of service for the ACSE and remote operations service element (ROSE) entities resting above it. Presently, five presentation services from the OSI Model are defined:

- P-CONNECT
- P-RELEASE
- P-U-ABORT
- P-P-ABORT
- P-DATA

LPP does not run with other application service elements such as the reliable transfer service element (RTSE). The presentation services primitives listed in the previous paragraph are chosen because they are used by CMIP for its operations.

Figure 9.19 shows the architecture for the LPP. It is organized around three modules. The *dispatch module* supports the presentation layer interface to the upper layer, which is called the *PS-User*. This

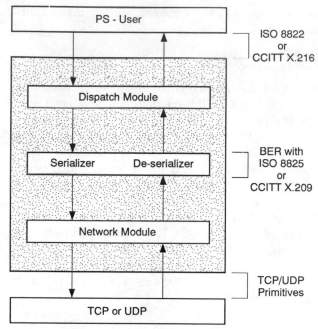

Figure 9.19   The LPP modules.

user is ACSE or ROSE. The interface is defined with either ISO 8822 or CCITT X.216.

The serialization module consists of a *serializer* and a *deserializer*. The serializer accepts an ASN.1 object and produces a binary stream based on the Basic Encoding Rules (BER) of ISO 8825 or its counterpart CCITT X.209. The deserializer performs an inverse operation.

The *network* module provides the interface to the lower-layer protocol; therefore, it manages a TCP or UDP port connection.

These modules are rather fixed in their capabilities. Therefore, unlike the upper-layer OSI entities, the LPP does not support any negotiation of services. This approach keeps the software simple.

Parameters used between LPP and upper layer.   LPP defines a subset of presentation layer parameters in its operations. Presently, it supports five sets of parameters:

- Presentation address
- Presentation context list
- User data
- QOS
- Session service version

ISO 7498-3 describes the structure for a *presentation address*. LPP uses four fields to define this address: (1) network address(es), (2) transport selector, (3) session selector, and (4) presentation selector. The three selector values are ignored by LPP. The network address(es) consists of a 32-bit IP address, a 16-bit port number, and a value indicating the transport service available below LPP (presently, either TCP or UDP).

The *presentation context list* is limited with LPP, which allows two presentation contexts only: (1) a presentation context for the association control (ACSE), and (2) a presentation context for the ASE using LPP (which is ROSE).

User data is passed to LPP from the upper layers as ASN.1 objects. Each object also has a presentation context identifier. LPP permits only two context identifiers to be used: the ACSE presentation context or the ROSE presentation context.

The QOS parameter is also limited by LPP. OSI QOS functions such as throughput, reliability, residual error rate, etc., cannot be used. Indeed, only two values are permitted in this parameter: TCP- and UDP-based services.

The *session service version* must have the value of 2 to be used with LPP.

Figure 9.20 shows an example of a portion of LPP's ASN.1 definition. This is the highest-level coding. The attributes in the CHOICE type define further the information passed between LPP and the upper-layer protocols.

The LPP defines the actions necessary for the presentation layer

```
RFC1085-PS DEFINITIONS :: =
BEGIN
PDUs :: =
CHOICE {
        connectRequest
          ConnectRequest-PDU,
        connectResponse
          ConnectResponse-PDU,
        releaseRequest
          ReleaseRequest-PDU,
        abort
          Abort-PDU,
        userData
          UserData-PDU,
        cL-user-Data
          CL-UserData-PDU }
```

Figure 9.20   LPP ASN.1 for the PDUs.

primitives to be used to give the ACSE and ROSE the view of a "real" presentation operation. The reader may choose to examine LPP to get a more detailed understanding of these operations. The author recommends that the reader review Section 10 of RFC 1085 if more detailed information is needed. In addition, Appendix A of RFC 1085 contains the abstract syntax definitions for the protocol.

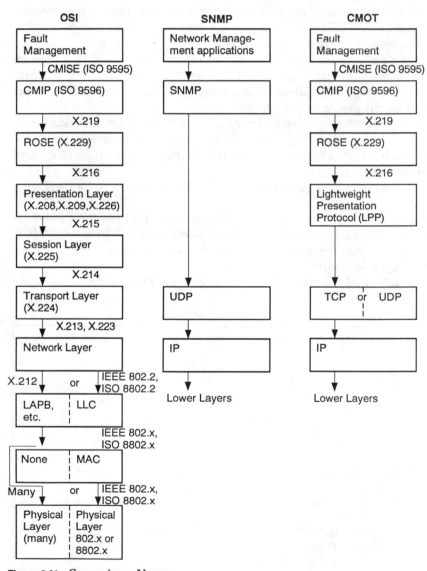

Figure 9.21 Comparison of layers.

Comparison of SNMP, CMOT, and OSI

Figure 9.21 compares the SNMP, CMOT, and OSI protocol stacks. It is quite obvious from a cursory examination of this figure that the OSI stack entails a considerable number of modules for its operations. In contrast, SNMP is a relatively lean stack, which provides the principal advantage of fast execution and the consumption of a relatively small amount of memory. Again, CMOT is shown in this figure to provide a full explanation of the network management protocols.

Because SNMP does not understand inheritance (see Chap. 1), it uses the get-next command to retrieve multiple instances of the same object. In contrast, CMIP allows one message to obtain all instances of an object.

Additionally, the CMIP CREATE and DELETE services allow an agent to dynamically create and delete objects in a network. In contrast, SNMP views network objects more as static entities.

Summary

The SNMP is the most widely used network management standard in the industry. It uses the TCP/IP interfaces, with support provided by UDP at the transport layer. It is designed to operate with the Internet protocols. The CMOT accommodates itself to the OSI lower layers and to the OSI applications service elements in the application layer of ACSE and ROSE. SNMP and CMOT employ ASN.1 and a modified ASN.1 to define the managed elements (OSI managed objects) in an internet.

Network Management Standards for LAN/MAN Protocols

Introduction

Previous discussions in this book have focused on the use of Common Management Information Service Element/Common Management Information Protocol (CMISE/CMIP) over the full seven layers of OSI network management. This approach can present significant problems for communications entities (workstations, gateways, etc.) that do not have the memory or Central Processing Unit (CPU) capacity to support these seven layers. CMISE/CMIP does not consume a lot of memory or CPU cycles, but a seven-layer OSI suite usually requires between 200 and 400 bytes of random access memory (minimum subset of OSI). This resource requirement precludes it being used on many devices—for example, DOS-based personal computers.

The approach taken by the IEEE in their local area network/ metropolitan area network (LAN/MAN) management standards (published as IEEE 802.1B/-15 dated March 8, 1990) is to implement a network management protocol at the lower two layers of the OSI Model. This approach is in conformance with the IEEE architecture in that it is a two-layer standard. The approach does not preclude implementing the full seven layers with CMIP for host computers that are managing a LAN.

This chapter discusses the approach taken by the IEEE which is generally referred to as CMIP over logical link control (LLC), or CMOL. Please be aware that the IEEE standard is not yet complete, and is still undergoing changes.

Before moving into the details of the protocol, the reader might wish to review Table 10.1, and Fig. 10.1, which contain common abbreviations used in this chapter and in the IEEE LAN management specifi-

TABLE 10.1   Common Abbreviations in IEEE LAN/MAN Management

LME	Layer management entity
LMI	Layer management interface
(N)-LMI	Layer management interface at layer N
NM	Network management
NMDS	Network management data service
NMDSI	Network management data service interface
NMI	Network management interface
NMP	Network management process
NMPE	Network management protocol entity
NM_LME	Network management layer management entity
NM_PDU	Network management protocol data unit (PDU)
PE	Protocol entity
RQ	Request
RSP	Response

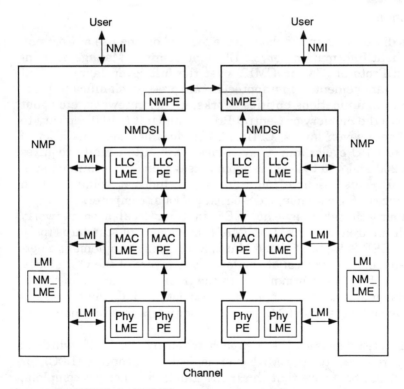

Figure 10.1   IEEE's LAN/MAN management protocols.

cations. The reader will probably refer to this table often during this discussion since the abbreviations are used extensively throughout this chapter.

Management Operations

The actual management operations of the IEEE LAN/MAN protocols are rather simple. These operations describe the accessing and manipulation of objects within an LME and are described with five operations. These operations are actually offered as a network management service at the NMI. The objects are not defined within the IEEE 802.1B specification; they are defined in the management section of the specific 802 standard. The layer object management operations are as follows:

- *Get operation:* The get operation is used to obtain a value of an identified object.

- *Set operation:* This operation is used to set a value on an object.

- *Compare and set operation:* This operation is used to perform a set of tests and, if the tests are successful, the object will be set to a particular value.

- *Action operation:* This operation is used to perform a sequence of operations on an object and/or to require the object to transit to an identified state. This operation requires that information be returned regarding the success or failure of the operation.

- *Event operation:* This operation is not initiated from a service user; rather it is an event that is locally initiated by the LME (something like an unsolicited message—an interrupt).

Two other operations are also defined. However, they do not require any actions at the NMI between the NMP and the end user. They are as follows:

- *Trace operation:* This operation is used to verify the existence and proper operation of NMP remote stations. This operation actually uses trace PDUs to obtain the service. Upon receiving the trace PDU, the remote NMP forwards a response. Both the reply and the response contain several fields of information that allow the NMPs to identify themselves and report status about their operations. The trace allows two or more stations to be involved in the operation. Therefore, it can cascade through a network to report on its topology.

- *Load operations:* This operation allows a transfer of a block of information, usually machine code, from a remote server to a LAN/

MAN station. The load operation is actually a rather involved protocol called the *system load protocol*. It is not described in the IEEE 802.1B standard. It is in the 802.1E/D6 standard. The idea behind this protocol is that stations may need to transfer a portion of their local addressable memory space to other stations.

The IEEE LAN/MAN Management Architecture

Figure 10.1 shows the architecture for IEEE's LAN/MAN management protocols. These many terms can be summarized by stating that the architecture is divided into two major parts: (1) the NMP and (2) LMEs.

Network management process

The NMP provides the user access to the network management operations. It receives the user information and performs actions internal to the workstation or communicates with other NMPs in other devices on the network. In conformance with OSI network management rules, the NMP can perform the role of a manager or an agent. As we learned earlier in this book, a manager acts on behalf of a network management user to request operations that are in turn carried out by the agent, which may be the remote NMP. From the view of the network management user, the agent is local (although it could be remote). We also learned that an agent, while servicing requests from a manager, maintains authority on how and if the operations are actually executed.

The NMI serves as the boundary between the NMP and the network management user. As the reader might expect, the NMI is effected through service definitions (primitives).

The NMP also contains two components that operate internally with an NMP. They are shown in Fig. 10.1 as the NMPE and the NMLME. The NMPE acts as the communications entity for peer-to-peer management communications through the exchange of PDUs between peer-to-peer NMPs. Its function is similar to that of a PE, which is described within each of the layers of the LAN station.

As illustrated in the figure, NMPE is allowed to access the underlying services of the LAN station by communicating to LLC through the NMDSI. This interface is provided through service definitions (primitives). These primitives are used to map directly to the LLC Type 1 unacknowledged, connectionless unnumbered information (UI) frames.

The NMLME is simply an instance of an LME. It is used to provide management operations relative to the local NMP. It also provides a few other functions (discussed later) such as event routing and access control operations for the management of the entire LAN/MAN station.

The layer management entity

The LME exists within each layer in the LAN/MAN station. It is used to provide layer-specific network management functions for the specific layer in which they reside. From the context of the IEEE standards, they are used to provide for local management of the layer. Their principal purpose is to provide status information about the operations of the layer and to permit the exercising of control over the operations in the layer. They are also used to provide information about the existence of certain operations within each layer. They communicate with NMP at the LMI. Again, this interface is defined through service definitions (primitives).

The protocol entity

Figure 10.1 also shows the existence of a protocol entity (PE) in each layer. As the reader should know by now, the PEs are used to provide for the specific functions of each layer, such as layer activation, layer coordination, error control functions, etc. These specifications are published in the IEEE standards through the LLC, medium access control (MAC), and physical sublayer descriptions such as 802.3 for Carrier Sense Multiple Access Collision Detect (CSMA/CD) and 802.5 for token ring, etc., and are not described in the IEEE 802.1 management standards.

Relationship of the protocols, interfaces, and entities

The operations in Fig. 10.1 consist of local and remote operations. With local operations, the NMP receives requests from the network management user at the NMI boundary and decides which local LME should service the request. In effect, NME performs routing operations by selecting the LMI. For remote operations in a peer NMP, the NMP invokes NMPE, which transfers a PDU at the NMDSI interface to the actual LAN station layers (LLC, then MAC, then the physical layer). At the receiving end, the PDU is passed up through the physical layer, the MAC, and LLC layers to the NMPE. It then passes the traffic to NMP, which makes a decision of how to route the request (if necessary) to the respective LMI to obtain the needed information.

Operations between PEs and LMEs

It should be emphasized that the IEEE 802.1 standards do not define the management operations between the PE and the LME. Several of the IEEE standards define a number of operations that exist between these entities. The effect of the operations between these two entities may be revealed at the LMI depending on the nature of the request issued by the end user and how it is handled by NMP.

Interfaces and Service Definitions

Three service definition interfaces are described in the IEEE standard. They describe the interfaces at (1) the NMI, (2) the LMI, and (3) the NMDSI. These service definitions are listed in Table 10.2. The next section provides a review of their functions.

Operations and Parameters Associated with the Service Definitions

This section examines the operations and associated parameters at each of the three interfaces. Remember that the network management services are invoked at the NMI, LMI, and NMDSI interfaces.

At the NMI interface

In general, the operations invoked by the primitives with NMI (again, see Fig. 10.1) entail the following actions. The only exception to these

TABLE 10.2   LAN Management Service Definitions

NMI
NM_SET_VALUE.invoke
NM_SET_VALUE.reply
NM_COMPARE_AND_SET_VALUE.invoke
NM_COMPARE_AND_SET_VALUE.reply
NM_GET_VALUE.invoke
NM_GET_VALUE.reply
NM_ACTION.invoke
NM_ACTION.reply
NM—EVENT.notify
NM_TRACE.invoke
NM_TRACE.reply

LMI
LM_SET_VALUE.invoke
LM_SET_VALUE.reply
LM_COMPARE_AND_SET_VALUE.invoke
LM_COMPARE_AND_SET_VALUE.reply
LM_GET_VALUE.invoke
LM_GET_VALUE.reply
LM_ACTION.invoke
LM_ACTION.reply
LM_EVENT-notify

NMDSI
NMDS_DATA.request
NMDS_DATA.indication

NMI operations is with the three primitives NM__EVENT.notify, NM__TRACE.invoke, and NM__TRACE.reply. These operations will be discussed after the discussion of the general operations.

The NMP, upon receiving an invoke primitive, will perform various editing operations to make certain the primitive call is correct. It then examines the destination address, and if it is local, it invokes the services of the appropriate LME through the use of the LMI service definition primitives. The appropriate LMI operation is identified by a resource identifier parameter in the parameter.

However, if the destination address is remote, the NMP must send traffic to another LAN station. Consequently, NMP is responsible for creating an appropriate PDU, discussed later in this chapter, and delivering this NM__PDU to the station via the NMPE. As we shall see later, the NMPE passes this PDU to the LLC PE through its primitive definitions at the NMDSI interface.

Conversely, the NMP sends reply primitives to the user by either receiving primitives from one of the local LMEs through the LMI interface or through the arrival of a PDU from LLC to NMPE through the NMDSI interface.

As mentioned earlier, three of the service definition primitives are handled differently from the previous general discussion. The NM__EVENT.notify is an unsolicited operation. It is given to the end user by NMP following the arrival of an event PDU from a remote station through the NMDSI interface to the NMPE. Alternately, this primitive could be given to the end user because a local event occurred and the NMP was so notified by an LME through an LMI primitive.

The last set of primitives deal with the trace operations. Upon receipt of an NM__TRACE.invoke, the NMP will form a trace PDU and transfer this to a remote station via the NMPE. In turn, an NM__TRACE.reply is sent to the end user upon receiving a trace response PDU from a remote station.

With this information in mind, we now examine the primitives and their parameters and associated operations in more detail.

Parameters in the primitives. Several parameters are associated with the NMI primitives. To simplify this analysis, the parameters are explained one time in the material that follows. Be aware that not all the parameters are used in all the primitives, and the standards should be studied if more detail is needed.

The *access__control__information* parameter provides access control information which can be used to grant or deny access to management information contained within network management entities or to grant or deny operations to be performed by the LMEs.

The *actual_quality_of_service (QOS)* parameter specifies the QOS which pertains to the information associated with the primitive. That is, it indicates the QOS that was actually provided as a result of an operation request. It is only relevant if the source_address is remote. This field is provided based on the quality_of_service parameter supplied in an invoke primitive.

The *destination_address* parameter is used to identify the NMP that is local to the value in the resource_identifier (discussed shortly).

The *exchange_identifiers* parameters are optional parameters that may be used in the invoke and reply primitives. They are used to match requests to responses and consist of a source identifier, which is used to identify the originating NM_user, and a transaction identifier, which is used to uniquely identify this individual transaction.

The *operation_status* is used to indicate the success or failure of an operation. The parameter is coded and used for one of the six actions as appropriate for the operation. Table 10.3 lists the status codes and the operations in which they are or are not used. The meanings of the codes are included in the table.

The *parameter_list* parameter is used in an invoke primitive to identify the elements that are to be associated with the requested operation. The parameter_list is also present in a reply primitive to indicate the operations performed. In addition, this parameter contains information relating to the success or the reason for the failure of an operation in relation to one parameter. Table 10.4 lists the codes for this operation and their relationship to the specific actions.

The *action_list* parameter is used to identify action operations on each object; it is present in the NM_ACTION.invoke primitive.

The *action_result_list* parameter is returned by an action reply primitive indicating which of the action operations were actually performed.

The *event_identifier* parameter is used with the event notify primitive to identify the type of event being reported.

The *event_value* parameter is also used in the event notify primitive to contain information about the state of the resource being reported.

The *report_address* parameter is used in a trace invoke primitive to provide information relating to what is known as the report address. This address is an indicator that identifies where a status re-

TABLE 10.3   Operation Status Codes

Codes	Get	Set	C&S	Action	Event	Trace
success: Operation performed correctly	X	X	X	X	X	X
badAccessRights: Access control value not acceptable	X	X	X	X		X
refuseToComply: Agent refuses for vendor-specific reasons	X	X	X	X		X
reqPDUtooLong: Request PDU too long to process by agent	X	X	X	X	X	X
rspPDUtooLong: Response PDU too long to process by agent	X	X	X	X	X	X
badResourceID: ID not known or supported	X	X	X	X	X	
badLayer: Specified layer not supported	X	X	X	X	X	
badSublayer: Specified sublayer not supported	X	X	X	X	X	
badResourceInstance: Specified instance not supported	X	X	X	X	X	
badResourceTypeID: Resource type ID not valid	X	X	X	X	X	
badSkipCount: Skip count not valid						X
badOperatorList: Encountered bad operation type field						X
badLayerEventInfo: Layer event information invalid					X	
negativeEventAcknowledge: Event PDU not accepted					X	

port pertaining to a trace operation can be sent (as stated earlier, more information follows on these actual primitives).

The *resource_identifier* parameter is used to identify the entity that is to examine resource-specific information that is contained in the primitive parameters. It would act on access control information, parameter_list, action ID, etc. It acts on the behalf of the destination address of the NMP.

The *resource_required_flag* parameter indicates if a receiving NMP is required to respond to an operation request.

The *source_address* parameter is used to identify the originator of the operation.

The *trace_operator_list* parameter is used in the trace invoke

TABLE 10.4 NM Parameter Status Codes

Codes	Get	Set	C&S	Action	Event	Trace
success: Operation performed correctly	X	X	X	X	X	X
badAccessRights: Access control value not acceptable	X	X	X	X		X
refuseToComply: Agent refuses for vendor-specific reasons	X	X	X	X		X
notSupported: Requested operation not supported	X	X	X	X	X	X
badParameterID: ID not known or supported	X	X	X			
badParameterOperation: Cannot operate on the parameter	X	X	X			
badParameterValue: Does not fit within a range	X	X	X			
badExpectedValueID: Invalid ID			X			
expectedValueMismatch: Some comparison operations do not make sense			X			
badExpectedValue: Does not fit within a range			X			
errorInPerformingAction: Action not completed				X		
badActionID: Indicated action not supported				X		
notAvailable: Various things not available	X	X	X	X	X	X

primitive to provide information about the *operator list*. The operator list contains MAC addresses of the stations that are to participate in the trace, as well as a description of the operation to be performed.

The *trace_report* parameter provides information in a trace reply. Its contents depend upon the parameters in the operator list that is contained in the trace invoke.

At the LMI interface

As shown in Fig. 10.1 and listed in Table 10.2, the LMI operations are restricted to the LME and the NMP. As such, trace operations are not performed since the purpose of the trace is to obtain information from remote stations. Consequently, the LMI to NMP operations are of a local nature only. As explained earlier in this chapter, many of the NMI operations previously discussed find their way to corresponding LMI operations.

The functions of the major operations, such as get, set, compare, action, compare, and set, reflect the overall management operations of this standard, discussed in the first part of this chapter. Therefore, they are not repeated in this section. However, it should prove useful to examine the specific parameters associated with the primitives. Again be aware that not all parameters are associated with all primitives.

Parameters in the primitives. The *parameter_identifier* is used to identify each existing parameter associated with a primitive. This parameter is used to determine which managed object has an action performed on it such as a get or a set. Although not stated in the standard, typically it would be associated with the parameter_list in the NMI primitives.

The *access_classes* parameter is used to perform the access control operations. Although not described in the standard, it is associated with the access_control_information parameter in the NMI primitives.

The *status* parameter indicates the success or failure of this operation. It is associated with the *operation_status* parameter in the NMI primitive.

The *parameter_value* is used to specify the current value of the identifier of the requested layer parameter. Of course, this value only has meaning if the operation was successful.

The *test_parameter_Identifier* and the *test_parameter_value* are used during testing operations at the LMI interface.

At the NMDSI interface

As shown in Fig. 10.1 and listed in Table 10.2, there are only two service definitions at the NMDSI interface, request and indication definitions. These primitives are generated when the NMPE is directed by the NMP to send a PDU or if the NMPE receives a PDU from another station.

Parameters in the primitives. The parameters for this interface are quite simple, which reflects the desire of the IEEE to keep the interface at the LLC upper-layer protocol simple. Only four parameters are associated with either primitive.

The *source address* specifies the data link address of the originating NM PDU. The *destination address* specifies the data link address of where the NM PDU is destined to go. The *priority field* indicates the priority associated with the QOS element of an associated NMI primitive. The *NM PDU* is simply the management information that is to be delivered to the destination address.

The Management Protocol

As with all IEEE and OSI layered protocols, the IEEE LAN network management standard includes a protocol that operates in conjunction with the service definitions. The purpose of the protocol is to allow the NMP to transfer PDUs to another NMP on behalf of an NM_user. The protocol defines the procedures for the managers (the NMPs that request an operation) and the agents (those NMPs that act upon the request or that generate an event).

This protocol is organized around the concept of *management exchanges* between managers and managers and/or managers and agents. There are five procedures defined for each management exchange, and they are as follows: (1) the *load* procedure is used to transfer information (program code usually) to another machine in the network, (2) the *request/response* procedure is used by managers and agents to inform each other about the operations, (3) the *private* procedure is not defined in the standard, (4) the *event* procedure is used by an agent to send unsolicited information to a manager, and (5) the *trace* procedure is used by a manager to direct an agent to test resources in the network.

To support these procedures, PDUs are exchanged between managers and agents. The PDUs are broadly classified as follows:

- *PrivatePDU:* This PDU is not defined in the standard and is implementation-specific. The reason a private PDU is included in the standard is to avoid the use of private tags.

- *LoadPDU:* This PDU is included within the System Load Protocol (IEEE 802.1EEE), which is explained shortly.

- *RequestPDU:* This PDU is sent from a manager to an agent to request something be done.

- *ResponsePDU:* This PDU is sent to the manager from the agent in response to the RequestPDU.

- *EventPDU:* This is an unsolicited PDU sent from the agent to inform the manager about something that happened.

- *EventACKPDU:* This PDU acknowledges the EventPDU.

- *TraceRQPDU:* This PDU is sent by a manager to an agent, which may send it to another agent. Its purpose is to allow diagnostic and troubleshooting operations to take place.

- *TraceRSPPDU:* This PDU acknowledges the TraceRQPDU.

TABLE 10.5 Operation-Level PDUs

RequestPDUs:	PrivateRQ, GetRQ, SetRQ, CompareAndSetRQ, ActionRQ
ResponsePDUs:	PrivateRSP, GetRSP, SetRSP, CompareAndSetRSP, ActionRSP
EventPDUs:	EventInfo
EventAckPDUs:	EventAckInfo
TraceRQPDUs	TraceRQ
TraceRSPPDUs	TraceRSP

Operation-level PDUs

Within an NM-PDU, the coding of an operation is known as an operation-level PDU. The net effect of this somewhat abstract concept is that the standard simply defines more specific PDUs. The relationship of the operation-level PDUs to the more general PDUs is shown in Table 10.5.

Examples of PDUs

This section provides several examples of the IEEE LAN network management standards PDUs. A brief explanation of these PDUs and their parameters follows.

The *get request PDU,* logically enough, is used to obtain information from an agent about managed resources. As shown in Fig. 10.2, the PDU consists of a *ResourceID,* which is used to identify the resource (entity, layer, etc.) that actually contains the objects being reported. For an event operation, it is used to identify the resource in which the event was generated. The *Exchange ID* field is used to correlate a response with a request. Typically it is a value (a number) that is the same for both the response and the request. The *AccessControl* field has been discussed previously in this chapter. To iterate briefly, it is used to determine what type of access control mechanisms, if any, are to be applied. For this PDU, it consists of a password and a value indicating what type of access is requested (read, write, etc.). The

```
--The Get Request PDU
GetRQ
      ResourceID
      ExchangeID                    (optional)
      AccessControl                 (optional)
      GetRQParamenterList
            DefinedParameterID      #1
            . . . . . .
            DefinedParameterID      #N
```

Figure 10.2   The get request.

```
--The Get Response PDU (no errors)
GetRSP
     ResourceID
     ExchangeID                              (optional)
     RSPParameterList
          ParameterStatus        #M         (success)
          DefinedParameterID                #M
          DefinedParameterVal               #M
```

Figure 10.3 The get response, with no errors.

GetRQParameterList contains unique identifiers of the parameters identifying information about managed objects which are being requested with the request.

The fields for the *get response* are quite similar to the fields in the get request PDU. The only difference, as noted in Fig. 10.3, is the *RSPParameterList,* which contains the parameters which were acted upon as a result of the get request. The *ParameterStatus* field within the RSPParameterList indicates if the operation on a particular parameter was completed without problems. If a problem occurs, the field contains a code indicating what type of error was encountered. For each parameter in the get request PDU, the corresponding parameter ID and the appropriate value is returned in the get response PDU. These are coded in the PDU as *DefinedParameterID* and *DefinedParameterVal.*

Summary

The IEEE LAN/MAN network management standards are based on the IEEE 802 architecture as well as the OSI Model. They are designed to operate with or without CMIP, although they are well positioned to use the common management information service element (CMISE) interface. While not stated in these standards, the Internet Simple Network Management Protocol (SNMP) can operate over them, as well as vendor-specific solutions. Indeed, they can be considered as a platform from which any network management application can be applied.

11

Directories and Network Management

Introduction

Directories have been in use in computer installations for over a decade. Organizations are now using them for network management operations. Some forward-thinking companies are now using directories to define the relationships of managed objects to each other, to manage agents, or to manage processes. The directory is used to check all key automated systems for accuracy and duplication, and it permits an organization to assess the impact of system changes to all the automated resources (managed objects). The directory has become a vital component in an organization's management of its automated resources. Since this book's focus is on network management standards, this chapter provides an overview of directories as they pertain to network management.

The OSI Directory

Several CCITT Recommendations and ISO Standards describe the operations of the Directory. It is designed to support and facilitate the communication of information between systems about *objects,* such as data, applications, hardware, people, files, distribution lists, and practically anything else that the organization deems worthy of "tracking" for management purposes. The Directory is intended to allow the communication of this information between different systems, which can include OSI applications, OSI layer entities, OSI management entities, and communications networks. *Nothing precludes the use of the OSI Directory with the Internet and IEEE standards as well.*

TABLE 11.1 Specifications for Directories

CCITT	ISO	Name of specification
X.500	9594-1	The Directory—Overview of Concepts, Models, and Services
X.501	9594/2	The Directory Models
X.509	9594/8	The Directory—Authentication Framework
X.511	9594/3	The Directory—Abstract Service Definition
X.518	9594/4	The Directory—Procedures of Distributed Operation
X.519	9594/5	The Directory—Protocol Specifications
X.520	9594/6	The Directory—Selected Attribute Types
X.521	9594/7	The Directory—Selected Object Classes

The Directory standards actually encompasses eight documents. Table 11.1 shows the designators for the CCITT and ISO Directory.

Directory Services to Help Manage the Network

As just discussed, the Directory places no requirement on the nature of the information stored in itself, and organizations most likely will use it to provide a wide variety of services. Table 11.2 contains a list of

TABLE 11.2 X.500 Directory Support Services (Likely Applications, Not All-Inclusive)

Service	Description
Configuration data	Description of network components and their status; information on active, passive, and best paths in the internet
Attributes	Characteristics of network resources
Names and aliases	Storage of user-friendly names as well as the mapping to network specific names with the ability to cross reference other names in other networks
DNs and RDNs	Storage of DNs and relative distinguished names (RDNs) for the OSI network management functions
ASN.1 code	ASN.1 coding for PDUs and macros
Alarm storage	Rules for network alarm measurement and severity analysis, and alarm clearing
Fault data	Storage of data on faults, and error logs
Accounting data	Information on usage, charges of network components
Security features	Rules for authentication, keys for encipherment, security logs
Performance	Rules for performance analysis, as well as statistics on network behavior
Application contexts	Description of the contents of each application context for network management
Syntaxes	Relationships of abstract syntaxes and transfer syntaxes for use by agents and managing processes

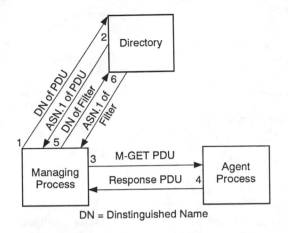

Figure 11.1 OSI network management and the Directory.

likely applications for the Directory. This list includes some management services described in the network management standards. Figure 11.1 shows a typical network management operation in which the managing process and the agent process exchange network management data units. This exchange is based on the managing process using the Directory to obtain the proper Abstract Syntax Notation 1 (ASN.1) definitions for the construction of the M-GET protocol data unit (PDU) and a filter operation.

This operation shows that the managing process obtains the ASN.1 definitions for the PDU by furnishing the Directory a distinguished name (DN) and a filter (from previous chapters, remember that a DN is an unambiguous identifier). The DN for the PDU definition is used to "construct" the M-GET PDU. It is sent to the agent process, which returns a response. Next, the filter is applied to the management information to determine if any further action is appropriate.

From the standpoint of efficiency and response time, an actual implementation would probably have some of the Directory information in cache. Moreover, events 1, 2, 5, and 6 in Fig. 11.1 would probably be established in a readily executable "cataloged procedure." Notwithstanding, the Directory still plays an important role in this operation.

Key terms and concepts

The information held in the Directory is known as the *Directory Information Base (DIB),* which is analogous to the OSI network management information base (MIB). The DIB contains information about objects and is composed of entries. Each *entry* consists of a collection of information on one object only. Each entry in made up of *attributes,* and each attribute has a *type* and one or more *values.*

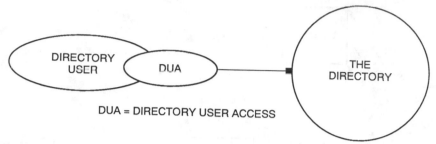

Figure 11.2   Functional view of the Directory.

The DIB is accessed by the Directory user through the *Directory User Agent* (DUA), which is considered to be an applications process. The DUA is so-named because it acts as an agent to the end-user vis-à-vis the DIB (see Fig. 11.2). Like the agent in OSI network management (which represents the user to network management), the DIB represents the user to the Directory.

Directory names.   A fundamental concept of the Directory is user-friendly naming. A name is stored in the Directory; the Directory then provides the services of verifying the name(s) by using its user name to retrieve addresses. These addresses can be any type of address, such as an ISDN address, an X.25 address, an X.121 address, etc.

Perhaps a good analogy to the use of the Directory can be made with the telephone system's white and yellow pages. For example, when using the white pages, a user-friendly name such as John Brown can be accessed through the white pages to obtain a telephone number and perhaps an address. This same idea holds true for the X.500 Directory services. Taking the analogy a bit further to the yellow pages, the user can browse on trade names or functional names, and the yellow page "directory" will yield the telephone number, address and, of course, the user-friendly name.

The ASN.1 OBJECT IDENTIFIER and the ISO/CCITT naming conventions are used as user-friendly names by OSI network management.

An approach to the use of names in the Directory is shown in Fig. 11.3. This figure illustrates that the Directory can be accessed at either the application layer or the network layer. At the application layer, the application process provides a name to the Directory, most likely an application title or another OBJECT IDENTIFIER registered in the ISO/CCITT network management naming hierarchy. In turn, the Directory uses the application title name to retrieve a presentation service access point (PSAP) address. At the network layer, a network service access point (NSAP) address is provided to the Directory by the network service

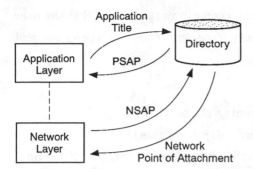

Figure 11.3 Mapping of names.

provider, which is then used by the Directory to retrieve a network point of attachment. In both cases, user-friendly names (well, somewhat user-friendly) are furnished to the Directory.

The Directory standards use the term *schema* in a different context than other directory and database systems. A schema is a rule to ensure that the DIB maintains its logical structure during modifications. It prevents inconsistencies in the DIB such as incorrect subordinate entries' class, attribute values, etc. It is the responsibility of the Directory to ensure that any changes to the DIB are in conformance with the Directory schema. Furthermore, controls are present to prevent a user from exceeding thresholds such as the scope of a search, the time spent on a search, the size of the results, etc.

Directory Services

The Directory standards define the operations listed in this section.

Service quality

- *Controls:* Establishes the rules for access and modification to the Directory
- *Security:* Defines the authentication, password, and other security procedures for Directory use
- *Filters:* Rules for defining one or more conditions that must be satisfied by the entry if it is to be returned in the result to the user

Interrogation

- *Read:* Obtains the values of some or all the attributes of an entry
- *Compare:* Checks a value against an attribute of a specific entry in the DIB
- *List:* Obtains and returns a list of subordinates of a specific entry in the DIB

- *Search:*   Using a filter, returns a certain part of the DIB to the user
- *Abandon:*   Causes the Directory to cease processing a prior request from a DIB user

Modification

- *Add entry:*   Adds a new leaf entry to the DIB
- *Remove entry:*   Removes a leaf entry from the DIB
- *Modify entry:*   Changes a specific entry, including the addition and/or deletion for replacement of attribute types and attribute values
- *Modify relative distinguished name:*   Changes a distinguished name of a leaf entry in the DIB

Other

- *Errors:*   Rules that describe how and why errors are reported
- *Referrals:*   Procedures for referencing other resources

Error-Reporting Services

The Directory defines a number of error-reporting procedures. It is quite important that they be implemented as part of the ongoing operations because they provide important diagnostic and troubleshooting services.

The Directory ceases to perform operations once an error has occurred and has been detected. It is possible that more than one error may be detected. In this case, the error is reported in accordance with a logical precedence list.

The higher entry in the following list means the error reporting has precedence over the next lower entry:

- NameError
- UpdateError
- AttributeError
- SecurityError
- ServiceError

The next list of errors do not use any reporting precedences:

- AbandonFailed
- Abandoned
- Referral

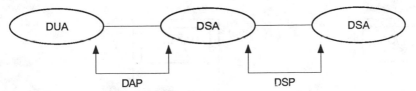

Figure 11.4 Distributed operations.

Operating a Distributed Directory

The Directory can be distributed across a wide geographical or organizational area. To support this environment, the Directory System Agent (DSA) provides access to the DIB from the DUAs or other DSAs. Figure 11.4 shows the relationship of the distributed Directory. A DUA is permitted to interact with single or multiple DSAs. In turn, the DSAs may internetwork with other DSAs through referrals to satisfy a request. The DSA is considered to be an OSI application process.

The DUAs and DSAs communications are governed by two protocols:

- *Directory Access Protocol (DAP):*   Specifies actions between the DUA and DSA in order for the DUA to have access to the Directory
- *Directory System Protocol (DSP):*   Specifies actions between DSAs

The Directory is administered by the *Directory Management Domain* (DMD), which consists of a set of one or more DSAs and zero or more DUAs. The DMD may be a country, a PTT, a network, or anything designated to manage the DIB.

The Relationship of the Directory to OSI

As discussed earlier, the Directory can be used at two layers of the OSI Model. At the application layer, it supports the mapping of application titles into PSAP addresses. At the network layer, it supports the mapping of NSAP addresses into subnetwork points of attachment (SNPA).

The Directory stipulates several directory-specific application service elements (ASEs) to support the DAP and DSP operations. These ASEs are involved in reading, comparing, searching, and other Directory operations. In addition, DSP and DAP make use of the remote operations service element (ROSE), the association control service element (ACSE) and the OSI lower layers. The relationships are shown in Fig. 11.5.

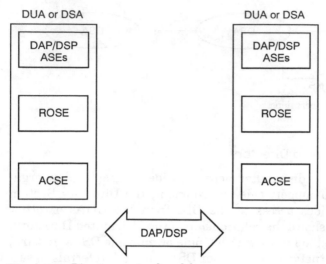

Figure 11.5 Directory protocol model.

Use of ROSE

The Directory ASEs are the sole users of the following ROSE services: RO-INVOKE, RO-RESULT, RO-ERROR, RO-REJECT-U and RO-REJECT-P. The operations of the DAP and DSP are class 2 operations [a ROSE category 2 is asynchronous and reports success (result) or failure (error)]. A DUA may choose to operate in class 1 [synchronous and report success (result) or failure (error)].

Use of ACSE

The Directory uses the ACSE A-ASSOCIATE and A-RELEASE services of the ACSE in normal mode. The application process uses the ACSE A-ABORT and A-P-ABORT services.

Use of the presentation layer

The Directory relies on ROSE and ACSE to obtain the services of the presentation layer. ROSE is the sole user of the P-DATA service. ACSE is the sole user of the P-CONNECT, P-RELEASE, P-U-ABORT, and P-P-ABORT services.

Use of other layers

The presentation layer uses the kernel and duplex functional units of the session layer. The use of the transport layer classes is optional, with one exception: CCITT stipulates that transport class 0 must be used. The use of X.213 for obtaining the network service is assumed. It is also assumed that a network address is used as stipulated in X.121, E.163-E.164, or X.200 (for the OSI NSAP address).

Summary

The Directory standards are published by both the CCITT and the ISO. It is a model to describe a repository of information for anything needed by an organization. Consequently, the OSI, Internet, or IEEE network management standards can use the Directory. However, since the Directory relies on the OSI upper layers for some services, its use in an internet environment requires the creation of some light-weight presentation and session layers as well as some ROSE and ACSE modules to support the Directory.

12

OSI Network Management Standards Implementations

Introduction

This chapter is a survey of some of the more prominent network management models published by network vendors. As such, the survey is not all-inclusive. Also, be aware that the network management products' market is not included in this chapter because of the volatility of the marketplace.

The OSI/Network Management Forum

The OSI Network Management Forum (OSI/NMF) is a consortium of companies whose goal is to foster OSI standards. The forum was organized in July 1988, with the intent of accelerating the use of international computer communications standards. The OSI/NMF develops its standards based on the OSI reference model.

The membership of the OSI/NMF consists of many of the major and large telecommunications companies in North America, Japan, and Europe. Organizations such as British Telecom, AT&T, MCI, Nippon Telegraph and Telephone, Northern Telecom, DEC, and Telecom Canada are examples of the voting membership.

The OSI/NMF has published a series of documents describing the implementation of the OSI network management standards. These documents are available from OSI/NMF at 40 Morristown Road, Bernardsville, NJ 07824, 201-766-1544, FAX 201-766-5741.

The Forum has published a seven-layer protocol suite, as well as numerous documents that define managed objects, protocols, functions, ASN.1 notations, rules for filtering and scoping, etc. Figure 12.1

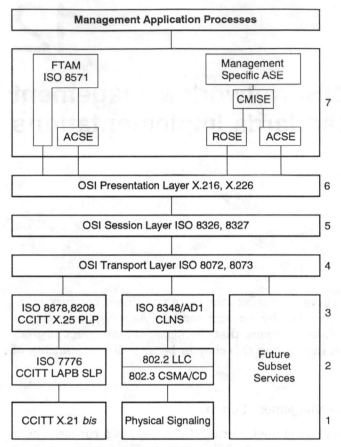

Figure 12.1 The OSI/NMF protocol stack.

shows the Forum suite. It is quite similar to other profiles that use the OSI layers.

OSI/NMF architecture

Figure 12.2 illustrates the general architecture of the OSI/NMF operations. The managed elements are actual network resources. They could be physical devices [such as private branch exchanges (PBXs), line cards, etc.] or logical entities (such as X.25 virtual circuits, transport layer socket connections, etc.). Managed elements may be either network or system resources.

The management solution is the complete set of management procedures and facilities used by an organization that implements the

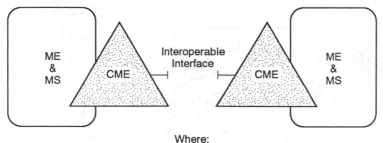

Where:
ME = Managed Element(s)
MS = Management Solution
CME = Conformant Management Entity

Figure 12.2   The OSI/NMF architecture components.

OSI/NMF architecture. The management solution may contain users, management systems, network management, and the conformant management entity (CME, discussed shortly). From a practical viewpoint, the general term *management* encompasses hardware, operating systems, database management systems, communications protocols, human interfaces, window managers, etc. The OSI/NMF does not require that all these components exist in each network management solution. They are configured to solve the specific network management problem.

The interoperable interface represents the point of demarcation for the exchange of messages within the OSI/NMF architecture. At this interface there is a set of protocols and procedures defined to meet the requirements of an object-oriented paradigm. Systems that are to exchange management information must support this interoperable interface, which represents the object-oriented design (OOD) realization. Therefore, the network management system itself is considered to be a black box.

The CME defines the real open system supporting the OSI/NMF interoperable interface. The central concept of this architecture is that the CMEs are used (at the interoperable interface) between one or two networks. The CME concept is designed to support communications between two vendors' products with standard formats and procedures at the interoperable interface.

Figure 12.3 shows the relationship of the OSI/NMF components. Network management is achieved through the CME, which acts as the boundary to the management solution (MS) and management elements (ME). In turn, these components communicate with the specific communications network. In essence, the outer rings of the communications networks are managed by a set of interoperable CMEs. A

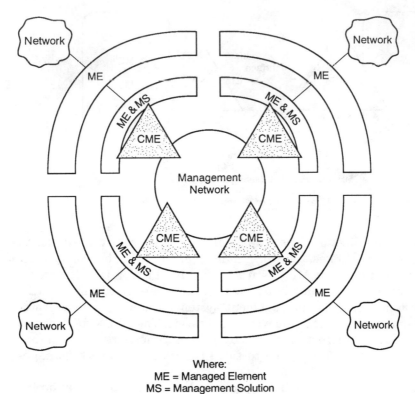

Where:
ME = Managed Element
MS = Management Solution

Figure 12.3   The OSI/NMF component relationships.

management network is modeled as a union of the CMEs and their interoperable interfaces. In this example, four unions comprise the management network.

In conformance with the OSI network management scheme, the OSI/NMF architecture operates around OOD and managed objects. As we learned earlier, a managed object is an abstraction of a resource in a network. It is managed at the visible boundary of an OOD system (which is an interoperable interface from the context of OSI/NMF architecture). As with the OSI architecture, the OSI/NMF managed object *represents* the actual managed resource. It is a view of the resource; it is an abstraction of a physical or logical entity. As Figure 12.4 shows, the managed objects are considered to be part of CME.

The managed objects can be made visible only by interoperations between CMEs through the interoperable interface. Therefore, the CME accepts or sends messages pertaining to the operations on a managed object.

A CME may act in the role of an agent or of a manager. If it acts in

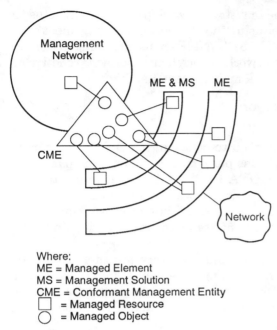

Where:
ME = Managed Element
MS = Management Solution
CME = Conformant Management Entity
☐ = Managed Resource
○ = Managed Object

Figure 12.4 Managed resources and managed objects.

the role of an agent, it makes objects visible at the interoperable interface. It is so named because it serves as an agent for the managed resources being represented by the managed object. The CME operates in a managing role if it manages objects in another CME.

The MIB

The OSI/NMF also uses the management information base (MIB). As discussed in earlier chapters, the MIB allows managed objects to be "seen" across the interoperable interface. The CMEs must share an MIB if they are to have a common understanding of the meaning and structure of information about managed objects. Moreover, the managed object can be "open" only if it is registered in the MIB.

The OSI/NMF has made notable progress in defining its MIB. It is a very positive and significant step toward the realization of open network management systems.

OSI/NMF influence in the industry

The OSI/NMF efforts are proving to be quite beneficial to international telecommunications standards. Because of the influence the organizations of the NMF have in the industry, its work provides an impetus for users and vendors to consider using the OSI network management standards. In addition, members of the OSI/NMF are participating in the various workshops throughout the world, which helps to provide cohesive interpretations of the OSI network management standards.

British Telecom's Open Network Architecture and Concert

British Telecom (BT) has been quite active in the OSI network management standards arena. It has published documents [as part of its Open Network Architecture (ONA)] on how it intends to use the OSI Model for its products. The BT ONA is well developed in comparison to some of the other vendors' profiles. BT has been working closely with the OSI network management standards groups and is a founding member of the OSI/NMF.

BT is both a network consumer and a network provider. Therefore, it views the use of the OSI network management standards as both a user and a provider. BT's ONA was conceived to meet BT's internal operations. However, it is now viewed as a foundation for several of BT's external products.

BT considers ONA to be a very important component for its future networks. Indeed, ONA and the OSI network management standards (through the coordination with the OSI/NMF) are closely aligned. BT is committed to the OSI Model, but like other organizations, it is not able to wait for all of the ISO specifications to be published. Therefore, in some instances, BT has moved forward with some of its own specific implementations.

Concert

The term used by BT to describe the network management aspects of ONA is *Concert*. The BT approach in designing Concert is to provide the customer with a portfolio of integrated, compatible products for network management. Concert is examined in more detail shortly.

British Telecom's view of network management architecture

BT's approach for network management is to divide its architecture into four subarchitectures:

- The *functional* architecture describes the functions that are to be performed by network management. It also describes how the management systems in Concert interact with each other.
- The *structural* architecture describes how the functions within the functional architecture are organized and how the layers in network

management interact with each other and pass information between them.

- The *interface* architecture describes the various layers of the seven-layer model.

- The *application* architecture describes the application service elements within the application layer that are used to support the end user.

Functional architecture. Even though ISO has divided its network management standards into five system management functional areas (SFMAs) BT's approach is to extend this scheme to seven functions. Figure 12.5 shows BT's seven functional categories. Some of the function names are the same as OSI network management standards and some differ. *Performance* management and *configuration* management are quite similar to the OSI SMFAs with the same name. *Event* management controls the events in the network. For example, testing, diagnostic operations, and alarm management are all handled with the event management function. *Resource* management is used to manage the physical and logical entities in the network. This function establishes and tracks the resources such as hardware, software, circuits, test equipment, etc. *Financial* management is similar in concept to the OSI accounting management SMFA, except the BT approach is both tactical and strategic and deals with items such as billing, depreciation, amortization, invoice reconciliation, and maintenance costs. The *access and security* management function, as the name implies, deals with authentication, security, encryption, and access operations. Finally, the *planning and design* management function is used to determine network topologies, network loads, routing strategies, fall-back operations, etc.

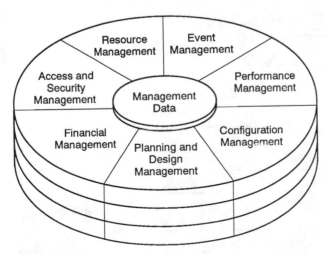

Figure 12.5   BT's functional architecture.

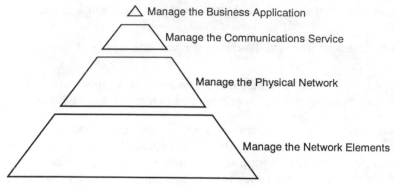

Figure 12.6 BT's structural architecture.

Structural architecture. BT has an interesting approach to the logical structure of its network management architecture. Recognizing that management systems tend to be hierarchical, BT has organized their architecture into four logical layers and emphasizes that an implementation of these logical layers may combine one or more of the OSI seven layers.

Figure 12.6 shows the BT scheme for the structural architecture. At the highest level, an enterprise must be concerned with managing the business application, such as an electronic messaging system. In order to support this system, it is also necessary to manage the underlying

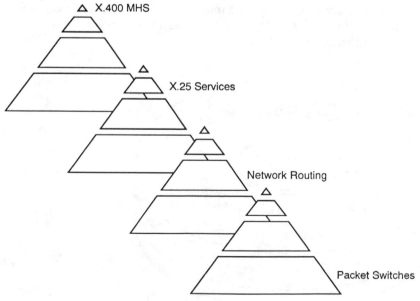

Figure 12.7 Recursive management framework.

communications service, such as the provision for a connection to a network. At the next level, the physical network must be managed in order for the connection to be supported through the network to the remote user. At this level, management of routing tables and acknowledgment protocols become important. Finally, the network elements, such as the packet switches, must be managed.

As shown in Fig. 12.7, the ideal is to provide a recursive aspect to network components and their management. For example, an X.25-based network may need a completely separate management hierarchy from the X.400 message handling system (MHS), but both management systems will contribute and participate in the overall network management system.

Interface architecture. The BT interface architecture is in conformance with the OSI/NMF specifications. BT emphasizes that the layers in Fig. 12.8 support network management systems as well as other systems such as packet networks, local area networks (LANs), etc. Indeed, the only part of BT's architecture that is specific to network management are the sublayers in layer 7 titled "Management Specific Application Service Element (ASE)" and "Common Management Information Service Element (CMISE) 9595/9596." A designer can use the BT stack to support other applications. For example, these two sublayers can be replaced with the X.400 sublayers to obtain the MHS services.

Application architecture. BT's application architecture is quite varied, but the Concert system uses the following platform:

- X 11 Windows
- Structured Query Language (SQL)
- Oracle databases
- OSI/NM communications interfaces
- UNIX V5 CX Open POSIX conformant

ONA components

As seen in Fig. 12.9, ONA describes three major components to support the end-user network management applications:

- *System Management Protocols:* This component establishes the permissible protocol stacks to support OSI network management.
- *Management Message Sets:* This component defines the application programming interface to (at this point) alarm surveillance, testing, and diagnostic functions.

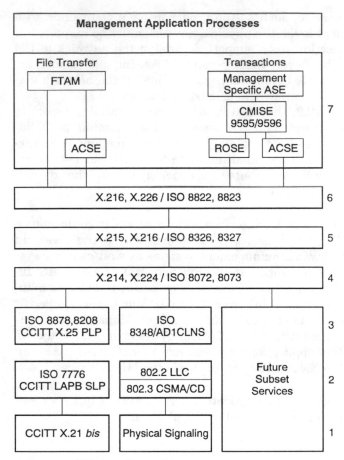

Figure 12.8 BT's interface architecture.

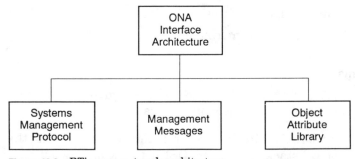

Figure 12.9 BT's open network architecture.

- *Object and Attribute Library:*   This component defines the rules on the use of templates and macros in the network management operations.

Figure 12.10 shows one example of BT's ONA architecture. This example highlights the network management stack. The ONA application rests above CMISE or file transfer and access management (FTAM), which in turn relies on the ONA lower-layer communication modules for the transmission of the network management message. The CMISE works with an application programming interface (API). This API has not yet been published for public consumption.

The ONA architecture relies heavily on descreminators and sieves for its operations. It uses the OSI/NMF convention of notifications, which pass through a filter. ONA also relies on the event report function to relay the management report to the proper entity.

AT&T's Unified Network Management Architecture

AT&T has developed an architecture for network management that is based on the OSI Model; it is the Unified Network Management Architecture (UNMA). It uses many of the concepts of the OSI protocols and interface specifications, plus features that AT&T has developed over the past several years with the use of UNIX operating system.

AT&T's UNMA is based on the network management protocol (NMP). The job of the NMP is to provide an interface to user components, such as telephones, modems, and workstations. These components arc known as element management systems (EMSs). The concept of EMS fits quite well with today's telecommunications environment in the United States, where communications networks are found in three distinct arenas: the customer site (customer pre-

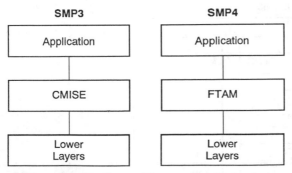

Figure 12.10 BT's System Management Protocols (SMPs).

mises), the local exchange network, and the carriers' interexchange network.

AT&T's implementation of its UNMA is centered around ACCUMASTER. ACCUMASTER uses NMP to manage the network. A user accesses AT&T's network management system through a workstation via ACCUMASTER. (In practice, the user is interfacing with X Windows.)

AT&T has worked with Cincom Systems Inc. to develop a module which allows the network manager to obtain information about SNA networks. In effect, the Cincom System integrates IBM's NetView capabilities with several of the ACCUMASTER modules.

The UNMA architecture is closely aligned with the OSI protocol stacks and OSI network management. Figure 12.11 shows the overall network management protocol structure. It is obvious from this figure that AT&T is committed to the use of the OSI management in their UNMA products.

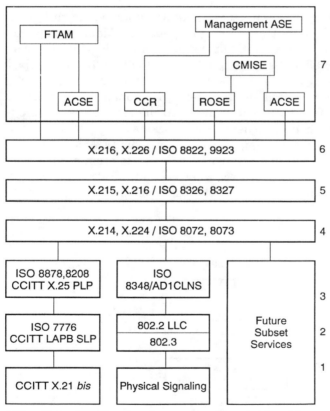

Figure 12.11 AT&T's network management protocol architecture.

The UNMA is grouped into six major categories, five of which closely align with the OSI network management functional areas:

- *Configuration and name management:*   Provides change, directory, and inventory management. It enables the network administrator to add and move managed objects and to obtain information through directories, such as vendor service contracts.

- *Fault management:*   Provides end-to-end testing, problem diagnosis, reconfiguration, troubleshooting, and repair services. It allows the network administrator to isolate problems or to reconfigure around the problem, if necessary. It also stores history about ongoing faults.

- *Performance management:*   Provides monitoring services such as tracking trends and thresholds. It measures network performance such as availability, usage, and overall network activity.

- *Accounting management:*   Provides bill-backs to customers. It supports budgeting processes, as well as verification of various billing operations and networks.

- *Security management:*   Provides access security and authorization security functions. It supports activities such as access based on authorization code, geographical location, time of day, function of individual, etc.

- *Network planning:*   Provides planning for growth, error resolution, and contingency factors.

AT&T's layers

As shown in Fig. 12.11, NMP uses the OSI seven-layer stack. AT&T intends the NMP to reside in the upper four layers and rest transparently on the bottom three. This approach means that the UNMA architecture is somewhat independent of the networks themselves. For example, layers 1, 2, and 3 could consist of a connectionless network, an X.25-based network, or an IEEE 802-based local network. The principal requirement is that the upper four layers connect to the lower three layers through the OSI service definition specifications and their complementary protocols. In case the reader is unaware of these standards, they are CCITT's X.214 and X.224 and ISO's 8072 and 8073 standards.

NMP includes CMISE and CMIP. AT&T states that if CCITT, ISO, or the T1M1 Committee changes the specifications for these OSI-based protocols, AT&T will make the changes to NMP in order to conform to the standard.

NMP variations from OSI network management

Most of the vendors discussed in this chapter have made additions and enhancements to the OSI network management standards. AT&T states where the changes occur:

- An enhancement is made to the SET service which allows the changing of values in a multivalued attribute. Changes include removals, replacements, and additions.

- Another enhancement to the SET service allows a user to establish attributes as defaults. In other words, AT&T will allow the SET service to have attributes without explicitly providing the values for the attributes.

- AT&T allows a user to cancel an M-GET service at any time.

- AT&T does not support the extended service functional unit.

DEC's Enterprise Management Architecture

Digital Equipment Corporation (DEC) has been a firm supporter of OSI standards for several years. In several recent product announcements, it states that it has brought the OSI protocol suites into its product line. At the corporate level, it has made several pronouncements committing itself to the use of OSI standards. Its network management scheme, Enterprise Management Architecture (EMA), continues this trend.

EMA is based on the OSI/NMF standards discussed in this book. For example, it uses the Common Management Information Protocol (CMIP) and CMISE. Like OSI network management, EMA is also organized around the concept of object programming and the managed object.

The structure of EMA is divided into a director model and an entity model (see Fig. 12.12). The combination of the directory and entity relationship defines the structure of DEC's management interfaces and interaction between management systems (directors) and managed objects (entities).

The EMA director model provides a modular architecture for the design of an open network management system. DEC's approach is to use the director model to provide easy interaction between the network management modules. As we shall see, these network management modules are "plugged" into the director components as needed.

The entity model is designed to provide network management information and network management interfaces without having to alter the managed objects themselves. It is an object-oriented model; thus it

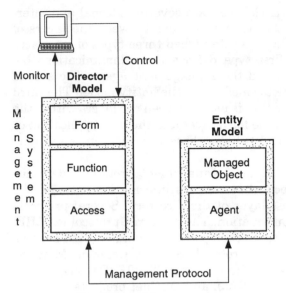

Figure 12.12   The EMA architecture.

fits well with the OSI network management architecture. In consonance with the OSI ideas, the entity model provides the means to define objects into object classes, which allows the sharing of properties within the classes and provides a set of rules for the management of the classes.

The director model consists of three layers: form, function, and access; and the entity model consists of two layers (which provide similar operations to that of the access layer): the management agent and the managed object.

- *Form:*   This layer supports the convergence of management information between a director and its elements. An example of the elements is users.

- *Function:*   This layer describes the services offered by management applications residing within the EMA director.

- *Access:*   This layer defines the operations for controlling and monitoring EMA's managed entities.

- *Management agent:*   This layer provides a remote interface to the managed object and performs procedures in response to the entity director.

- *Managed object:*   This is an entity (hardware or software) that provides a service to a client.

The director and entity models contain several external and internal interfaces to support the communications between the layers of the director and entity. DEC has established three types of interfaces for these activities. The first type defines the communications between the managed object and the management agent. The second type rests between the director model and the entity model. The third type is an internal interface that is used between the layers within the director model and between the form layer and the user application or user workstation. Figure 12.12 shows these interfaces in the shaded areas.

The path in Fig. 12.12, labeled "Management Protocol," identifies the communications protocol that conveys information between the entity agent and the access layer of the directory. Several protocols can be used to carry this information. The preferred protocol is CMIP, although DEC establishes that other protocols could be used such as Simple Network Management Protocol (SNMP), Common Management Information Services and Protocol over TCP/IP (CMOT), or Systems Network Architecture's (SNAs), and DECnet products.

EMA is designed for the director to manage any type of entity. The simplest approach is for an organization to define and develop a managed object in accordance with DEC's entity model. However, if the entities are not designed in accordance with the entity model, they still must be presented to the director by the access layer. In this situation, the access layer acts as a convergence protocol and must handle the translation from the entity model. Like many approaches today, this practice requires consistent interfaces to the director model, regardless of what exists outside the management layers.

The entity model

The DEC entity model closely parallels the OSI network management architecture. It supports the framework that is consistent with OSI's structure for management information (SMI) documents. The entity model identifies entity classes based on attributes, attribute groups, directives, and events.

- *Attributes:*   Like the SMI, attributes are specific pieces of data that provide management information about managed entities. For example, an attribute could be an operational state on a line card with values describing this as disabled, enabled, active, or busy.

- *Attribute groups:*   Attribute groups closely resemble the SMI's concept of instances. An instance is the managed object of the same class; that is to say, attribute groups deal with like sorts of attributes that contain common identifiers, names, etc.

- *Directives:* Directives describe the requests from a director to an entity. The entity receives the directive and returns a reply. This is similar to the notifications and operations in the OSI Model.

- *Events:* This models the OSI notifications, which allows unsolicited information to be sent to a director from the entity's agent.

The entity model also allows subordinate entries where one object class can be a member of another object class; thus DEC's approach allows inheritance and the sharing of behavior between objects and superior object classes.

The EMA is organized around object-oriented models. Therefore, actions presented through the agent to the managed object can include the CMISE service definitions described in previous chapters, as well as the specific operations defined in other OSI network management services.

The director model

As discussed earlier, the director's role is to coordinate network management activities and to initiate management operations at the request of end-user applications. It also responds to the events sent from the entity model.

The director of EMA is based on the types of modules implemented in the software. Figure 12.13 shows an example of the director components. They consist of the Management Information Repository (MIR), management modules (presentation, functional, and access modules), and the executive.

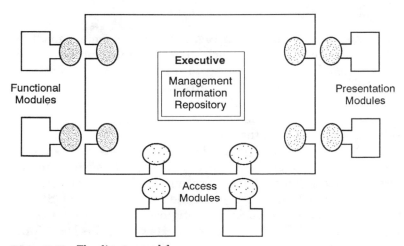

Figure 12.13   The director model.

The executive.   The executive acts as a coordinator for the execution of the EMA software. It provides scheduling for the work, sets up remote procedure calls (RPCs), coordinates dispatches for local and remote calls, etc.

The MIR.   The MIR is a repository that stores the management information. It is designed to store four types of information about a managed environment:

- *Class data:*   This type of data contains information about managed entities that share the same properties. Therefore, it permits hierarchical definitions in which subordinates can be used to group related entity classes through the containment approach.

- *Instance data:*   This type of data contains network management information relating to actual occurrences of entities within a class. It contains information such as network identifiers, packet names, and other identifiers used for system configuration. DEC's approach for instance data is to allow this information to be used for network management to determine the representation of a network regardless of the state of the network.

- *Attribute data:*   This data type contains information specifically about entity instances. Attribute data can be used to provide a profile of a managed object or a snapshot of a particular point in time. Typically it is stored in some event log where it is time stamped and used for analytical purposes.

- *Private data:*   This data type is used at the discretion of the network manager and has no structure imposed upon it by the enterprise model.

Management modules.   As shown in Fig. 12.13, management modules "plug into" a director. This approach divides management services into logical pieces (logical layers). As with any layered concept, this approach allows operations to be separated from each other and to provide services independently of each other.

The *presentation modules (PM)* are used to support the interface of the director components with the end user. Several presentation modules may exist if a user chooses more than one interface. For example, a personal computer or a graphics workstation could be supported by two different presentation modules operating as a service to a director.

Functional modules (FM) are responsible for the specific OSI network management services, such as configuration, performance, accounting, security, and fault management. However, the DEC functional module allows for more than one OSI network management function to be placed inside the functional module. The functional management module uses data stored in the MIR to perform many of its activities.

Access modules (AM) provide a key service for DEC network management. They allow the director to interface with any entity model (e.g., a different vendor) by performing conversion of formats between two different systems. DEC encourages the use of CMIP for consistency. However, other formats could be used by implementing an access module to resolve syntax and coding differences between the model and the agent. This process is achieved through the CCITT/ISO Abstract Syntax Notation 1 (ASN.1). The use of ASN.1 allows an access module to translate a managed object's network management information into a format that can be used by the director.

An access module is much more than a presentation layer protocol. DEC has given the access module considerable intelligence. For example, a remote managed entity need not contain the functional modules. The access module has knowledge about the entities it supports. Therefore, it can translate specific network management information into a data format. But it should be emphasized that this approach requires a great deal of knowledge about the specific event occurring at the managed object. In effect, with DEC's approach to the access modules, they assume a number of the functions of the OSI functional management areas as represented in EMA by the functional modules.

This approach can be seen in Fig. 12.14. The network management center at the bottom of the figure supports the presentation modules (PMs), as well as the configuration management (CM) and fault management (FM) functional modules.

The presentation modules are used by the director for interfacing with the network operator's console, printers, and database event logs. Notice that the remote directors do not contain any of the functional management modules; rather they use the appropriate access module to provide support and event notification coming from a managed object in the network. The access modules at the remote directors (in the top part of the figure) report about faults and configuration events to the center's configuration and fault management modules.

The EMA concept is still evolving. Notwithstanding, EMA contains actual operating modules. For example, the terminal server manager is used to manage terminal servers across a DEC-based Ethernet LAN from a central location. It is used to isolate, diagnose, and correct problems. It is a very user-friendly system which requires relatively little training for the personnel to use it.

DEC provides a very flexible and powerful LAN traffic monitor for its Ethernet-based LANs. This system is called the *LAN traffic monitor (LTM)*. It provides the network manager with timely information

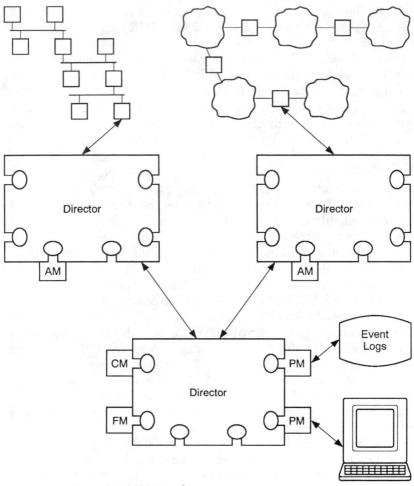

Figure 12.14 Example of EMA topology.

on the performance of the LAN in relation to throughput, delay, and error conditions.

IBM's Open Network Management and NetView

IBM has made several announcements regarding its Open Network Management (ONM) architecture. The ONM plan provides an insight into IBM's strategic plans regarding network management.

ONM supports IBM's strategic movement to the OSI Model. It includes the use of CMISE/CMIP.

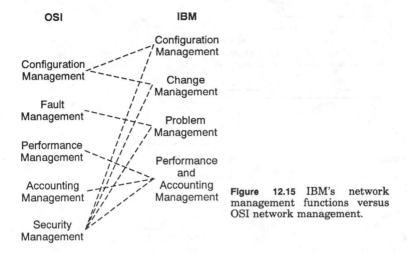

OSI   IBM

Configuration
Management

Configuration
Management

Change
Management

Fault
Management

Problem
Management

Performance
Management

Performance
and
Accounting
Management

Accounting
Management

Figure 12.15 IBM's network management functions versus OSI network management.

Security
Management

ONM does not map directly to OSI network management. However, similarities can be found between the OSI functions and the ONM functions. Figure 12.15 shows a general comparison of the OSI functional areas and the current SNA network management protocols. IBM's philosophy is to develop network management solutions which manage both non-SNA and SNA resources.

NetView

Much of the activity of IBM vis-à-vis the OSI network management standards focuses on NetView. The reasons are obvious. Many vendors are committed to NetView interfaces, and NetView is steadily integrating more OSI network management functions. NetView has developed some very powerful and user-friendly graphical displays. Moreover, NetView now supports interconnections into TCP/IP networks. Finally, IBM is developing its OSI/CS (communications subsystem) product to allow an IBM machine to communicate with an OSI-based network.

IBM has designed some interesting features into NetView. As shown in Fig. 12.16, the structure is built on focal points, entry points, and service points.

The focal point allows the network control center to take a global view of the network. Like many of IBM's approaches, it provides for centralized network management. It receives network management information from entry points and service points; it also consolidates and organizes this information for the network manager. Entry points focus on the support of SNA-type network devices. They manage resources that have SNA addresses. For example, entry point compo-

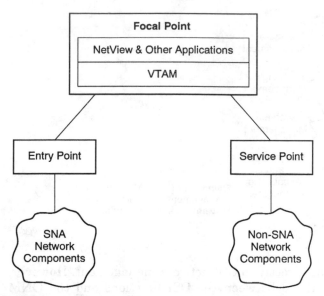

Figure 12.16 Focal points, entry points, and service points.

nents would include Systems 36, 38, and 88; 8100 Series computers; the Series 1 computer; 3710, 3174, and 3274 devices; as well as the 43xx machines. Service point features allow NetView to bridge into non-SNA and non-IBM components. At this point, it also supports voice-oriented services. It works in a similar fashion to DECnet's enterprise access module in that it performs presentation layer functions with format and syntax conversion between SNA and non-SNA interfaces.

Figure 12.17 shows yet another view of how NetView operates. It uses the services of the virtual telecommunications access method (VTAM) for the definition of several services (VTAM, for example,

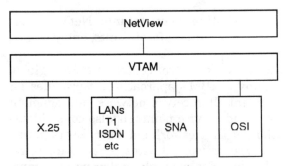

Figure 12.17 NetView implementations.

provides a powerful macro language that supports configuration management). VTAM has optional modules that allow it to interwork with other systems, such as X.25, LANs, etc.

Hewlett-Packard's OpenView

Hewlett-Packard has long-supported OSI standards. Indeed, Hewlett-Packard was one of the first large companies to establish a corporate policy supporting the OSI Model. Hewlett-Packard has continued this approach in the OSI network management area with its OpenView system.

OpenView supports network management activities in both LANs and wide area networks (WANs). It consists of four major components:

- *Network command interpreter:* This component supports the remote command execution, the management of remote resources, and the analysis of performance of managed objects. The network command interpreter also has a number of security support operations.

- *Status and diagnostic monitor:* This function is similar to an OSI log control activity in that it collects performance and status information and uses this information for diagnostic work as well as fault isolation activities.

- *Transmission impairment measurement:* This function provides the monitoring and measurement of problems and impairments through other Hewlett-Packard software modules.

- *Bridge manager:* This component is responsible for problem analysis and diagnostics for problems that occur in bridges.

Summary

A number of organizations have developed their own network management models. Some of these models are proprietary in nature and others are founded on the OSI network management model. In the future it is likely that the network vendors will bring more CMIP and SNMP products into their marketing plans, but it is unlikely that proprietary solutions such as EMA and NetView will go away. Rather, it is more probable that the vendors will support dual stacks.

13

Conclusions and Summary

Introduction

It is clear that standards for network management are needed in the industry. It is equally clear that proprietary-based systems have fared well in the marketplace. For example, IBM's NetView has enjoyed considerable success. IBM claims that over 10,000 NetView licenses have been sold and that over 70 percent of all Systems Network Architecture (SNA) sites use NetView. In a sense, NetView has become a de facto standard. However, the long-term solution is a set of network management protocols which are independent of specific vendor's architectures. The OSI, Internet, and IEEE network management standards are the best choice among the options.

The large carriers, such as AT&T and British Telecom, will continue to refine their products. They are also integrating the network management standards into their products.

Many organizations are developing their network management software with the use of the Internet Simple Network Management Protocol (SNMP) standards. SNMP has gained considerable support in the industry because it is relatively simple to install and use, and it operates on the Transmission Control Protocol/Internet Protocol (TCP/IP) suite, which is one of the most widely used sets of protocols in the world.

It should be recognized that no standard will be able to satisfy all specific requirements. Consequently, the best approach to network management is to consider the standards as a platform from which to develop other network management capabilities.

Do I Migrate to Network Management Standards?

If an organization chooses not to use network management standards, it will by default adapt proprietary protocols (which, in the author's opinion, will eventually migrate to the standards discussed in this book).

On the other hand, if an organization decides to use the standards, it should decide if it will (1) migrate to the OSI standards, (2) migrate to the Internet standards, or (3) migrate to the IEEE standards. The advantages and disadvantages to these options are summarized in the next paragraphs.

The OSI standards are not complete and have not achieved widespread use. However, vendors are now placing these standards in their product lines and their use is increasing. These standards are more complex than the Internet standards, because they are richer in function and take advantage of object-oriented design (OOD) concepts of inheritance and polymorphism as well as instance creation. The Internet concepts are widely used. They are easy and simple to implement. While they do not have all the capabilities of the OSI standards, the Internet is broadening their applicability by defining management information bases (MIBs) for DS1, DS3, local area networks (LANs), and the X.25 objects.

The IEEE standards are a given. They fit well with the IEEE 802 model and can be used with or without the Common Management Information Protocol (CMIP).

Planning for a Migration

The development or implementation of a standardized network management system requires an organization to adhere to the following:

1. A plan to use network management standards is meaningless until a fairly accurate assessment of the impact on the organization is known. If an organization chooses to integrate these network management standards into its network architecture, careful consideration must be given to the impact of the standards' integration into the current systems.

2. This impact can only be known after it is determined which automated systems (applications software, systems software, database software, communications software, databases, files, hardware) must be changed, replaced, or added.

3. The plan must also take into account any possible personnel and facility changes.

4. An assessment must be made of the effect of the use of the network management standards on the organization's mission.

5. Once these bases of knowledge are known, an organization can then begin an evaluation of the time and money required to mi-

grate to the standardization. From this evaluation, the organization can make trade-off decisions, develop a detailed plan, and begin staffing accordingly for the effort.

An organization stands to benefit from the use of network management standards. Indeed, an organization's nonuse of the standards will most likely place the company in an untenable position in the future with regard to interoperability and interconnectivity with a large number of organizations that are committed to the use of network management standards.

The major risk in committing to the change now is that the network management standards are still undergoing substantial changes. Another major factor to be considered is the resources that must be committed to the project.

Summary

Network management standards are a must in today's complex networking environment. The issue is in choosing which network management software to install in an organization's network. The recommendation of this author is to use the Internet standards now and to migrate to the OSI network management standards (as they mature). But be aware that many of the OSI system management functions are embryonic, and related products are few.

To repeat, if an organization is dependent on TCP/IP, an additional recommendation is to adapt the Internet network management standards. There should be no hand-wringing about the issue. Productive products are available to assist the manager in the difficult task of network management; take advantage of them.

Proprietary systems such as NetView are excellent packages that have become de facto standards. These packages will serve the customer well.

The long-term options favor the OSI network management standards. They are designed by organizations and individuals who have a broad base of practical experience in network management. Additionally, they are organized around object-oriented techniques. Therefore, they have a solid conceptual and theoretical foundation.

The transition from a current environment to a new environment in any information system is often arduous and painful. But the transition can eventually reap significant cost benefits and productivity savings to an organization.

A Tutorial On Object-Oriented Design and Object-Oriented Programming

Object-oriented design (OOD) and object-oriented programming (OOP) (hereafter referred to generically as OOD) are new buzz words for this decade. They are receiving extensive examination in the industry and scores of organizations are training their programming staff on these techniques. OOD is in contrast to the usual practice of procedural programming, which consists of a step-by-step coding of a program to perform a required set of tasks.

OOD owes its origins to the accepted practice of modular programming and the structured programming techniques which became popular in the 1970s. It differs substantially from these earlier concepts, however, in the way it organizes data and the code that operates on the data. To get an idea of how OOD works, we need to understand several key terms, which are summarized as follows:

- OOD operates on the concept of *objects*. An object is an entity that has both data and associated actions that operate on the data.

- To take the idea a step further, the object is actually an "encapsulation" of the data (which are usually called *instance variables*), with the code (which are usually called *methods*).

- A *message* is a request that is sent to an object in order to perform an action. In turn, the method is the action performed on the object. It implements the message it receives.

- Every object belongs to a *class*. The class describes the object's data and the message(s) it responds to. In effect, the class is the implementation of an object. From the constructs of programming, a class could be considered a *compile-time entity* and an object could be considered a *run-time entity*.

■ A *subclass* inherits the instance variables and methods of a parent class, which is also known as a *superclass*. However, it is important to understand that subclasses can define additional instance variables and methods and even override superclass methods.

All these terms may seem a bit confusing. Perhaps a simple example will clarify their meaning. (I would like to thank the Symatec organization for this example. I have been using Symatec's THINK-C in my work with object-oriented C.)

Figure A.1 shows that class Employee contains instance variables Name and Birthdate. It accepts messages GetName, GetAge, and GetWkPay. It also contains the methods returnName, return(Today-Birthdate), and return 0. The figure also shows two subclasses, HourlyEmployee and ExemptEmployee, which are a subclass of Employee.

```
Class: Employee
Superclass: None
Instance variables:   Name, Birthdate
Messages                               Methods

GetName                                returnName
GetAge                                 return (Today-Birthdate)
GetWkPay                               return 0
```

```
Subclass:   HourlyEmployee
Superclass:   Employee
Instance variables:   HourlySalary

Messages        Methods

GetWkPay        return (HourlySalary * 40)
```

```
Subclass: ExemptEmployee
Superclass: Employee
Instance variables:   YearlySalary

Messages        Methods

GetWkPay        return (YearlySalary/52)
```

Figure A.1 OOD example.

We can see in the figure that the subclasses HourlyEmployee and ExemptEmployee inherit all the instance variables from the employee superclass. In addition, a new instance variable is described for each subclass (HourlySalary, YearlySalary), and the method return is over-ridden for the two subclasses.

Index